A 1,000-Mile
Great Lakes
Island Adventure

A 1,000-Mile
Great Lakes
Island Adventure

by

Loreen Niewenhuis

"Life should be an adventure!"

CRICKHOLLOW BOOKS

Crickhollow Books is an imprint of Great Lakes Literary, LLC, of Milwaukee, Wisconsin, an independent press working to create books of lasting quality.

Our titles are available from your favorite bookstore.
For a complete catalog of all our titles or to place special orders:

www.CrickhollowBooks.com

A 1,000-Mile Great Lakes Island Adventure
© 2015, Loreen Niewenhuis

Cover photograph by Loreen Niewenhuis was taken on Flowerpot Island, located in Lake Huron near the Bruce Peninsula.

Back cover photograph: Author on Isle Royale, Lake Superior.

Cover design: Philip Martin.

Original Trade Softcover

ISBN: 978-1-933987-23-1

To Ben & Mary, and Lucas

May your lives

be filled with adventure.

Contents

Introduction

This is my third Great Lakes Adventure. The first was a 1,000-mile hike around the perimeter of Lake Michigan. This journey allowed me to fully explore my favorite place, the lake I got to know first as a child. I returned to the shoreline as an adult and encircled it step by step, recording it in my muscles and bones. It was a transformational experience: it reshaped me, tuned my senses to nature, and expanded my sense of what I could accomplish. And I learned so much about Lake Michigan along the way. I interviewed people living along the edge of the water and experts whose life's work was to understand the lake. I visited museums and fish hatcheries, historic sites and even a "schoolship" that is a floating Great Lakes classroom for kids. The book about that first adventure, *A 1,000-Mile Walk on the Beach*, connected with many readers who love Lake Michigan as much as I do.

That first undertaking gave rise to my second adventure, this time a 1,000-mile journey exploring key shoreline stretches of all five Great Lakes. I discovered the unique personalities of each lake, walked the geological layers exposed at the water's edge, and also hiked some of the watery connections between the lakes. My second book, *A 1,000-Mile Great Lakes Walk*, gave a broader picture of the Great Lakes.

On this journey, I hopped out to several islands and began to get a sense of how special those bits of land surrounded by the lakes were. Those brief excursions led to the conception of yet a third adventure – this one – a 1,000-mile journey exploring the islands of the Great Lakes.

My initial concept was simple: I would visit islands in each of the five Great Lakes – hiking, kayaking, boating and biking on and around them – until I accrued 1,000 miles. But as I began my research, I soon realized the magnitude of the challenge. It turns out that there are around 35,000 islands in the Great Lakes and their connecting waters. Yes, I had to choose from *tens of thousands* of islands in the Great Lakes Basin. How would I select which islands to visit?

Some of the choices were obvious:

The St. Lawrence River – the most downstream portion of the flow of the Great Lakes – is loaded with islands (the **Thousand Islands**), and I wanted to kayak among them. And some of the youngest islands in the Great Lakes are located in Lake Ontario just offshore from Toronto.

American tall ships gathered at **South Bass Island** before sailing to clash with the British Royal Navy during the War of 1812. On the bicentennial of the bloody Battle of Lake Erie, there would be a reenactment coinciding with my adventure. I marked it on my calendar and planned to be aboard one of the tall ships for this historic event.

Manitoulin Island in Lake Huron is the largest in the Great Lakes. In fact, it is the largest island on fresh water anywhere in the world. Limestone flats there still bear scrapes and gouges from the glaciers that encroached thousands of years ago to form the basins for these waters.

The **Manitou Islands** in Lake Michigan are part of the Sleeping Bear Dunes National Lakeshore. I knew from my past travels that the largest population of the endangered Great Lakes piping plover nests on these islands, and I applied as a volunteer to help monitor the birds as part of this island adventure.

I had never been to **Washington Island** off the tip of Wisconsin's Door Peninsula, and I was also determined to explore there. This island has a permanent population of 600 people, many descended from hearty Icelandic and Scandinavian immigrants.

Isle Royale in Lake Superior is a National Park. Moose and wolves inhabit this remote island, and scientists have observed their interaction for over 50 years. I discovered that I could be part of a team of hikers tasked with collecting moose bones.

These choices were intriguing and seemed a good foundation to the adventure. After that, there were other factors that appealed to me, things I wanted to explore to fully understand the story of the islands. I wanted to make sure that I traveled to both remote islands and inhabited island communities. I wanted to visit both near-shore islands and isolated landmasses accessible only by a long boat ride. I was also interested in getting out in a kayak wherever possible, so I searched for places where islands were grouped together, giving safer passage to small watercraft.

If I didn't get to your favorite island, I apologize. Visiting all 35,000 of them would have taken several lifetimes. And a number of these islands could have inspired an entire book on their own. This account threads together the story of the connections between the islands, while revealing the unique qualities defining each island I visited. I hope that my glimpse into each of these watery-edged places encourages you to perhaps seek out an island adventure of your own.

In all, I passed by thousands of islands on this odyssey, setting foot on more than 30 of them. The islands I explored varied in size from less than an acre (unnamed island in the Toronto Island group, Lake Ontario) to almost 700,000 acres (Manitoulin Island in Lake Huron). Only seven of these islands were attached to the mainland by bridges. Most were accessible only over water. Some of the islands I visited are large enough to contain their own small lakes. Both Manitoulin Island and Isle Royale are punctuated with dozens of them. Some of these island lakes, in turn, have islands poking out of them.

This odyssey took place between May of 2013 and October of 2014. The islands are grouped here by the lake in which they reside. This book is more episodic than my first two, which were accounts of long hikes: the first a long circular journey around Lake Michigan, and the second linking long sections of shoreline on all five Great Lakes.

But islands are different. They are isolated landmasses, surrounded by water. They are, by their very nature, episodic.

Conjure an island in your mind. Picture it sitting there in the lake, gentle waves lapping at its edges. Now take a glacier a mile tall and run it over your island, scrubbing and crushing it under the weight of the slow-moving ice for several thousand years. Then melt the glacier and create an era of storms that crash mighty waves onto the island. Raise the level of the water fifty feet, then drop it back down.

Did your island survive? All of the islands in our Great Lakes survived this and much more.

The geology of the Great Lakes Basin is unusual because there are rock ridges that exist in narrow bands running through the region. These rock layers are varied – sandstone, limestone, dolostone, granite, shale, slate. Where these layers persisted in the basins that became our lakes, islands poked up above the level of the water.

The Niagara Escarpment, a grand arc of dolostone (a type of limestone hardened with magnesium), underpins most of the islands in Lakes Michigan and Huron. The islands in the southern part of Lake Superior have a base of sturdy sandstone, while the islands of the St. Lawrence River are granite. Lake Erie's islands are pedestals of limestone. Lake Ontario has few islands, but my journey took me to some unusual landmasses near Toronto that began as sand bars and evolved into islands long after the retreat of the glaciers.

Here is a general island rule: The larger the island, the greater the diversity of life. This makes sense. Larger islands have more habitats supporting a greater variety of creatures. Scientists love to examine life on islands because they are relatively isolated systems. Birds and bats – and even some insects – can come and go, but other life is more restricted. Fewer species visit, and those on the island are connected in a tight web of life. So the variables in the system are fewer than they would be in comparable studies done on mainland environments.

Darwin formulated his theories of species diversity and natural selection after his journey to the Galapagos Islands. From his studies, he came to see that creatures had adapted to the specific conditions on each island. Each rocky piece of that archipelago had a unique set of inhabitants who survived and procreated because they had some slight difference that gave them a competitive advantage over the rest of their kind. Over many generations, these differences were "selected" by the constraints of the environment leading to new, emergent species unique to each island.

All creatures in island communities must adapt, respond, and find a niche in which to thrive. On islands, sub-species of creatures develop, like the Lake Erie Water Snake that has adjusted to life on a small group of islands. There are some plants found on Great Lakes islands that are found nowhere else on earth. Some islands act as an oasis, a place where plants or animals threatened elsewhere may thrive. Isle Royale, for instance, is host to over 40 species of plants that are endangered or threatened.

And what about the people who make islands their homes? On islands hosting human settlements, I met people who had chosen a life with watery edges, a way of existence rooted in isolation and self-reliance. Why are certain people drawn to living on an island? Is it a conscious choice? Or is it the island that chooses and shapes the people? I sought answers to these questions.

This journey challenged me personally in new ways. Kayaking and biking used different muscle groups from the ones honed during my hiking adventures. There were weeks when I would hike, kayak, and then bike. The result was, at first, discovering that I could experience soreness in virtually every muscle in my body simultaneously.

But most of all it was a journey that led to new perspectives for me to explore the Great Lakes, from the surface of the water, or from the vantage of an island landmass rooted in these great inland seas, a place to look back at mainland stretches I had walked. I recalled how often I had paused on the shoreline to look out at a distant shadowy island, wondering what might be found there. Now, I would find out.

Water is the natural element that islands a landmass. It is the inescapable, defining, surrounding feature of these special places. Water has a myriad of moods as it interacts with the environment: wind, light, ice, rain, and current can alter the appearance of water in endless, ever-changing ways. Humid or cold air may cause molecules to leap upward, to rise as fog. Over open stretches, sky and clouds are reflected and distorted. You can see the weather coming, then experience its effect amplified by the lake, as the water acts out the forces of air and wind sweeping across and around the island.

My time on these islands allowed me to fully experience these waters and their many moods.

Join me, won't you?

Walk, kayak, bike and boat with me once again on this island adventure. . . .

Lake Ontario Islands

&

The Islands

of the St. Lawrence River

My story of the Great Lake islands begins on the St. Lawrence River. Did you know that all of these inland waters are on a journey of their own? That they flow persistently to the sea? The St. Lawrence River conveys the mingled waters of the Great Lakes to the North Atlantic Ocean.

Lake Ontario funnels into the mouth of the St. Lawrence, then the waters flow to the northeast. The river courses through the Thousand Islands, then past Montreal and Quebec City, finally mixing with the North Atlantic in the Gulf of St. Lawrence. This river's journey is nearly 750 miles long. While there is proof of Viking expeditions to North America around the year 1000 A.D., lasting non-native settlements in the Great Lakes Basin began with exploration by the French in the mid–16th century. European explorers used the St. Lawrence as a great highway, entering the Great Lakes Basin using this waterway.

Jacques Cartier was the first French explorer to see the Gulf of St. Lawrence in 1534. He ventured upriver the next year. He visited large native camps, some with fortifications and lush gardens growing corn, beans and squash. Cartier asked the natives what they called the river and they expressed the name as "A river without end."

Cartier claimed what is now Ontario for France, calling it New France. He was also responsible for kidnapping two sons of a First Nations chief named Donnacona, who was head of a large village located on the site of present-day Quebec. Since he had promised King Francis that he would find a passage to the Orient – or at least some gold – and had found neither, he presented the two native men as proof that he had at least found something: an exotic place that Europeans would call the New World. On his second excursion, Cartier returned the men to their father. The information they gave guided Cartier's upriver exploration. The chief, understandably, forbade his sons from accompanying the French explorer any farther.

When Cartier arrived at the site of modern Montreal, he discovered that the river was wild with rapids to the west. The river drops 250 feet on its course from Lake Ontario to the Gulf of St. Lawrence, and moving upriver past Montreal was impossible at this time. Lake Huron was actually the first Great Lake to be seen by the French as they explored other routes overland. Lake Erie, surprisingly, was the last Great Lake to be sighted, but this was primarily due to the warring Iroquois who controlled the region.

As I looked over maps of the St. Lawrence, I focused on the archipelago in the western part of the river. Located between the Ontario cities of Kingston and Cornwall and, on the American side, from Oswego to Massena, New York, this region is called the Thousand Islands. I bought a couple of nautical charts. Spreading them on the floor of my home in Battle Creek, Michigan, I matched up the map edges to view miles of island-studded river. I learned to read the charts, which showed not only what was above the water but also what was below: changes in depth, locations of shoals and wetlands, and, of particular interest to me, safe places to launch a kayak.

I have used many types of maps during my adventures. Satellite images were essential to my long walking treks, allowing me to examine the edges of the Great Lakes in great detail. Obstacles like power plants or water-treatment facilities hugging the lakeshore were easy to spot in these images. But on this island adventure I would take to the water more often, in kayaks or other vessels, so I became acquainted with the language of the nautical charts. Online maps were still my favorite tools, though. I could view the entire Great Lakes Basin one moment, then with a few clicks, could zoom in to study the intricate shoreline of a small remote island.

As I viewed the Thousand Islands region on one of these computer maps, I kept drifting downriver, downriver, looking at the hundreds of islands the river flowed through. And then I reached the city of Montreal. Zooming in, I realized that Montreal itself is on an island, sliced from the mainland by the Riviere-des-Prairies. Early native peoples called this waterway "River behind the island."

How lucky for me, I thought, *that I'm exploring the islands of the Great Lakes Basin, and I get to choose which islands to visit. . . .*

So, as I organized my gear for travel to the islands of Lake Ontario and the St. Lawrence, I also packed for a few days of exploring the French Canadian island metropolis of Montreal. I drove through Toronto and then to the far eastern end of Lake Ontario. From there, I followed the St. Lawrence River to the city of Brockville, where I left my car at the train station.

My new journey was underway.

Island of Montreal, Quebec

New York meets Paris

The Island of Montreal is the easternmost and most "downstream" island I explored on this adventure. Clearly it is not a remote outpost where wild animals roam (I'll get to those soon), but a highly urbanized landmass surrounded by flowing rivers, a place often described as a cross between New York and Paris. While I love the wilderness, I also enjoy the cities of the Great Lakes, and I've spent many happy weeks in Chicago, Milwaukee, and Toronto. I'd never been to Montreal, though, the exotic, French-flavored, Great Lakes Basin metropolis.

Taking the train from the station at Brockville to Montreal was fast and relaxing. Wooden electrical poles, now obsolete, ran parallel to the tracks. The wires were broken in places, dipping down to the ground. Glass insulators studded the cross poles – some sky blue, but most were clear – like translucent birds roosting.

We passed cornfields and grazing cows, fields of solar arrays, riverside wetlands, and forested land. The trees were mixed. Birches, maples, and poplars mingled with mighty conifers. This latitude is the southern limit for many of the conifers, and the deciduous trees are nearing their northern limit. The land by the river was flat, the soil rich from the river occasionally spilling over its banks, reinvigorating the soil with nutrients.

Soon, the train sped into the city of Montreal and submerged underground. When the train stopped at the terminal station, I gathered my bag and checked my city map to confirm I was close enough to walk to my hotel.

The Island of Montreal is the second-largest island in the St. Lawrence River. Anticosti Island is the largest and is found 500 miles downstream from Montreal, far past Quebec City. Montreal Island has the distinction of being the most populous island located on fresh water in the world. Nearly 2 million people live there. Some say the island is shaped like a boomerang, but I think that's a strange description for a city with such a vibrant French culture. I would suggest it looks like a snail – escargot – that has left its shell behind. The island is thick in the middle, tapers near the ends, and is about 140 square miles in area.

There is such rich history here – both human and geologic. Two significant natural features that define this island are the river and Mont Royal. Ships coming from the Atlantic Ocean heading up river could easily navigate the wide expanse of the St. Lawrence to Quebec City, then continue west another 150 miles. But here, at Montreal Island, the rough and wild Lachine rapids prevented further upriver travel. It was a logical place to found a settlement. The river insisted that the city be positioned here.

Montreal served as the central hub of the fur industry for nearly a century. Alternating French and British powers governed the city through its early years. These power shifts along with various waves of immigration led to a diverse population that has also helped define this great island city.

It was Cartier who named the mountain here, Mont Royal. Hence, *Montreal* became the name of the city. This geological feature was caused by an ancient volcano that deposited the magma dome. Over time, the surrounding sediments eroded away faster than the dome, exposing it as a basalt mountain. There are three peaks in the formation. The tallest is 764 feet above sea level. The mountain park is inextricable from what it means to be a Montrealer today.

Beware of raccoons

Before Montreal became a city of skyscrapers, the Mountain (as Montrealers call Mont Royal) was visible from everywhere along the flat riverfront. Today, modern buildings block the sightlines inland. As I hiked through glass and concrete towers mixed with stores and historic churches, I wondered when I'd finally see it. The street I was on began to gently climb, then, as I turned west, a rock wall studded with trees loomed in my path. I had found the Mountain.

Landscape architect Frederick Law Olmsted (responsible for designing some of the finest parks in North America, including New York City's Central Park) was commissioned to turn the Mountain into a park. Parc du Mont-Royal opened in 1876. It protects almost 500 acres, a permanent and beloved green space in the heart of this city.

On my hike to the summit, I saw a sign warning visitors about the raccoons. On it, a raccoon face was near a hand holding three dots. The universal slashed red circle was over this and the text read: *Ne me touchez pas, ne me nourrissez pas, je suis porteur de maladies!* Now, I know very little French – often struggling to come up with enough French to convey my inability to comprehend it – but I could figure out the meaning here. "Don't touch! Don't feed! Raccoons carry diseases!" People were happily feeding the squirrels, though. There were no squirrel warnings.

I hiked to the Chalet du Mont-Royal. This massive stone and wood structure was built during the Great Depression as a public works project to provide much needed employment. The chalet, with its surrounding stepped and rounded plaza, replaced old pavilions on the site. Frederick G. Todd, Canada's first landscape architect, assisted Olmsted with the plan for Parc du Mont-Royal. Todd said this about the type of structure that should be built on this site:

The mountain itself is so lofty and so ruggedly picturesque, and the views are so grand in their proportions, that any structure erected by man, on top of such a wonderful creation of Nature, must unite itself with, and accentuate these strong natural characteristics, if it is to be truly successful. It must be simple in order not to detract from the grandeur of the views, and it must be picturesque to harmonize with the park.

The chalet embodies Todd's requirements. It fits the park. The stone structure rises out of the stone mountain. The plaza here has the best vantage to look back on the city and river. It is odd to look down on skyscrapers, but the elevated plaza allows this unique vantage point. The wide ribbon of the river mirrors the sky, the rapids swirling like fast-moving clouds on its surface. Montreal had the International and Universal Exposition in 1967 and also hosted the 1976 Olympics. Some structures from these events remain on islands in the river – like the Olympic stadium and an enormous geodesic dome – and are visible from this overlook. In the distance, several small mountains in southern Quebec rose from the river plain, tall enough that low clouds were torn by their peaks.

Inside the Chalet du Mont-Royal, the main hall is enormous and bright because the wall facing the city is lined with French doors topped with windows. The vaulted ceiling is supported by thick wooden beams bracketing the roof to the walls. On each bracket there is a horizontal post supporting a statue of a squirrel with a nut. There are dozens of these statues. All squirrels, no raccoons. Apparently, the squirrel is king of this mountain.

Parc du Mont-Royal is part of life for Montrealers who walk, run, or exercise there, often with their dogs. Many go to feed the squirrel kings. Some climb the 400 steep wooden steps to the mountain top, others take more gentle winding paths through the park. Benches wait alongside for the weary.

Taming the St. Lawrence

In 1825, the rapids were still untamed, but city engineers finally devised a way to get around them: the Lachine Canal. This waterway sliced through the bottom of Montreal Island with a series of locks to allow boats safe transport. Before the canal, goods coming up-river had to be off-loaded at Montreal and warehoused before being transported overland. With the canal, boats and barges could safely circumvent the rapids and continue westward, and the warehousing industry quickly dwindled.

By the 1830s, Montreal was the most populous city in Canada. In the years that followed, Montreal had the busiest Canadian port – even busier than New York City for a time – and was also a major railroad hub. Grain grown in Canada's middle plains was transported here, ground, and then shipped, making Montreal the leading exporting port of flour for decades.

In 1959, the St. Lawrence Seaway opened, making the Lachine Canal unnecessary. The Seaway created a series of new locks and wider channels to circumvent all of the rapids between Montreal and Lake Ontario. Lake freighters and even ocean-going vessels were finally able to safely navigate the full length of the St. Lawrence River.

Today, the historic Lachine canal corridor is being transformed. Old warehouses are being rehabilitated into condos and shops, and dilapidated industrial sites are being erased, making room for new development. A green corridor with paths for pedestrians and bikes runs the length of the canal, and I decided to rent one of the BIXI bikes found all over the city to explore there.

The eastern end of the canal is called the "flour basin" because of the towering silos here once filled with flour. These complexes today are fascinating industrial ruins. One concrete silo was twenty stories tall. Rusting metal machinery capped the edifice. With each rainfall or snowmelt, rust streaks down, staining the concrete. Some other decaying substance causes lighter streaks that mingle with the reddish ones. Nature conspires to create art on these ruins.

I began at the flour-basin end and biked the length of the canal. The paved pathway follows the waterway, often hopping from one side to the other on one of the many bridges. Construction zones punctuated the route where new was replacing old, or old was being remade to new.

I pedaled along, cursing the bike for not having more gears as I struggled to keep my momentum. Reaching the end of the canal, I parked the bike and walked to the river's edge. The St. Lawrence is nearly a mile wide here and frothed with rapids. As I watched the movement of the water, I tried to erase the modern buildings and busy bridges to imagine the river in the years before Cartier's arrival. The river is still mighty today, even though canals and dredging have tamed portions of its flow.

A cormorant paddled near shore. When she saw me, she flew out to the middle of the river and landed. The current swiftly swept her downstream.

Pedaling back toward the flour basin, I found myself enjoying the ride, gliding for long stretches. What I hadn't realized during the first half of my day's ride was that the path was slightly uphill heading west, following the natural rise of the river. The spillways alongside the locks should have tipped me off that the canal was stepping upward. Going back to the east, I felt it. The return ride was easy and fun.

Old Montreal next to new

For my remaining time in this great city, I walked and wandered. This is a perfect city to explore on foot, and, like New York, it doesn't sleep much. Like any great continental city, it is a place for people from all points on the globe to mix and mingle. While French has been the official language of Quebec province since 1977, the people I spoke with were kind about switching to English when I asked. Many times, they would switch mid-sentence when they saw my wide eyes, even before I could put together the phrase: *je ne comprends pas francais.*

In Montreal, I heard the best line from a person on the street asking for money: "All my boyfriends are in jail. Spare some money for bail?" This plea was from a young woman sitting on the grassy yard of a stone church. I burst out laughing. It was pure poetry.

I walked the narrow cobbled streets of Old Montreal, passing churches and statues of heroes long dead. I saw the remains of the original stone walls of the city behind the Hôtel De Ville (Montreal's City Hall). And I toured museums like the Château Ramezay (former home to the city's governor in the 18th century, later used as headquarters for the fur trading business) and Musée Pointe-á-Calliére where the basement is an archeological dig revealing literal layers of history. Walking from the river inland on the Boulevard St. Laurent, I felt history underneath my feet and all around. The storefronts reveal the waves of immigrants landing here. I strolled past Chinatown grocers selling dragon fruit and lychee nuts, butcher shops featuring smoked meats from Eastern Europe, and French cafes.

To satisfy my craving for art, I visited the Musée des Beaux-Arts de Montréal. There, I saw a vibrant Gerhard Richter "squeegee painting" and a magnificent triptych by Joan Mitchell called "View from the Seine." The deep blue slashes across Mitchell's three paintings evoked a mighty river, and I was glad this work had found a home in a great river city like Montreal.

I explored the city piers jutting out into the river. Some are open spaces with parks and monuments, while others have entertainment complexes like the Montreal Science Centre. One even has a skating rink in the winter.

Past the flour basin, a long manmade peninsula pokes out into the river, perpendicular to the piers. Originally constructed to shield the city's waterfront from ice floes drifting downriver, this point was used for Expo 67, and a unique apartment building called Habitat was built here as a pavilion. This structure is a famous example of the Brutalist architecture movement (the term sounds unpleasant, but comes not from the word "brutal" but from the French *béton brut,* or "raw concrete"). This modernist offshoot uses concrete to create fortress-like structures. Habitat was designed by Israeli-Canadian architect Moshe Safdie as his master's thesis while at McGill University in Montreal.

After the Expo, Habitat was converted to apartments. The structure is made of over 350 identical pre-fab concrete forms that are stacked and staggered and rotated, a giant precarious fortress of squared-off Fred Flintstone houses, reaching 12 stories tall in places. In a city with so much rich history, this modern architectural gem was delightfully playful in contrast.

I strolled the city at night, mingling with people speaking not only French and English, but languages from far-flung places. I saw a fountain that spewed water and flame. I ate steak and frites at an elegant French bistro, excellent Chinese food in Chinatown, crepes in Old Montreal, and walked some more.

Montreal is a city of contrasts: old next to new, river flowing around mountain, fountains with water and flames, and a vibrant French-Canadian society swirled with the cultures of the world. The river made this city take root. The impassable rapids, channeling the entire outflow of all five Great Lakes, forced people and goods to stop here. But it is the people, both past and present, that have made Montreal the world-class Great Lakes Basin city it is today.

Miles for Montreal Island:
Bike   Hike
15   29

Thousand Island Region of the St. Lawrence River

After my visit to Montreal, I followed the St. Lawrence back upstream about 150 miles to the Thousand Islands area, hoping to get in a few days of kayaking in this scenic, island-crowded section. But on the first day I planned to kayak, strong winds were blowing and the kayak outfitter cancelled all rentals for the day. Instead, I opted for a boat tour among the islands. The winds were so strong that even the tour boats were delayed on their schedules, and whitecaps frothed the river.

When our small group of windblown people finally boarded the vessel, we settled in for the long cruise to Boldt Island. I had read that there are 1,864 islands in this region of the St. Lawrence River, but on the tour I learned there was now one more. Someone had dumped crushed rock on top of a shallow shoal, and that manmade island increased the number to 1,865.

Some of the islands are in the U.S., some in Canada. The Treaty of Ghent spelled out the terms for ending the War of 1812, including dividing the Thousand Islands between America and British-controlled Canada. This treaty gave the majority of the islands to British Canada, though actual landmass is about equal. Some of these islands are large enough to support sizable permanent communities with schools and stores. Others barely meet the requirements to be counted as an island: an area greater than 1 square foot that is above water level year round, and supporting at least one living tree.

The base of these islands is Precambrian granite. This ancient rock (also called the Canadian Shield) was formed over a billion years ago, and it underpins a vast area of the North American continent, including the St. Lawrence and Great Lakes Basin up to the Canadian Arctic territories circling Hudson Bay. This stone is incredibly erosion resistant. The rounding of the islands by persistent glaciers and flowing water give some indication of the forces wearing away at these rocks for eons. Pink granite is found on several islands in the Thousand Islands area, a prized form of the rock quarried for ornate gravestones and shipped as far away as Chicago.

Raiders, rumrunners, and revolutionaries

As our small boat chugged through the marked channels between the islands, it was clear that the markers were essential to navigation. The wide river was a maze, with so many islands that it was difficult to differentiate between true riverbanks and just another string of islands in the distance. This confusing archipelago has given refuge to raiders, rumrunners, and revolutionaries. It is easy to hide here, and just as easy to flee with the flow of the river when pursued. The idea of a hideout on a river island has long been an image of freedom, of life lived beyond rules of normal society.

Bill Johnston was the first lighthouse keeper on the river. Johnston led a pretty exciting life prior to this posting. During the War of 1812, he captained a gig – a fast rowboat holding six men – to help the Americans against the British. With his gig, Johnston and his men could slip into shallow areas or even carry the lightweight craft across an island to escape patrolling British ships. The islands served as a slippery in-between place, the perfect base for stealthy strikes on the enemy. Johnston spied on the British forces, attacking when he saw an advantage. After the war, he settled in New York, but kept active with a side business smuggling tea and rum across the river to Canada.

Johnston's quarrel with the British didn't diminish after the War of 1812. By the 1830s, anti-British sentiment in Canada generated a revolutionary wave. Johnston joined William Lyon Mackenzie, a former mayor of Toronto, in this uprising. (This proves that Toronto mayors had the "bad boy" image even before recent Mayor Rob Ford.) The rebels successfully captured a steamer, *Sir Robert Peel,* but their men who were skilled in operating such a vessel never arrived. With the steamer drifting downriver with no control, Johnston and his men set it on fire, abandoned the steamer, and fled in their small boats.

Since this raid happened on the American side of the river, both British and American forces pursued the renegade rebels. Although some were captured, sympathetic juries refused to convict them. Johnston evaded capture by hiding in the Thousand Islands, assisted by his daughter who brought him supplies. The rebellion was finally quashed. By 1847 Johnston was living on the right side of the law – a less exciting life, perhaps, as keeper of the light on Rock Island.

Millionaire's Row

We rounded Wellesley Island, the largest on the American side of the zig-zagging, watery international border. It is on Wellesley Island that the Thousand Islands International Bridge has planted a huge tower to support its elevated crossing to the American shore. The bridge span is 150 feet above the river. This height allows even large ocean freighters to slip underneath the steel span as they navigate between the Atlantic and the Great Lakes on the St. Lawrence Seaway.

Something fascinating happens submerged in the river here. The water on the upriver side of the bridge is around 50 feet deep, but the water on the downriver side is five times that depth. In other words, there is an *underwater* waterfall here. With this abrupt change in depth and the narrowing of the river, the current is powerful and confused. The surface of the river roiled and boiled as proof of these forces. There were places where two swirling currents butted up against each other, causing a small standing wave to form.

Many famous and wealthy people built mansions on these islands around the turn of the 20th century, including the Bournes of Singer Sewing Machines, the Pullmans of the train car enterprise, and the Wycoffs of Remington Typewriter Company. There were so many estates here that one stretch of the river was named "Millionaire's Row." The mansions were grand, and the parties thrown on the islands were often epic. I want to give special recognition to Marjorie Bourne for her creativity in island party life during Prohibition. She purchased a second island not far from Dark Island where the immense Singer Castle was located. This second island happened to be in Canadian waters, where alcohol was still legal. When she threw a big party, libations would be rowed across the watery border when no one was looking. Afterward, the empty bottles were tossed gleefully into the river and swept away.

Though there are many mansions here, no one had a grander vision for an island estate than George Boldt. Boldt was born on an island in the Baltic Sea and immigrated to America in 1864 when he was a teenager. In Philadelphia, he began working in kitchens but soon rose to hotel manager. From there, he purchased hotels, then built the largest one Philly had ever seen, the Bellevue-Stratford. When William Waldorf Astor built the Waldorf Hotel in New York, he hired Boldt as proprietor. Boldt helped to merge this property with the Astoria Hotel and managed them together as the famous Waldorf-Astoria. Under Boldt's management, this hotel was the first to develop room service. A management genius, Boldt earned a lavish annual salary of over a million dollars.

In the late 1890s, Boldt bought Heart Island and, with a flair for the literal, had it re-shaped into a heart. He purchased a quarry to source stone for the many buildings he had planned. The grandest of all was the 127-room castle that would serve as the main house. It was to be a gift to his wife, Louise.

As the home was nearing completion in 1904 – over 300 craftsmen were on the island working on the interior of the structure – Louise died suddenly of pneumonia at the age of 42. Boldt sent a telegram instructing the workers to lay down their tools. It is said that Boldt never again set foot on the island.

The property was untended for over 70 years until the Thousand Islands Bridge Authority acquired the island and the nearby yacht house on Wellesley Island. Restoration continues today, with revenues from tours used to continue the work and upkeep of the property.

Shortly after passing underneath the Thousand Islands International Bridge, we docked at Heart Island. I pulled out my passport. Since my boat was from the Canadian side of the river, I had to go through customs (a hut with a border guard) before stepping onto the American island. I walked the perimeter first, taking in the view of the castle from all angles and also stopping in at some of the smaller structures – the powerhouse and the Alster Tower – open to visitors.

Entering the castle through its double wooden doors, I found an enormous entryway with marble floor. A grand staircase flowed from opposite sides of the open second story to merge into a wide, marble staircase. Several stories up, the space was crowned with a stained glass dome.

I smelled wood smoke and was surprised to find a fire burning in the entryway fireplace. The first floor had been finished according to period details, the ballroom being the most recent space to be completed. There was a reception room and a billiard room on this level, along with the dining room, ballroom, library, and Mr. Boldt's office. The second floor had finished bedrooms and bathrooms. While the rooms were furnished with period-appropriate décor, the place smelled new, and the floors were shiny and unworn.

Heading to the uppermost level, I was surprised to find it unfinished and vandalized. The wet plaster walls were broken and crumbling in places, smattered with graffiti from the many years that the castle was untended. Couples wrote their names here, vandals fractured white plaster walls to reveal wooden lath. The floors were wide, rough, substructure boards. Many had gaping knotholes, some of which had been covered over with pieces of tin nailed at the edges.

The contrast between the finished and unfinished parts of the castle was stunning, and gave a unique perspective into the construction of the place. It also revealed the abuse it has endured through the decades. I went outside on the upper level terrace, where there was scaffolding erected on a section where restoration was taking place.

From that high perch, I had a dramatic overlook of the river. When boating earlier in the day among the hundreds of islands, I often felt claustrophobic in the narrow channels. Now, from several stories above, the river view was splendid. A tour boat maneuvered up to the dock, swirling the water behind it. I looked upriver and thought I saw a huge building through the treetops, but then I noticed it was moving. A freighter was slipping through the narrow passage between the island and the riverbank. The ship turned out to be a geared bulker, the *Federal Elbe,* managed by a company based in Montreal. When I researched the vessel later, I discovered it had most recently docked in Belgium and the Netherlands. This "saltie" (the nickname for ocean-going vessels) looked too big to navigate the Thousand Islands portion of the river, but there it was, gliding smoothly by Heart Island.

I later found out that Boldt Castle wasn't the only grand edifice in these islands associated with an untimely death. When William O. Wyckoff finished his mansion on Carlton Island in 1893, he moved in and tucked himself in for a good night's sleep in his new summer home. Wyckoff never woke again. Today, his mansion still occupies a peninsula of Carlton Island, deteriorating into ruins. It is for sale at around a half million dollars.

The sun descended as we all returned to the tour boat. The sky turned golden, backlighting the castle as we pulled away from Heart Island. Motorboats sped past us, rushing up and down the river to reach their home docks before sunset. On open stretches, the golden red sunlight shone in a broad streak on the water, swirling like molten fire afloat on the river.

An uncommon woman

After touring Heart Island, I wanted to take a longer hike on a larger island. I drove over the Thousand Islands International Bridge from the Canadian side of the river, hopping onto Hill Island for a short stretch, then another short hop over to Wellesley Island. Even though I was still on the river, I had crossed the international border and had to stop and show my passport.

Wellesley Island has a large state park with trails. My walk began skirting Eel Bay, a large shallow bay on the west side of the island, named for the American Eels that were once abundant here. The species is now rare due to over-harvesting and declining habitat. There is still some good fishing here, though, especially for yellow perch and bullhead.

I hiked the winding paths through the open woodlands with exposed mounds of granite. I found a hickory tussock moth caterpillar climbing on one of these outcroppings. This mostly white caterpillar has decorative black dots down the middle of its back and tufts of white bristles along the edges. Some spiky, longer bristles extend out from each end. These longer barbs are connected to glands that will excrete a mild irritant if you disturb them. I didn't disturb them.

On the trail, a sign pointed to a side path leading to two geologic formations called potholes. I hiked to the water's edge and found two large holes drilled into the granite slab by water swirling and wearing away at the stone over time. One was 6 feet deep, and the larger one 15 feet deep. I had seen these formations in limestone before, but never in granite. The force needed to carve granite is much greater, since this stone is up to 40 times less porous than limestone. The formation of these potholes was caused by the whirlpool action of water swirling small chunks of granite in a small depression in the stone. Stone-on-stone action grinds away until it forms the deep, polished cavity – the pothole – in the granite slab.

Later, I found a historic photo that helps confirm this theory. It shows a woman standing in a pothole holding a rounded and smoothed rock that she has lifted from the bottom. She was not any woman passing by, though. The woman in the photo was Minna Anthony Common, an extraordinary naturalist who grew up spending her summers on Wellesley Island. She became a regional expert on the flowers and fauna here. For twenty-five years, Common wrote and illustrated a twice-weekly nature article for New York's *Watertown Daily Times*. Other newspapers and prominent magazines also published her work. She left her name – literally – on the island, as the nature center in the park is named for her.

A different kind of walking stick

The day was warm, and each time the trail got close to the calm water, I wanted to sit down with my back against a tree and look out at the river. So, finally I did. I found a vantage about ten feet above the river with a slanted tree. A patch of thick grass grew at its base. I sat.

The water was so clear that I could see rocks and water plants on the bottom of the bay. There were smaller islands nearby, and the channels in between were shallow enough to slow the few boats that passed. I could hear them throttle down to carefully navigate the passage, barely causing a ripple. Mostly, the water was calm and quiet.

It was too calm for me. I am used to much larger bodies of water with waves and currents or at least a constant, gentle sloshing.

When I stood up, I noticed a small stick had fallen onto my shoulder. When I went to brush it off, it climbed onto my hand. It was a walking stick. This is a cleverly designed bug that is fairly common, but it is difficult to spot because it does such a great job of looking like a stick. As it crawled up my forearm, I noticed that the long body bulged slightly where the pairs of legs attached. The body was light tan. The front legs were green like new shoots, but the middle and back legs were striped tan and brown like a shadow had fallen across them. Each foot ended in a series of delicate hooks that adhered to my skin. The small head was the attachment point for two antennae that were almost as long as the insect's body. This creature is a master of camouflage.

When it reached my shoulder once again, I carefully transferred it back onto the tree against which I had rested.

Paddling the Frontenac Arch

I finally got out on the river in a kayak on my last day in the region. Each fall, a group in Brockville has a "Paddle the Arch" kayaking day on the river. "The arch" refers to the Frontenac Arch, a geologic ridge of granite that rests between Montreal and Toronto, joining the Canadian Shield to the eastern Adirondack Mountains. A billion years ago, this formation, along with the Canadian Shield, was a rugged mountain range. Over those billion years, the mountains have been worn away, leaving only their bases in the landscape today. These granite hilltops form the islands in the river.

With the meeting of the geological formations and the overlapping growth zones, this area has incredible biodiversity. In 2002, the arch area was designated a World Biosphere Reserve by the United Nations Educational, Scientific and Cultural Organization (UNESCO). This designation signifies the global significance of the region. National Geographic also identified the area as a place of significant "geotourism," a term created to denote the connection of tourism with the geographical character of a place, where the connection "should sustain or enhance the environment, culture, aesthetics, heritage, and well-being of its residents." The Frontenac Arch was the ninth region in the world to get this recognition.

I met up with the group at a riverside park. Thousand Islands Kayaking Company brought the equipment for the paddle, along with two of their guides. The mayor of Brockville, Dave Henderson, joined the group. It turns out that the city of Brockville owns 16 of the islands here and maintains them for recreation. As the sun climbed into the sky, our group of about a dozen people got into kayaks and paddled upriver.

The St. Lawrence River narrows to less than a mile near Brockville, so the American side of the river was easily visible. While this seemed like a placid stretch to paddle solo, the main shipping channel goes through the narrows, so I preferred to paddle with an experienced group that was used to dealing with freighters slipping by their little kayaks. This region also draws many boaters, and if you're going to be in a low-profile kayak with zippy speedboats nearby, it's safest to be in a flotilla.

Ice paddling

The day was gorgeous, in the upper 70s and calm, the sky nearly cloudless. One local man, Murray Golledge, joined the group. He had been building and paddling kayaks out of Brockville for decades, and he came along to tell stories of the river. When we paddled into a sheltered cove, Golledge told us about a winter's paddle he had taken there a few years ago. At the head of the cove, he discovered a group of boys playing hockey where the ice was thick. But where he was paddling, the ice was thin and cracked into shards as he advanced. The boys stopped their game to watch him cut an arc in the ice.

One of the women in the group said she owned a cottage on one of the islands. I asked her what was special about having it on an island versus the riverbank. "I like that I can paddle all the way around it," she said.

"So your island is completely knowable?" I offered.

She smiled. "That's it. Exactly."

Because islands are outlined by water and self-contained, they are a place apart from normal life. And with these plentiful small islands, some people own a personal oasis with water rushing by, a separate land made distinct by the river.

Where the current strengthened, Golledge guided us to stay in the eddies where the paddling was easier. It was clear that he knew the river intimately. Some of the islands had sheer faces of granite over two stories tall that fell straight down into the water. We passed by islands named Harvey, Chubb, Stovin, and Snake, along with many smaller, unnamed islands. In one cove, we gathered our flotilla to look down at a submerged ship, its timbers furry with algae. Later in the day, we passed a boat filled with diving gear that was anchored above another sunken vessel.

We ate lunch on Stovin Island, then paddled back to Brockville. Our bevy of colorful kayaks was festive on the deep blue water of the mighty river. It was wonderful to be out on top of the water, to feel the river moving beneath my craft, to paddle hard against the current streaming between the islands.

The water of the five Great Lakes eventually flows down the St. Lawrence, and as I slipped my paddle into the current and pulled, time after time, I thought about where the water beneath my kayak had been in the past decades. Some of the water, surely, had been in the wilds of Lake Superior. Some droplets had helped to float a freighter in Lake Michigan. Some had slapped against limestone shoals in Lake Huron. Some had surrounded schools of walleye near the Lake Erie Islands. And all of this river's water, coming together in a roiling surge, had recently tumbled over Niagara Falls and rushed to Lake Ontario.

Miles for Thousand Islands:

Hike	Kayak	Ferry/powered boat
5	9	34

Toronto Island, Ontario

Are you going to Scarborough . . . Bluffs?

The final group of islands I explored for this section was in Lake Ontario near the city of Toronto. In order to understand this collection of sandy islands (locals refer to the islands in the singular, "Toronto Island"), we must first look at a fascinating area of Toronto's shoreline called Scarborough Bluffs.

During my second 1,000-mile adventure, I had explored much of Lake Ontario's northern edge. I had begun near the mouth of the St. Lawrence and hiked nearly 150 miles west into downtown Toronto. When I hiked into the Scarborough Bluffs area with its almost 300-foot tall earthen pinnacles, deep ravines, and high overlooks out onto the lake, it was like I had hiked into another world. These weren't the massive perched sand dunes or even limestone or sandstone bluffs that I had seen on the other Great Lakes. These were sand mixed with clay in compressed layers stretching almost ten miles along Toronto's eastern shoreline.

The Scarborough Bluffs have been slowly eroding. The edge abutting the lake has been sliced open, and no vegetation grows on the almost vertical faces of the bluffs. Rain and waves and many creeks cutting steep ravines through this formation wash sand into the lake, and currents swirl it offshore from Toronto.

Centuries ago, a large sandbar had formed from this flow of sand into the lake creating a natural harbor. John Graves Simcoe, the first Lieutenant Governor of Upper Canada, liked the look of the sheltering harbor and settled here in 1793, naming the new city York (which evolved into the city of Toronto). It was his wife, Elizabeth, who named the nearby bluffs after the white limestone cliffs in Scarborough, England.

If you take a boat out onto Lake Ontario and look back at the exposed faces of these bluffs, you'll see horizontal stripes denoting the various sedimentary layers that stacked up in the past. Here scientists can delve into the complete record of the ice age. This area doesn't just contain layers from the most recent encroachment of the Laurentide ice sheet (85,000 to 10,000 years ago), but as far back as the Illinoian ice sheet that covered the area around 135,000 years ago. This oldest layer holds the fossil record of the creatures that thrived here during periods when the ice retreated for a time. Excavations have exposed the bones of bison, moose, mammoth, and bear that once roamed here. The fossilized bones of giant beaver have also been recovered. You'd have to glue about ten modern beavers together to equal one of these giants. They weighed over 200 pounds, and their front teeth were six inches long.

My interest was in islands, not hills, but the erosion of these Scarborough Bluffs was the foundational ingredient for the genesis of Toronto Island.

The islands offshore from Toronto are some of the youngest islands in the Great Lakes Basin, formed after the retreat of the continental ice sheets. And they are rather dynamic because they are based on shifting sand. In fact, this landform was not an island but was attached to the mainland until the mid-1800s, when a strong storm severed it from Toronto's shoreline.

This peninsula that evolved into an island was an important landmark to native peoples along the lakeshore. Explorers, fur traders, and missionaries also used this sandbar as a navigational marker as they paddled or sailed Lake Ontario. Natives in the area – members of the Huron tribe, followed later by the Mississaugas – hunted this sand spit and fished the harbor and inlets between the islands. The Mississaugas in particular were known to consider the area as a special place, one that could bring healing to the sick.

Navigating the harbor was tricky, so in 1809 a lighthouse was constructed on the island's southwest corner. Soon, the lighthouse keeper was joined by a handful of fishermen and their families who came to live on the islands. Even with the lighthouse guiding ships in the area, though, many wrecks still occurred here.

A hero born from tragedy

In 1862, William Ward was just fourteen years old when he took his five younger sisters onto Toronto Bay for a sail. His father had warned him to stay on the island that day because the wind was so strong, but William was confident in his sailing skills and went anyway. His youngest sister was only four years old when she climbed into the little sailboat. Unfortunately, as they were making the final turn to return to the island, the rigging became tangled and the sailboat capsized.

The girls wore dresses made of heavy cloth, which weighted them down in the water. Somehow William righted the boat and had pulled all of his sisters back into it when the wind caught the sails again, rolling the small craft a second time.

Only William survived that day. Four of the little girls' bodies were laid out for several days while the search continued for the fifth. When she was finally found, all five girls were laid to rest.

During the remainder of his life, William Ward dedicated himself to pulling people from the raging and often icy waters of the bay or lake, often at great peril to himself. The first opportunity arose in 1868 when the *Jane Anne Marsh* went aground at night in a blinding snowstorm. The accident wasn't discovered until the next day. Ward teamed up with Robert Berry – another islander and also a champion boxer and rower – to row a skiff out to the stranded vessel. The lake was so wild that the skiff capsized several times on the way out to the steamer. The crew had been out on the lake so long that the men gripping the mast for dear life had several inches of ice built up on their clothing. Ward and Berry used loose pieces of cordwood from the steamer to strike the ice from the men, freeing them. Since only two survivors could be rowed back at a time, the heroic men had to make many trips to the doomed vessel. They saved every soul on board.

Ward was later presented with Britain's highest honor for bravery – the Royal Humane Society's gold medal – for saving everyone from another foundering ship, the schooner *Olive Branch*. Ward also received as a gift a lifesaving boat that he captained and crewed for thirty years. Over his lifetime he was credited with saving over 150 people from certain death in these waters, Ward's generous penance for his inability to save his little sisters.

An oasis

In the mid-1800s, small hotels were built to encourage more people to enjoy this outpost from city life. In April of 1858, though, one of the hotels was swept away when the peninsula was separated from the mainland in a storm, permanently "islanding" the landform. A month later, the new channel was wide and deep enough to allow small boats safe passage.

Another fascinating person shaped by the islands was Ned Hanlan. The western end of the island, Hanlan's Point, bears his name today. Hanlan was an expert rower, having grown up on the islands where rowing was a primary form of transportation. He began competing in professional sculling matches and was soon Canada's first internationally famous athlete. He was one of the first rowers to adopt the sliding seat in a sculling boat, and he perfected its use. During his career, he won 300 consecutive races and was the singles sculling champion of the world four years running. He was so much better than everyone else that he often took a break during a race – even to the extent of dramatically faking a seizure – allowing the competition to catch up. He'd then smile and take off like a shot, beating everyone to the finish. In one race, he was so far ahead that he had time to cross the finish line, then back up a bit and cross it a second time, effectively beating his opponents twice.

In 1880, Hanlan was given a lease to build a hotel on the islands. A nearby amusement park featured a diving horse, an attraction that drew crowds in this era. William "Doc" Carver came up with the idea, according to legend, when he was crossing a bridge on his horse, and the wooden bridge began to come apart underneath them. His horse leapt to the water below, and they both miraculously survived the plunge.

Carver trained a few more horses to dive and promoted them as attractions. There were several locations where people would pay up to 50 cents to watch a horse jump from an elevated platform into water. The steel pier in Atlantic City had a diving horse for many years, usually doing the stunt with a woman rider on its back. One of these women, Sonora Webster, was on a horse that stumbled on its takeoff, causing an uncontrolled dive. Webster hit the water with her eyes open, and her retinas detached, blinding her. Astoundingly, she continued to dive with the horse even after that, when she could no longer see.

While most diving horses had riders, the one on Hanlan's Point jumped solo. I found a photo of the white horse that catches it in mid-air a split second before it enters the water. The horse has great diving form: nose down, front legs bent, rear legs and tail extended behind it. While the other diving horses plunged into a pool of water, the Toronto Island horse vaulted from a platform about forty feet high into the channel and had to swim back to the island after each performance.

Today, a pony named Lightning in Lake George, New York, claims to be the only diving horse in the country. Lightning "dives" into a pool from a height of about ten feet. It's more of a jump than a dive, and he's more of a pony than a horse. After swimming across the pool and climbing out using a ramp, Lightning is rewarded with a bucket of oats.

Chosen by the island

As more people visited the islands, many of them decided they wanted to live there. Some wanted to spend the mild months as islanders, others felt chosen by the watery outpost and desired to make it their permanent home. By the late 1940s, several thousand people had made the leap to live on the island, many of them fleeing overcrowded Toronto. A great mix of people gathered there, from Toronto's upper crust living in huge summer homes to a tent community of poorer people during the warm months. Many artists, writers, and poets relocated there permanently. Toronto's society could be stuffy, and the island promised more freedom of thought and expression, and the island lifestyle of a relaxed, interconnected community.

In the 1970s, the city of Toronto stopped renewing leases for island residents with the goal of transitioning the entire outpost to parks and recreation. The communities on Hanlan's Point and Centre Island were quickly erased, but the remaining neighborhoods on Algonquin and Ward's Island organized and resisted removal. After a decade of battles in court and a tense standoff between the sheriff holding eviction notices and residents blocking bridge access to their communities, the remaining islanders were finally permitted to stay.

Pink bike on a green, green island

Today, Toronto Island Park is a short ferry ride from the docks on Bay Street. I walked through downtown Toronto to the water's edge and bought a ticket for the ferry. Though the ride to the island was smooth and quick, that disconnecting glide over the waters of Toronto Harbour allowed the friction of city life to dissipate.

When the ferry docked, everyone lined up to disembark – many with bikes or strollers and kids – into a verdant and calm world afloat on the lake. There are no cars allowed on the islands, so the pace is gentle and human. The tension that one must maintain to move safely through hectic city streets falls away here.

I began walking the winding, paved paths. There are restaurants, marinas, open park spaces filled with mature trees, and an amusement park scaled for little kids. Bridges hop over waterways to smaller islands in between the larger ones. In all, eleven islands nestle together, some too small to have names.

Some of the most impressive trees were willows, and they gave a gentle grace to the island setting. I found the bike rental and hopped on the one-speed, fat-tired, pink bike. Since it was past the summer season and a weekday, there was only a scattering of people dispersed across the hundreds of island acres. I cruised the long boardwalk on the Lake Ontario side and didn't see a single person the entire way. Gentle, blue-green waves splashed against the boardwalk's retaining wall.

On the other side of the island, I was struck by the gorgeous views of the Toronto skyline. Because the waterfront has been built up over time, it's easy to forget that the lake splashes at the edge of this great city. In comparison, Chicago has preserved more of its lakeshore for public and pedestrian access, so the presence of Lake Michigan is more palpable there. Here, Toronto Island has the best perspective to appreciate that Toronto is a city with a watery edge.

I rode the pink bike all over the islands, past the amusement park and petting zoo, through the neighborhood on Ward's Island with its funky houses and overgrown hedges, along the paths tracing the edges of the islands where I could look past the shipping docks and up the shoreline to the east. I passed the beaches, deserted for the season. There is a "clothing optional" beach at Hanlan's Point, another indication that life often has different rules out on an island.

Miles for Toronto Island:

Bike	Hike	Ferry/powered boat
5	7	3

LAKE ERIE ISLANDS

Surprisingly, the other four Great Lakes were seen by Europeans some decades before they knew about the existence of the fifth lake, Lake Erie. This lake is named after a tribe of native people, the Erie Tribe, meaning "long tail" or "cat people," a probable reference to the cougars that once inhabited the area. The fierce Iroquois wiped out this tribe, and it was the reputation of the Iroquois that made European explorers avoid the southern Great Lakes Basin region. It wasn't until 1669 that Louis Joliet made the first journey to these waters.

Lake Erie's islands are grouped in the western quarter of the lake. There are about 20 here, poking out of this shallowest Great Lake. The international boundary line bisects Lake Erie east to west, dividing this archipelago almost exactly in half between America and Canada. Canada claimed the largest, Pelee Island, and Ohio got the grouping near its shores. The largest here is Kelleys Island. These islands are the high points in a ridge of

Devonian Era limestone that runs vertically through Lake Erie, roughly on a line between Port Clinton, Ohio, and Leamington, Ontario.

Western Lake Erie is a boater's delight. The lack of sandy beaches and prevalence of lush wetlands on the shoreline necessitates that people get out on the lake to enjoy it. Fortunately, the islands are near to the shore and have recreational opportunities like hotels, restaurants, bars, historic sites and interesting geologic features. Rich fishing waters surround these islands. Even during the middle of winter, fishing continues through holes drilled in the ice to catch the abundant and delicious walleye.

For this adventure, I explored some of the islands off the northern shore of Ohio and one tucked inside Sandusky Bay. I also took part in the largest naval battle reenactment ever done in America, commemorating the Battle of Lake Erie.

Johnson's Island,
Sandusky Bay, Ohio

Johnson's Island is about a half mile from the open waters of Lake Erie, situated behind a peninsula in Sandusky Bay. This island has a history tied to the Civil War, and a connection to my family, as I have cousins who own a summer cabin there.

The first owner of the 275-acre island was Epaproditus Bull, so it was first named Bull Island. Which I think was a missed opportunity. If your first name is Epaproditus, you might want to slap that name on your island. Bull's family abandon the island because of attacks by Native Americans at the onset of the War of 1812. Forty years later, Leonard B. Johnson bought the island, renaming it Johnson's Island.

Exile, isolation, imprisonment

Throughout history, islands have been places of isolation and seclusion. Sometimes, this is forced: a matter of exile and imprisonment. It took two islands to hold Napoleon: he was exiled to the first, Elba, in 1814, a pleasant island in the Mediterranean. He was allowed a personal escort of 1,000 men, a household staff, and was even given the title Emperor of Elba, ruling over its 110,000 people. But Napoleon was a bit of a, well, "Napoleon," and it was not long before he returned to the mainland to gather an army once again. Soon recaptured, he was exiled again, this time to the more remote and desolate island of Saint Helena in the South Atlantic – "questa piedra maladetta – this cursed rock" – where he died.

Lepers were similarly shipped off in forced exile to the Hawaiian Island of Molokai, a colony established in 1866 that persisted for over a century. On the American west coast, dangerous prisoners were ferried to Alcatraz just a mile and a half from shore in San Francisco Bay, a high-security federal prison from 1933 to 1963 known as "The Rock," home to felons like Al Capone, "Machine Gun" Kelly, and Whitey Bulger. Societies have long "islanded" such individuals deemed unfit to dwell with the rest of their law-abiding citizens.

Johnson's Island was similarly chosen as an ideal location for an island prison. Early in the Civil War it became clear that the bloody conflict would not be easily ended, so sites were scouted to build prisons to hold captured Confederate soldiers and officers. It was thought that these should be far away from battle lines to discourage raids attempting to free the prisoners. In 1861, the Federal government leased forty acres of Johnson's Island in Sandusky Bay and built a prison camp to hold captured Confederate officers. Several features made this a good place for the prison: the island was easily re-supplied (unlike islands farther offshore that might be cut off in the winter). The prisoners could be transported efficiently by rail to the nearby city of Sandusky and then ferried to the island. And, foremost in the minds of the planners, escape was less likely from a prison surrounded by water.

The island stockade was built to hold 3,000 prisoners, and more than 9,000 captured soldiers spent time interred there at one time or another throughout the war. The 128th Ohio Volunteer Infantry helped secure the prison. One unit of this group was called the "Gray Beard Brigade," made up of octogenarians who had long, gray beards. There were a number of attempted and several successful escapes from the prison, which may have been encouraged by the advanced age of the guards.

The captured officers – including fifteen Confederate generals during the war – were treated well on Johnson's Island early in the war. They ate pretty much the same food as the guards, though prisoners got the lesser cuts of meat. There was even a store where prisoners could buy extra food and supplies if their families sent money. As the war dragged on, though, stories about the horrific conditions in southern POW camps like Andersonville reached the north. In retaliation, rations were cut on Johnson's Island and the store was closed.

Horace Carpenter, a Confederate officer, wrote about his 16 months interred on the island. The decline in rations happened during his stay, and he noted that the once-plentiful rats slowly disappeared as the prisoners ate them. He said he was never lucky enough to kill one, though not for lack of trying. Carpenter said the bunkhouses were comfortable in the summer since they allowed a breeze to pass through, but in the winter they offered little protection from the bitter cold. Carpenter slept on the upper level of the bunk beds. During the winter, he often awoke to find a layer of snow covering his thin blanket.

In January of 1864, five prisoners plotted to escape the camp during a bitterly cold night when the temperatures plunged to 26 degrees below zero. It was so cold that oil in lanterns placed along the perimeter of camp would not ignite. The guards did not stand watch that night. The captives scaled the 14-foot fence and scurried across the ice, but two of the men, nearly frozen, ended up giving themselves up. The other escapees reached Port Clinton, made off with a couple of draft horses, and rode to Detroit. There, they found the Detroit River flowing with large slabs of ice. Abandoning the horses, they made the treacherous crossing by jumping across the ice floes. After three days on the run, they found safety in Canada.

Canada played a strange role during the Civil War. The citizens were anti-slavery and would welcome and shelter escaped slaves. At the same time, the country was still under British rule, and Britain bought much of the cotton exported from the South. Naturally, they backed the South in the war. So if Confederate soldiers escaped a POW camp and made it to Canada, they, too, would be welcomed, just like the runaway slaves.

The Confederate Cemetery

Today, the only indication that there was once a Civil War prison on Johnson's Island is the cemetery. Winters at this latitude were especially hard on men from the South. Some of the prisoners had never seen snow before their time on Johnson's Island. With harsh winters and so many men packed in tight quarters, diseases easily spread. Most of the men buried there died of pneumonia.

The island has been a quiet vacation community since the 1970s. Prior to that, it had a brief heyday as a recreation spot, before the nearby Cedar Point Amusement Park prevailed as the star attraction in the area. Today, Johnson's Island is a gated community, but visitors who wish to see the historic graveyard can access the island via a causeway.

I visited my cousin Gina's cabin on the island on Memorial Day. We went down to the nearby Lake Erie Beach where some brave people splashed in the still frigid water. The rest of us wisely enjoyed the sunny day on the sand.

After dinner, I walked around the island with a small group. Several deer in a stand of trees watched us pass by. Johnson's Island today is an island retreat, a pleasant summer place where families have cabins that are filled with memories of annual getaways. Gina and her husband, Ted, had assembled their log cabin from a kit. It was spacious with an upper loft area with room enough for their four kids and their friends, sleeping on sets of built-in bunk beds.

Most houses on the island were similarly "cottagey," but as we approached an old quarry, the cabins were replaced by massive homes. A channel cut into the island allows boats to get in and out from the quarry lake with its steep, limestone walls, to Sandusky Bay and Lake Erie. Mansions ringing the interior lake had private docks for their large boats. Metal staircases bolted into the limestone at the bottom spiraled their way to the houses on the top.

"The developer wanted to put restaurants and bars here," Gina said, "but that wasn't what most people wanted, so we fought it."

The mansions had a different feel from the cozy cottages found else-where on the island. I've seen this type of evolution of waterfront property during my hikes. There is only so much land with water access, and over time, that land becomes more valuable, and the most desirable places become more restricted and exclusive.

Islanded

We soon reached the cemetery on the north end of the island. It was sur-rounded with a low, wrought iron fence. Mature trees shaded the 206 marked graves. Most of the white Georgia marble headstones were inscribed with the name, age, regiment and company of the captured soldier. If remains were unidentified, the white marker was simply engraved with the word "UNKNOWN." Modern tools like ground-penetrating radar have been used to locate additional unmarked remains, bringing the total number interred here to 267.

The tombstones line up in seven long rows stretching toward the water. A small, American flag was stuck in the ground near each headstone for Memorial Day. Near the water, large slabs of granite are inscribed with the story of the prison.

A bronze statue of a Confederate soldier stands atop a stone pedestal. It was placed here in 1910, and hundreds of people from both the North and South traveled to Johnson's Island for its dedication. This was 45 years after the end of the Civil War, and many of the men in attendance were veterans of that conflict, including George Washington Gordon from Tennessee, who was one of the youngest brigadier generals in the Confederate army. He was wounded and captured at the Battle of Franklin in November of 1864 and spent the rest of the war as a POW on Johnson's Island. Gordon, who in 1910 was one of Tennessee's Representatives in Congress, gave a speech on Johnson's Island the day the statue was dedicated. His feelings of returning to the site of the island prison, now as a representative of the reunited country, were surely complex.

The statue soldier carries a musket in his right hand. The bayonet is fixed. His left hand is raised to shield his eyes as he looks out over the water. The men held here were cut off from their homes, their families, from most of their comrades, from the mainland, from the south.

Johnson's Island had utterly islanded them.

We strolled the site quietly, respectfully, for those men never returned.

Miles for Johnson's Island:
Hike
3

Kelleys Island, Ohio

Messages from the past

Kelleys Island is the largest of the American Lake Erie Islands, and the one closest to shore. Car ferries loop out to both Kelleys Island and nearby South Bass Island until late in the year when the lake freezes. These ferries make the islands convenient vacation destinations.

The first thing I noticed when the ferry entered the harbor on Kelleys Island was a slab of limestone on the shoreline. An open structure with a roof sheltered the rock. After the ferry docked, I walked along the curve of the harbor to this unique piece of Native American history: Inscription Rock.

The surface of the thick slab of limestone measures around 600 square feet. Native Americans carved pictographs into the surface of the rock. Estimates suggest the stone was inscribed in the early- to mid-1600s. Today, the messages are faded; the rock has worn away over the centuries.

Nearly two hundred years ago, the Bureau of Indian Affairs charged Captain Seth Eastman with documenting this rock and the location of Native American villages and burial mounds in the region. His sketch of Inscription Rock as he saw it is reproduced on a bronze plaque on site to help visitors pick out the messages nearly erased by time. His drawing shows human and animal figures; some are arranged in little scenes with wavy lines conveying the concept of water.

Historians think this rock was a kind of message board used by Native Americans to pass along information about hunting and fishing or signifying where their travels would take them next. At a time where the water was the best way to travel in the region, islands were convenient places to stop and resupply. Native American bands were often nomadic, flowing with the seasons to familiar spots where food was most accessible. They would have fished here during the same mild months that vacationers today are ferried to this island retreat.

I continued hiking west along the lakefront road curving with the edge of the island. On this side of Kelleys, I could look out over the few miles of Lake Erie to South Bass and clearly see the Perry's Victory and International Peace Memorial sticking up from that nearby island. This massive Doric column is visible even from the mainland on clear days.

Walking near the northwestern-most part of the island, I passed the Lafarge limestone quarry. Limestone has been mined on Kelleys Island for most of the past 200 years. The stone here was prized as superior to other limestone on the market in the 1800s. Early on, it was mostly used for building structures like many of the breakwalls around Cleveland and Cedar Point. One of the massive shipping locks in Sault Ste. Marie, Michigan, was constructed with this stone. Later on, much of the quarried stone was shipped for use in the great iron smelters in the Great Lakes Basin. Limestone is mixed in the smelting process with molten iron ore, where it binds to impurities, separating them out. The resulting compound – the limestone mixed with impurities – is called slag, and it is sometimes discarded, but other times is ground up and used in the production of cement.

The grooves of the glaciers

Since Kelleys is an island vacation destination, the few cars that passed me drove slowly, taking in the scenery. At the docks, visitors can rent bikes or golf carts. Many leave their cars on the mainland and use these island transports. This made for a leisurely hike along the roadside flanked by woods as I headed to the north side of the island. Soon, I was at the site I most wanted to see: Glacial Grooves State Memorial.

I had often seen distinct glacial scrapes in rocky areas where I'd hiked on my earlier adventures around the Great Lakes, but the grooves on Kelleys Island are famous for being some of the most pronounced and easily accessible in the world. I have a friend who lives nearby on the shores of Lake Erie on the mainland. She once met a French geologist on a cruise who –

when learning she was from Ohio – asked if she had ever been to Kelleys Island. She explained that it was only a few miles from her house and, of course, she had been there many times. He was quite pleased, and began a conversation about the wonderful glacial grooves. My friend was delighted that someone living on the other side of the world would know so much about her little island retreat in Lake Erie.

The prominent grooves once ran several miles on the island, but today only a small portion is evident and protected. Much of the rest was destroyed by mining activity. How distinct are these grooves? In places, they are an amazing 15 feet deep. They are so remarkable here because the glaciers grinding their way over the terrain were studded with rocks from farther north, increasing their efficiency at carving away the limestone. The ice sheets easily moved over nearby soft shale deposits, so they gained power and speed as they scoured the Lake Erie Islands.

Glacial Grooves State Memorial protects just over three acres of the island. Much of this area was covered with glacial till deposited by the retreating glaciers. In the early 1970s, a large section was revealed by carefully removing these deposits. Today, a 400-foot-long stretch is exposed, around 25 feet wide. It is a long, gouged-out slab of limestone, and on it, the glaciers and meltwater from their eventual retreat carved beautiful patterns into the stone. In places it resembles huge columns lying side-by-side in the scooped-out site. In others, the patterns look like a master craftsman carved elaborate, swirling undulations in the stone.

For many years, these features were not protected. As I walked around the site, dozens of other people circulated in a slow route around the top of the fenced-off grooves, looking down at the stone shaped by towering slabs of ice.

I overheard the family in front of me talking:

Grandma to her daughter: Remember when we came here when you were little?

Daughter: We climbed all over these rocks.

Grandma: (disappointed) Now it's all fenced off.

Young Granddaughter: Can I climb down there?

Daughter: No. I'm so sorry, honey. They put up a fence.

I heard another conversation taking place on the other side of the grooves:

Teenaged Granddaughter: Why is this here?

Grandpa: Glaciers.

Teenaged Granddaughter: What? When?

Grandpa: Long time ago?

Teenaged Granddaughter: When? How did they do this? I don't understand.

Grandpa wanders away from granddaughter without answering.

The scientist in me wanted to jump into these conversations, but it was interesting to let them play out. Would the first group recognize the importance of protecting this site? Would the grandpa in the second group be able to explain how this area was once under a towering slab of ice grinding away at this stone?

I was surprised to discover that many of the natural wonders or historic sites I encountered on the Lake Erie islands had lacked protection for so long or were privately held instead of the land having been conferred to the state. Here, decades of visitors had scampered over and chipped away at these remarkable glacial grooves before the fence was erected. And I came across a photo of Inscription Rock from the early 1900s where three men dressed in suits and hats sat on the face of the rock.

On my hike back to the dock, I cut into the interior to hike around the North Pond State Nature Preserve, then the interior quarry. The nature preserve had a loop of boardwalk weaving through the wetland site. The pond here actually merges with Lake Erie when the barrier beach periodically opens, then becomes an inland pond again when it closes. The movement of the beach depends on the wave action of the lake and precipitation levels. It's a dynamic system, which makes it an area of great biodiversity.

The interior quarry had a pleasant system of trails. I hiked a loop around Horseshoe Lake, which is the deep portion of the quarry now filled with water. The day had warmed up considerably, and on the occasional welcome breeze, I thought I heard the cadence of a marching band. I'm prone to heatstroke, so I drank more water and took a rest break.

But as I resumed my walk, I still heard the thumping drums and brassy overture of a marching band. I then remembered that the festivities for the reenactment of the Battle of Lake Erie were beginning. Sure enough, the eminent Ohio State Marching Band was giving a concert on the island. The drums and brass floating over the rubble of the abandoned limestone quarry were an odd echo of the past, a tribute to the military clash of the War of 1812 in which Lake Erie played such a central role. The outcome of this war would ever divide the Great Lakes between the two bordering countries sharing its shorelines.

Miles for Kelleys Island:

Hike	Ferry
11	6

South Bass Island, Ohio

The Island Snake Lady

The most famous Lake Erie Island is probably South Bass. It was here in the harbor of this island – called Put-in-Bay – that Commodore Perry gathered his ships before launching out to meet the British fleet in the Battle of Lake Erie. This naval clash resulted in an unexpected win for the Americans during the War of 1812.

Soon after my visit to Kelleys, I took the ferry to South Bass to meet with the Island Snake Lady. South Bass is a summer destination, and the ferry was jammed with people ready to enjoy their vacation, while I had a strange, snake-centric agenda.

I wanted to explore the Perry Victory and International Peace Memorial, the two caves on the island, the town of Put-in-Bay, and, of course, meet the Island Snake Lady, Kristin Stanford. The day I arrived on the island was going to be hot, so I rented a bike to cover more ground without getting heatstroke.

South Bass (many people refer to the island as Put-in-Bay, so there are two terms for the same island) is a place, like Kelleys, where people can rent a golf cart or a bike, or they can bring their car over on the ferry. There is more vehicular traffic on South Bass, but the main roads have wide bike lanes, so riding or hiking is quite safe.

When I got to the Snake Lady's lab, she was out, so I toured the nearby fish hatchery. This historic hatchery has been transformed into an informational site about the waters surrounding the island. It is worth a visit.

Fifty years ago, Lake Erie was declared "dead." This was the hatchery that raised the fish to re-stock Lake Erie and revive the fish population, so that now it is self-sustaining. If you talk to people fishing this Great Lake, they'll tell you about the walleye, a sport fish that's excellent to eat. I've met some fishermen who will toss back anything they catch but the walleye, including salmon.

I spoke to Jason, one of the workers at the hatchery, who told me about the walleye. "Back in 2003 we had a mega-hatch. There were around 80 million that year," he said. "The numbers have stabilized at around 17 million now."

I asked about round goby in these waters, an invasive species that is quite aggressive.

"They love it here," Jason said. "It's estimated that there are 35 goby per square meter in the waters around the islands. They eat the small bass, so the bass numbers have gone down, but the ones that do survive grow up and eat the goby, so the bass that are around are bigger than before."

We chatted a little more, then I walked around the facility. There are mounted fish on display, tanks with live fish, and information about all things Lake Erie. One problem plaguing this Great Lake is *microcystis*. When this microorganism blooms, it forms a bright green particulate in the water resembling algae, but it is a bacterium (cyanobacteria). While the blooms muck up the water, the more dangerous feature is the toxin this bacteria produces. It can harm or even kill mammals, including people. Toledo, Ohio, made national news in 2014 when the water supply became unsafe for several days because of high concentrations of toxin. Phosphate feeds these blooms, so to combat the problem, stricter regulations are being enforced that dictate how and when farmers can fertilize fields in the Lake Erie watershed. This, hopefully, will reduce phosphate run-off into the lake.

When I reached the display with several round goby, I stared into their unblinking, bugged eyes. These fish are native to the Black Sea and were transported to our Great Lakes unintentionally in ballast water. Ships will take water into their ballast tanks for stability, then expel that water when they take on the weight of new cargo or when entering shallow waterways. The majority of invasive species in the Great Lakes Basin were given a free ride here in these tanks.

Recent laws mandate that vessels rinse their tanks with salt water before entering the Great Lakes system. This measure, alone, has drastically reduced the number of invasive species entering our lakes.

Some forward-thinking ship designers are conceptualizing vessels without ballast tanks. Instead, they have a chamber in the hull of the ship that water streams through. Stability is maintained by adjusting the flow. This concept uses water the ship is moving through as flowing ballast, instead of transporting water – and creatures – to far-off places in ballast tanks.

The round goby hangs out on the bottom of the lake. It has buggy eyes and a wide, sad, downturned mouth. The body of the goby is elongated, with a suggestion of a stripe down the side. The fish in the tank rested on rocks and looked pretty relaxed, but this is not a laid-back fish. It is aggressive and can out-compete many fish – like native bass species – for food and territory.

As I exited the hatchery, the Island Snake Lady approached me. I know you're expecting a description of a woman covered in snakes, or at least a medusa hairdo, but Kristin Stanford looked pretty normal. She wore blue jeans and a pink tank top. Sunglasses perched on top of her snakeless head held back her blonde hair.

I know. I was a little disappointed, too.

Stanford works with the Lake Erie Water Snake (LEWS for short). This distinct sub-species, *Nerodia sipedon insularum,* differs from the snakes commonly found on the shores of the mainland here, especially around Marblehead and Lakeview. The mainland snake is the common Northern Watersnake, *Nerodia sipedon sipedon.* These snakes differ in their coloration and in some habits, especially what they eat.

Stanford took me to see her new laboratory. Lab tables with their thick, black tops were plentiful, and all the drawers and cabinets were bright red. Large windows looked out on the harbor.

"I don't have any snakes here right now," she said. Again, I hid my disappointment. Seriously. I wanted to hold one of these snakes.

I had heard that the snake population had made a comeback. I asked why this had happened. Stanford explained that in the late 1990s, there were as few as 1,500 of this species left on the islands, and the Lake Erie Water Snake was listed as threatened. But they've now rebounded to a population of at least 10,000. In 2011, they were removed from the list of threatened species.

She took me over to a shelf filled with jars of preserved specimens and said that the round goby was partially responsible for the snake's comeback.

I peered into the jars. Sure enough, they were filled with partially digested gobies. "Snake dinners?" I asked.

"Yes. The snakes are eating gobies almost exclusively now. And since the gobies are so plentiful, the snakes don't have to work so hard to find food. We take measurements of each snake we catch, collect the contents of their stomachs, and put a tracker on them before releasing them."

I pictured snakes slithering around the island with little radio collars. "Tracker?" I asked.

Stanford lifted up a vial with a tiny metal slug in it. "A microchip. Like they put under the skin of dogs. We do the same with our snakes. That way we can identify individuals when they are recaptured." Stanford was a graduate student when she first came to the islands to work with these snakes, and she has stayed to help protect them. She is in charge of the important educational component of this work, speaking to groups that come to the islands.

This unique sub-specie developed in the isolation of these islands and is found only on this Lake Erie archipelago. This means the LEWS has the smallest range of any snake – and one of the smallest of any vertebrate, for that matter – in the world. Islands isolate life, and on these outposts life forms that persist may genetically diverge and become unique.

I thanked the Island Snake Lady for the tour, her time, and her important work.

To the top of the memorial

I jumped on my bicycle and rode around the harbor to the Perry Victory and International Peace Memorial. If you look at South Bass Island from above, it has two distinct parts joined by a narrow tract of land, like the smaller part of the island was being pinched off from the rest of it. On this narrow isthmus, the Perry Memorial was erected almost a century ago.

After parking my bike, I stopped at the visitor center to see the exhibits about the Battle of Lake Erie. The island was gearing up for the bicentennial of this battle, which involved staging a full-scale reenactment. I was thrilled to be participating in this event, standing in the place of Private Josiah Briggs who served on America's lead ship in the battle, the *Scorpion*.

The visitor center had an enormous display filled with miniature ships. Each was a scale reproduction of the vessels that clashed on Lake Erie two centuries ago. Moving slowly around the exhibit, I took note of the relative sizes of the ships, how many masts they had, and how many cannons poked from their sides. I finally reached the *Scorpion*, a two-masted schooner, rather humble in its design. That was the vessel that Josiah Briggs crewed.

I kind of wished for a bigger boat.

I walked to the massive Doric column that towers above everything else on the island at 352 feet tall. It sits on a slight rise in the land, with steps leading to the main entrance. The column, steps, and plaza around it are all constructed of granite. The base of the column is 45 feet in diameter and tapers a bit to about 35 feet across at the top.

I passed through the bronze doors into the chilled stone space within the column. The inscription on the marble floor read: "Beneath this stone lie the remains of three American and three British officers killed in the Battle of Lake Erie, September 10, 1813." This monument was not only a memorial. It was also a crypt for some of the fallen.

The limestone walls were inscribed with the names of all the Americans killed in the battle. I found the name of my ship, the *Scorpion*, and read the names beneath it: John Sythammer and John Clark. My soldier, Josiah Briggs, the one I'd be standing in for during the reenactment, survived the battle. He fought by the side of the two shipmates killed in the battle, and one of these men John Clark, Midshipman, was one of the three American officers buried in the memorial.

I walked the curving steps to the next level and waited in line to buy a ticket to ride the elevator to the observation deck. On this level, there were immense bronze plaques on the walls. These listed the names of all the sailors who were in the battle that day. I scanned the hundreds of names until I found Josiah's.

The elevator ride to the top was slow, and a National Park ranger gave us a talk on the way. "This is the fourth-tallest national monument," she said. "It's taller than the Statue of Liberty." She told a bit about Oliver Hazard Perry, the American Commodore for the battle, concluding, "So be thankful for your freedom that Perry helped secure for you so long ago."

I thought about that as the group shuffled off the elevator and out into the bright sunlight.

Freedom? True, if we had lost the war of 1812, the British would likely have taken some of the Midwest as their land. So maybe my home state of Michigan would today be part of Canada, which won its gentle, bloodless separation from British rule in 1867. But Canadians are pretty "free."

On the other hand, if the British had won, they had promised part of Ohio as a homeland for the Native Americans who fought on their side. Maybe these tribes would not have been pushed west, mostly annihilated, and forced onto reservations. So, granted, America might be different today if we had lost the War of 1812. But to say we gained our freedom in that war is a bit of an overstatement. And the conflict was not concluded until a year after the September 1813 Battle of Lake Erie with the 1814 Treaty of Ghent, a paper ending to a bloody war that lacked a decisive conclusion on the battlefield.

As I took in the view from the top of the grand column, I lost the desire to argue history with the ranger. This is the tallest Doric column ever constructed on earth. The harbor – crowded with boats in anticipation of the reenactment – and village lie at the foot of the column. The dark-green, tree-covered island was distinct against the blue-green of Lake Erie. Many other islands in the archipelago were also visible from the top: Kelleys, Middle Bass, Green, and Rattlesnake Islands (where no rattlesnakes now live), and the edges of more islands beyond.

Above the observation deck, the column is crowned with an eleven-ton, bronze urn with snarling lions and ornate patterns on the metal. It has taken on a rich patina from being out in the weather and is now tinged green over the brown metal. Spotlights glow upward at night, illuminating the urn in the dark.

The memorial had recently undergone a $6 million restoration in preparation for the Bicentennial of the Battle of Lake Erie. This wasn't just an effort to spruce it up. The monument was showing signs of serious weathering and was starting to shed pieces of its granite sheathing. Several years ago, a slab of granite plunged from near the top of the column. It penetrated through the plaza and into the lower level. Thankfully, no one was on site at the time.

On the top of the restored column, there was an enjoyable, cooling breeze that wasn't blowing down below, but I soon descended to find my bike. I wanted to have time to tour the island caves.

To the caves

The two caves are conveniently located across the street from each other. I considered visiting only one since I assumed they were probably geologically similar, but it turned out they couldn't be more different. The Crystal Cave is owned by a winery on the island, so for a single price of admission you can tour the cave, visit the winery, and then have a free tasting. Since the day was so hot, though, I declined the tasting and gave my wine token to the pleased gentleman in line behind me.

The Crystal Cave is actually an underground geode, comprised of strontium sulfate crystals (also called celestite, a name that refers to its blue color). You've probably seen small geodes, the golf ball-sized rocks for sale in gift shops that you can bash open with a hammer, exposing the interior crystals. Well, this geode is over 30 feet in diameter. It easily held our group of 15 people. The sparkling hollow space was discovered while drilling for water in the late 1800s. The drill tip struck the geode, then the landowner dug out a way to access it, naming it the Crystal Cave (*cha-ching*).

The largest crystal here is 18 inches across and at least 20 inches long. This single crystal weighs almost 200 pounds. The cave was studded with massive, cloudy, light-blue crystals sticking randomly off of the ceilings and walls into the empty center of the cave. Amazing.

Next, I walked my bike across the street and bought a ticket to Perry's Cave. After many of Perry's men became sick from drinking Lake Erie water, they switched to sourcing their water from this cave. Once they drank only cave water, most of the men recovered enough to go to battle against the British.

Unfortunately, an early owner of the land had plundered the cave in the late 1800s. He was interested in making a quick dollar, so he broke off most of the stalagmites, selling them as souvenirs. The cave still has many thin stalactites hanging down from the ceiling, but the butchered floor of the cave detracts from the tour. The current owner has tried to gloss over the carnage by naming the remnant bumps on the floor after things they resemble: a lion, an egg, and even Homer Simpson in profile.

The caves were both around 50 degrees, and it was a pleasure to get out of the heat. After the second cave, I rode my bike to the nearby state park and wandered the shoreline looking for a Lake Erie Water Snake.

I saw one in the water, but it swam away before I could introduce myself.

Miles for South Bass Island:

Bike	Hike	Ferry
6	2	6

The Bicentennial Reenactment
of the
Battle of Lake Erie

My exploration of the Great Lakes islands coincided with the 200th anniversary of the Battle of Lake Erie. This was a pivotal naval battle during the War of 1812. The American fleet launched from Put-in-Bay on South Bass Island to clash with the British fleet on Lake Erie in September 1813. Commodore Oliver Hazard Perry commanded the American ships, while the British were under the more seasoned command of Captain Robert Heriot Barclay, an experienced Royal Navy officer who had fought alongside Lord Nelson at Trafalgar in 1805.

The evening before the reenactment, I had dinner with my friend Mickey, her cousin Marcia, and her husband, Dave. We talked about the naval battle, and I told them that I would be standing in for Josiah Briggs, a private on the schooner *Scorpion*.

"Did he survive?" Mickey asked.

I explained that he had. But that was about all that I knew about this man. I had tried to find more details about Josiah's life, but had been able to discover nothing other than the fact that he was a private on the *Scorpion*. Knowing that he got off the ship at the end of the day, that he saw the outcome of the battle, was important to me, though, as I contemplated standing in his shoes. I felt more able to imagine Josiah's thoughts and feelings, looking back two centuries, knowing that he survived the battle.

In the following pages, I'll give the historic factual account of that fateful battle in September 1813, followed by what I imagined Josiah Briggs went through (passages in *italics)*, and, finally, my experiences during the bicentennial reenactment in September 2013.

September 1813: It had taken Perry nearly a year to build the main ships in his fleet and then gather all of his vessels at Put-in-Bay. The larger ships, the *Niagara* and *Lawrence,* were built at Presque Isle, Pennsylvania. They were so large that they were trapped in the harbor when completed, as prevailing winds and currents had formed a submerged sand bar at the mouth of the harbor, reducing the water depth to less than five feet. Fully rigged, the *Niagara* and *Lawrence* drafted twice that depth. To free the two ships, all cannons and rigging were removed, then complicated floats called "camels" were used. These watertight, wooden collars could be filled with water and submerged, then the ship was maneuvered over it. The water was then manually pumped out, making the camel buoyant, helping to lift the ship.

Josiah had arrived on Lake Erie in time to assist in the work to get the larger ships out of the harbor at Presque Isle. He didn't think it was going to be possible to get the mighty ships over the shallow sandbar. British ships had passed close enough to the harbor to be seen with a spyglass. If they had trained their guns on the ships while still at anchor, they would have been easily destroyed. It took hours of backbreaking work at the pumps to finally get the Lawrence high enough in the water to float carefully out to Lake Erie. The Niagara went a little faster. All of the cannons that Josiah and the other sailors had removed from the tall ships then had to be put into rowboats, rowed out, and re-installed.

Josiah and his shipmate friend Henry Cook were surprised to learn that these grand ships were built using green wood. They overheard the supervisor of their construction, Noah Brown, say that they would endure no more than one battle. This made Josiah feel a little more confident being assigned to the smaller and more seasoned two-masted schooner, the Scorpion.

September 2013: Fifteen tall ships gathered on Lake Erie for the reenactment of the Lake Erie engagement. Many were from Canada or America's East Coast. The one that came the farthest was from Norway. While many of the ships were recreations from the general period, only one of the American ships was a true reproduction of a vessel that battled that day. Two hundred years after the original two-masted brig, the *Niagara,* took sail on Lake Erie, its replica (built in 1988) would launch out onto the lake once again. Another ship, the *Friends Good Will,* was a reproduction of one of the British ships. I had seen this vessel at its homeport in South Haven, Michigan, many times.

In fact, since I had spent so much time on the shorelines of the Great Lakes, I was familiar with many of the tall ships gathered at Put-in-Bay for the reenactment. The *Pathfinder* and the *Playfair* are from Toronto, Ontario. The *Denis Sullivan* has a homeport of Milwaukee, Wisconsin. The *Madeline* docks in Traverse City, Michigan. The *Appledore IV* makes its home in Bay City, Michigan. And the *Windy* docks in Chicago, Illinois, at Navy Pier where I began and completed my first 1,000-mile hike.

Seeing these ships gather on Lake Erie was like meeting up with old friends in a new place.

September 1813: The evening before the historic battle, Commodore Oliver Hazard Perry called his officers to his flagship, the *Lawrence,* to plan his strategy against the British fleet. Perry's ship was named after his fallen friend, Captain James Lawrence, recently killed in a naval battle in the waters near Boston. Perry had an enormous blue flag sewn with his friend's dying words: "Don't Give Up the Ship."

Perry told his men that when he hoisted this banner it was the signal to commence firing on the British.

Josiah was nervous when the officers left the Scorpion *to go to the* Lawrence, *but he tried not to show it. He and the other men completed their tasks and then went below to get their rations for dinner. They came up on deck and sat in a group as they ate. They speculated about the coming battle and how they would fare against the British Navy. While the men liked Perry, they weren't too sure about him leading the fleet into battle because he was only 27 years old. And they knew that Captain Elliott, who was slightly older and in charge of the* Niagara, *resented Perry's leadership. As they ate, the men speculated that their ship, the fast* Scorpion, *might be ordered out in front during the battle since it could be maneuvered more easily than the larger ships. This worried Josiah, but his friend Henry assured him that the British would train most of their fire on the* Lawrence, *especially after Perry hoisted that big blue flag.*

September 2013: I was so excited the night before the reenactment that I hardly slept.

September 1813: The morning of the battle, at 5:00 a.m., Perry's lookouts sighted the British fleet nine miles from Put-in-Bay.

The men hadn't slept well the night before the battle. Josiah wasn't assigned to the night watch, but he spent some of the dark hours on deck anyway since he couldn't sleep. The stars were brilliant over the lake that night. When the call went up at dawn that the masts of the British fleet could be seen just beyond Rattlesnake Island, all of the men scurried to make the Scorpion *ready. Josiah, just 18 years old, followed the lead of the older sailors, especially Henry, doing his best to complete his assignments as quickly as possible. They would soon sail out to meet the enemy.*

September 2013: The morning of the reenactment, I was awake by 5 a.m. and on the ferry to South Bass Island at 6 a.m. The sun hadn't lifted out of the water yet, and the ferry was jammed with people heading to the event. Many wore period dress – serious reenactors – with tall hats and vests. I was not so historically clad. I wore my hiking pants, a long-sleeved T-shirt, and carried a raincoat and my GPS unit and two cameras in a small red backpack. For footwear, I had chosen a pair of tennis shoes that would give me good traction on deck. They were mostly pink with a flower pattern and were very cool – certainly not accurate to the period, but I hoped Josiah wouldn't mind a bit of flair as I stood in his symbolic shoes.

After the ferry off-loaded us on the island, we boarded a shuttle that took us to the conference center where we got our credentials and shirts with our sailor's name and rank on the back.

In the middle of handing out the hundreds of packets, there was a brief explanation of the battle plan. Then actor Billy Campbell was introduced. He was the celebrity VIP, the star of the movie *The Rocketeer,* who had been brought in to depict Perry during the reenactment. He said a few short sentences, then confessed to having imbibed too much tequila on the island the previous night. As someone who is prone to motion sickness even in calm seas, my sympathies went out to this guy who was going to be on a Great Lakes tall ship all day with a hangover.

We were then grouped by our assigned vessel and shuttled off to the docks. By 10:30 a.m. I was wearing my gray, long-sleeved tee shirt with:

Josiah Briggs
Private – 1813

lettered on the back.

My friends Mickey, Marcia, and Dave arrived at the dock just before I boarded my ship. They took photos of me in my Josiah shirt and wished me well in the battle. When everyone was aboard the *Appledore IV* (the two-masted schooner standing in for the *Scorpion),* we left the dock and maneuvered out of the harbor. The larger ships were still taking on passengers and would soon follow. The day was overcast with leaden clouds that sprinkled us with rain and threatened to do more.

September 1813: When Perry ordered his squadron to leave the harbor and sail out to meet the enemy, they knew that the odds were against them. The British had never lost a naval battle. The British squadron numbered only six ships, but they were well armed with 63 cannon, some of which could toss a cannonball a full mile, and be accurate within a half mile. The Americans had nine ships, but had only 54 guns, with half the range of the British guns.

And Perry needed more than 700 sailors to fully man the vessels of his fleet, but had only 500 fit to sail. He was glad that they had at least found a cleaner source of drinking water in the island cave, or many of his 500 might still be ill. Even with the recovered men, most of his ships would sail short-handed that day.

Josiah and the other sailors had to be in charge of several tasks because the Scorpion *would sail with a light crew. They only had two guns, so manning their smaller ship was not as important as the ships with more firepower. Josiah understood the logic, but he couldn't help feeling more vulnerable, especially after Midshipman John Clark confirmed that they would be the lead ship in the battle. Josiah was ordered to spread sand on the deck, and when he whispered to Henry to ask why, the answer was short: "So the deck does not get slippery with our blood."*

September 2013: The clouds began to break up as we headed into the open waters of Lake Erie. The captain instructed the crew to hoist our mainsail, and it quickly filled with the steady breeze. Seven miles out into the lake, a hummingbird zipped around our mast, then flew quickly out of sight.

I turned to the young man next to me who wore a dark blue Coast Guard uniform. "Did you see that? A hummingbird!"

He looked around. "Way out here?"

I pointed to the east. "Yes. It just zipped away."

Our ship was crewed by several able hands, but I was glad we had an extra sailor on board for the battle. On his forearm, there was a beautiful tattoo of the Great Lakes based on a historic map of the region.

"What year is that map from?" I asked pointing to his forearm.

"The mid-1700s," he said.

It looked like a map I had seen on display in a museum on Mackinac Island, and he confirmed that his tattoo was of that very map. He used to be stationed on Mackinac Island, but was now in Cleveland as a public relations officer.

"Do you miss the bigger lakes?" I asked.

"I did at first," he said. "But I've grown to appreciate Lake Erie."

September 1813: For two hours Perry tacked his fleet, trying to get positioned with the wind at their back, in order to have the advantage as the battle commenced. This would allow his ships to bear down more quickly on the British, but the wind would not cooperate. Just as he was about to give up and go with the wayward wind, it shifted, finally filling their sails.

Josiah's arms burned from hoisting the sails and then repeatedly trimming them against the wind as they tacked back and forth with the fleet. The only sounds on deck were of the flapping sails during each turn and the subtle grinding noise of the sailors' boots on the sand as they moved efficiently to each task.

September 2013: We sailed 13 miles out into the lake. On the way we were given a sack lunch: turkey or ham sandwiches, a drink, an apple, and a candy bar. Over 2,000 private boats gathered out on the water to watch the reenactment. Vessels of all size – from many small speedboats and one pontoon boat all the way up to triple-decked ferries – sped out to the battle site and ringed it for the show. Coast Guard and police vessels zipped back and forth, warning the spectator boats to stay clear of the battle zone, to give a wide berth for the tall ships to maneuver in the steady wind. The PR officer with the Great Lakes tattoo carried out his assignment, taking photos of the Coast Guard vessels in action.

As I've mentioned, Lake Erie is a boater's lake, and it seemed that nearly everyone owning a watercraft was on the lake that day. I had never seen so many vessels converge on one place.

September 1813: As Perry's flagship made its way out onto the lake, his men also sprinkled sand on the decks of the mighty *Lawrence.* One sailor later reported that the crew was silent, even though no order had been given to be quiet.

Josiah watched in surprise as a hummingbird buzzed up to the sail he was manning. It looked down on him, hovering, then zipped away over the water toward the British fleet. The line of enemy ships grew larger with each passing moment.

September 2013: A computer program was used to draw up various battle plans for the reenactment. Wind and currents were entered along with the capabilities of each ship sailing that day. Updated plans were radioed to the fleet in real time, and we sailed using GPS coordinates to get us to the battle site. It was a historic reenactment with high-tech coordination. Still, it was not until afternoon when our line of ships was finally in place and the enemy reenactors had organized their ships opposite us.

September 1813: Only the two lines of warships were on Lake Erie that day 200 years ago. Perry finally raised his "Don't Give Up the Ship" flag, and the tension broke momentarily as the men of his fleet gave up a battle cry.

Perry's line of ships closed in on the British around noon that day. They trimmed their sails and sped into the open lake toward the British line. The longer-range British guns could fire on Perry's ship, the *Lawrence,* for several minutes before his own short-range cannons could return fire. The American commandant and his men sailed into a storm of death unleashed from enemy guns. The British fleet trained most of their cannons on the *Lawrence,* shredding its sails, shattering the green wood that was planking its sides and causing carnage on and below the decks.

The Scorpion *was out ahead of the* Lawrence, *and Josiah had dutifully tied off his sail and now helped man one of the guns, waiting for the order to fire when they were close enough for their shot to reach their target. Most of the British guns were firing on the* Lawrence, *and Josiah feared for the lives of the men on that ship.*

September 2013: My ship, the *Appledore IV* (standing in for the *Scorpion),* was outfitted with a tiny cannon for the mock battle. This brass miniature cannon took a shell about the size you'd load in a shotgun. The sailor in charge called out, "Lock and Load!" then "Fire in the hole!" before pulling the cord that fired the shell. Even though it was tiny, it gave a big bang and a billow of smoke. I plugged my ears for each shot.

When we fired our first shot, a hearty cheer went up from our ship, and the battle was underway. The ship directly behind us in the line, the *Windy* (standing in for the *Lawrence),* had a huge American flag with only 15 stars (as the U.S. flag looked in 1813) flying off her rear mast. It unfurled with the wind, making a beautiful sight. Since we were the first ship in the line, we could look back over the other eight vessels standing in for the American fleet. With their sails filled with wind, the splash of waves on their hulls, it was like looking back two centuries.

Broadsides from the larger ships thundered, and the thick smoke from the cannons drifted over the lake.

September 1813: When the British ships were finally within range, the *Scorpion* fired the first shot for the Americans from one of its 24-pound guns. With her sails full of wind, the *Lawrence* trained her guns on the enemy ship *Detroit* under the British captain Robert Heriot Barclay.

Barclay was a veteran of the Battle of Trafalgar. He had lost his left arm combating the French at sea and was a determined and confident commander in charge of the British squadron. Before the first shots were fired during the Battle of Lake Erie, Barclay ordered that his flag be nailed to the mast so it could not be lowered in surrender. Barclay had the smaller fleet that day, but he had more guns and they could fire farther than the Americans'.

The minutes passed agonizingly slow until the order was finally given to fire. Josiah watched Henry site down the bore of the cannon. He timed the swells of the lake to aim the shot at the mast of the closest British ship. Henry pulled the lanyard to engage the gunlock, firing the cannon. The shot took a chunk of wood from the mainmast on the British ship, spraying the sailors with huge, piercing wooden shards. The report of the cannon left Josiah's left ear buzzing, but he was able to hear Henry yell for him to reload. Josiah realized that they had fired the first shot for their side.

Smoke billowed from every gun after it fired, and soon the watery battlefield was shrouded in smoke. Shouted orders and report of cannons were interspersed with screams from the wounded. The sand on the decks was necessary.

September 2013: To enhance the scene, a barge filled with pyrotechnics was anchored near the battle site. It added the sounds of explosions and billows of smoke to the panorama to be captured on video of the reenacted naval battle.

September 1813: Within two hours, Perry's flagship was out of action, battered to a state of near-wreckage. Every gun on the *Lawrence* was rendered useless under the barrage from British guns. Most of his men – 83 out of 103 – were wounded or dead. Things had not gone well on the *Scorpion,* either. One of its cannons had exploded, injuring many men on board.

When Perry could no longer fight from the *Lawrence,* he took down his flag and boarded the one skiff that would still float. He ordered a few of his remaining able men to row him to the *Niagara.* This was a dramatic and risky move. Even though the British fired on the rowboat, all aboard made it safely to the *Niagara.*

The *Niagara,* under the command of Captain Elliott, was supposed to fire on the British *Queen Charlotte,* but, inexplicably, had hung back from the battle. Perry boarded the unscathed *Niagara,* took command, raised his blue flag, and ordered it to sail into the enemy line.

All was chaos after the explosion on the Scorpion. *Josiah thought an enemy shot had found its target, but then he turned and saw the other cannon was twisted and smoking. It had exploded. Josiah caught a small piece of shrapnel in his wrist, but it was his right one and he was left-handed. He tore a strip from his tattered shirt, bound the wrist, and moved to help the wounded men fallen around the other gun. But Henry grabbed him by a shoulder and hauled him back to his post. Josiah lifted a cannonball as best he could with his one good hand and stuffed it down the hot barrel.*

As Henry sited the shot, Josiah looked at the men lying on the deck. Two of the officers were mortally wounded. Both were missing limbs and quickly bleeding out. He glanced over at the nearby Lawrence *as Henry fired the cannon. All seemed lost, as the many guns on the* Lawrence *had gone silent. The buzzing in Josiah's ears now obscured most of the thunder of the cannons and the screams and whimpers of the wounded. Josiah thought it would not be a bad thing to go deaf at this moment.*

September 2013: We watched hungover Billy Campbell gamely clutch a black hat fringed with white as he climbed down a rope ladder to a waiting motorboat. At some point he had changed into period dress and now wore white pants and vest, a light blue coat with red cuffs, and tall, black boots. The two men in the small boat waited for him to gather the "Don't Give Up the Ship" flag handed down to him, then motored him over to the *Niagara,* splashing through the choppy waves.

We cheered when his blue-and-white flag was raised on the *Niagara.* The ship slowly turned toward the British line.

September 1813: Now under the command of Perry, the *Niagara* crossed the British line and released both broadsides simultaneously. The British returned fire, resulting in more carnage on both sides. Those who didn't suffer direct hits from the cannons and guns often fell victim to the massive wooden splinters exploding from hits on the vessels. When Barclay tried to turn his ship, the *Detroit,* it crashed into the *Queen Charlotte* and their rigging tangled the ships together into one hulking wreck, completely vulnerable to further broadsides. Barclay was hit in his one remaining arm at the shoulder. Two different enemies maimed this man in two different wars on two continents.

By 3 p.m., the largest British ships had surrendered, and the rest of the fleet soon followed.

Josiah couldn't believe it. Where had the Niagara *come from? And where had she been during the battle so far? She looked undamaged while all the other ships were shattered, their sails shredded. Then, he saw Perry's flag flying from her, and he gave up a cheer that was more of a croak since he was parched from the heat and smoke. Perry had taken command of her after the* Lawrence *was shredded. With renewed vigor, Josiah reloaded the cannon, and Henry fired once again on the British ships.*

September 2013: The recreated *Niagara* sliced through the ships standing in for the British line and opened fire from both sides. The smoke from this dual broadside was impressive, and another cheer went up from my ship.

After the dramatic transfer of Billy Campbell and the *Niagara's* crossing of the British lines, our ship fired off our last shot.

September 1813: Barclay, wounded in his thigh and arm, sent his officers to present his sword in surrender to Perry. Perry allowed them to keep the sword. When he learned that Barclay was wounded, Perry expressed concern and regretted that he didn't have an extra doctor to send to him. Barclay would survive this battle.

Perry, miraculously, was not injured even though he had been at the center of the entire battle.

Josiah's ears still buzzed when all the cannons finally went silent. Henry took the cannonball from Josiah's good hand and set it down on the deck. Josiah noticed the gray in Henry's hair that he hadn't noticed before. Did war do that to men, he wondered? Josiah felt older than his 18 years. He leaned on the gun for a moment, but the metal barrel was still hot and he staggered away to find a coil of rope on deck to sit on, exhausted. Henry came around with a bucket of cave water and scooped a cupful for him. Josiah drained it, then dipped it again and poured it over his head. He wiped the water across his face to cover the tears streaming from his eyes.

"No shame in that," Henry told him before moving on to offer the water to the other sailors.

September 2013: The winds had lightened during the battle, and there was a general sense that, by 3 p.m., things were done. The boats ringing the site motored off to their homeports. We watched them speed away and I, for one, felt a little abandoned out there.

Now, all that was left was for the ships to sail back to Put-in-Bay. Ours was the first ship to head out, so we would be one of the last to dock.

September 1813: Perry took a moment on the deck of the *Lawrence* to write his famous report to General William Henry Harrison:

> *We have met the enemy and they are ours.*
> *Two ships, two brigs, one schooner and a sloop.*
> *Yours with great respect and esteem,*

> *O.H. Perry*

The captured sloop he mentioned was the *Friends Good Will.*

Josiah helped bind the wounds of his fellow crewman. The two dead officers were covered with tattered sailcloth until their hammocks could be retrieved from below deck.

On the return sail, Josiah thought about setting foot on the firm ground of the island once again, of the leaves that were just beginning to change on the trees, and of the smell of land. Josiah used to love the lakes. Now, with the smell of burnt gunpowder and fresh blood filling his nostrils, he longed for the safety of the island.

Josiah watched Henry expertly sew the hammocks closed around the bodies of the fallen officers. When Josiah's wrist bled through the dressing, he re-bound it with a shredded piece of sailcloth that was no longer needed.

September 2013: As we returned to the island, private crafts hurried well ahead of the fleet of tall ships. Several people on my ship talked on their cell phones. One guy complained about how long it was taking to get back. While he was talking, I saw a moth flying with our ship. It soon sped up and left us behind.

The day had warmed, though, and the lake had calmed, so it was a gentle day to take a long sail. I enjoyed the ride and chatted with people on the ship. I asked them if the reenactment "was all you imagined?"

"And so much more!" most of them replied.

One of the reenactors had brought a harmonica along and he played historically accurate tunes on the leisurely sail back to the island.

Some people were on the ships because they were history buffs. Some were avid Lake Erie boaters or sailors. Some loved tall ships. One young woman had recently decided that she wanted to learn how to sail, so this was a first step toward that goal. The people on my ship came from as far away as New York to take part in this historic reenactment.

September 1813: The sailors who died during the battle were sewn into their hammocks, weighted with a 32-pound iron shot, and buried "at sea" in the waters of Lake Erie. The officers were buried with honors on South Bass Island. This battle is infamous for having one of the highest casualty rates in the history of naval warfare.

Josiah was ordered to help transfer their extra cannonballs to other ships. He asked Henry why they were doing this since the battle was over. "To weight the dead," Henry answered.

Josiah didn't understand until he saw the body of the first private go over the side of the Lawrence. *The dead man was sewn into his hammock with one of the cannonballs to weight his body to the bottom of Lake Erie.*

The two men killed on the Scorpion, *John Sythammer and John Clark, were both officers, so they were taken to land for burial along with the other fallen officers, both American and British.*

Remains

From the historic battle: The very "Don't Give Up the Ship" banner has survived and is on display at the U.S. Naval Academy in Annapolis, Maryland.

Pieces of the original *Niagara,* mostly the metal deck spikes, still exist. Even one of Perry's epaulettes (those ornate decorations on the shoulders of the uniform) survives. Various museums and private collections have swords and shot from the famous battle. Walking canes were carved from the timbers of ships involved in the naval clash, and some of these survive.

From the reenactment: My long-sleeved tee-shirt with

The Battle of
LAKE ERIE
Bicentennial

over the heart and:

Josiah Briggs
Private – 1813

on the back.

I also saved my official "Reenactor" badge and lanyard, along with a commemorative pin featuring the silhouette of a tall ship and the date, September 2013.

This historic battle site is ever-changing; it is the shifting surface of Lake Erie. There is no floating marker, no monument to the fallen where they fell. But on South Bass Island, the fallen officers are interred. And the immense column rises from the land to mark this victory for the American side and to commemorate the lasting peace that persists to this day – despite the ferocity and carnage of that day's battle – between America and Canada.

Miles for The Battle of Lake Erie Reenactment:
Tall ship
31

Belle Isle, Michigan

Water from the upper Great Lakes (Superior, Michigan, and Huron) eventually flows south through the Detroit River, to fill Lake Erie. I explored one island in that river, Belle Isle, and I'll include it in the Lake Erie section as Erie is the nearest Great Lake.

Belle Isle is just shy of 1,000 acres. It is located in the Detroit River near the center of the city of Detroit. It used to be a grand city park – and is the largest city-owned island park in the nation – but it has seen rough times as Detroit has recently succumbed to bankruptcy. In 2014, Detroit conferred the island to the care of the State of Michigan under a 30-year lease agreement.

I visited the island with my sister, Leslie, and cousin, Milene, shortly after this transition.

Let's go to the Detroit Zoo!

One of the foundational stories told in our family of Leslie and Milene growing up is about the day in the late 1970s that Leslie (only 16 with less than a year of driving experience) decided she'd pick up Milene (then 13) to go to the Detroit Zoo.

Leslie, being a worldly teenager, figured that the Detroit Zoo was in Detroit. It is not. The Detroit Zoo is located in the city of Royal Oak, a suburb. This is probably why both of their parents didn't even blink at their request to take this daytrip.

The two girls blithely headed into the metropolis of Detroit, Leslie at the wheel, Milene riding shotgun, with the conviction that the zoo would reveal itself. There must be signage for such an important place, they reasoned. For hours, they crisscrossed the city, and stopped to ask for directions several times from people, who all tried to convince the girls that the Detroit Zoo wasn't in Detroit.

Leslie was insistent, though, and they were finally directed to the much smaller zoo on Belle Isle.

Looking back, they were astonished that their younger selves had dared to blindly venture into the city in that time before GPS and cell phones. Still, Leslie triumphantly points out that all turned out well and that they did, in the end, visit a zoo in Detroit.

Downtown! Things will be . . . well, kind of rough

In 2013, Detroit had deteriorated to the point that it was forced to declare bankruptcy. The city is broke. And as we drove from the suburbs into the heart of downtown on our way to Belle Isle, it was pretty clear that most of the city is also broken. Decay and destruction is evident along the highway. Many structures are abandoned or gutted by fire. There are efforts under-way to erase this blight, but once-grand monoliths like Michigan Central Station – when completed a century ago it was the tallest railway station in the world – have been abandoned for three decades.

Before I am accused of "Detroit-bashing," let me say that I have a deep affection for the city. I lived and/or worked and studied there for nearly a decade. Pockets of the city are regenerating, especially around the anchors of Wayne State University, the headquarters of the Quicken Loans company, and the nearby stadiums where the Tigers and the Lions play. I am hopeful that the city will continue to bounce back.

Les and I drove to Milene's house to pick her up, then took the high-way into the heart of Detroit, emerging at Hart Plaza on the Detroit River. The Renaissance Center is nearby; its retro-futuristic group of mirrored towers stand at river's edge. We passed the famous disembodied fist sculp-ture honoring the fighter Joe Louis, floating in the median of Jefferson Avenue. Cables from a supporting structure suspend the arm in mid-air. To me, "The Fist" always resembled a medical display, the severed arm dan-gling there for everyone to study the bulging muscles and tendons beneath the bronze skin.

Past the hanging arm, on the corner of Woodward and Jefferson, is where my favorite sculpture in the city is located. "Spirit of Detroit" is a

26-foot bronze man seated on a marble base. In his right hand he holds a family, in the other a golden orb. Art and sports don't usually mix, but when Detroit has a team in the playoffs, the team's jersey (in giant size) is placed on the statue. I recall seeing him wear a Red Wings jersey; it was delightful that this Detroit icon was cheering on the Wings.

We headed upriver on Jefferson Avenue to the MacArthur Bridge that connects Belle Isle to Detroit. When we crossed over onto the island, the first thing we noticed was how the grass and weeds were a lush green, almost shocking in their rich color after driving past block after block of scruffy, struggling vegetation in the nearby city lots gone feral. We parked on the west end of the island and moved toward the sound of cascading water.

Donald Trump plus Charlie Sheen

Silenced for many years after vandals stripped out the copper pipes from the structure, the Scott Fountain had recently been restored. It is located on a raised site accessed by broad white marble steps leading to a brick plaza encircling the structure. The large fountain – more than 500 feet wide – fills the plaza with the sound of splashing water from numerous spouts. As we drew closer, we saw that the spouts were coming out of sculpted bronze turtles in the lower pool, and flowing out of the mouths of white marble lions along the middle level. A central, raised bowl shot water skyward in a plume. The effect of the frothy white water and the bright white marble in the sunshine was brilliant.

The fountain was built in 1925 with the fortune bequeathed to the city by James Scott, a wealthy real estate developer. Scott died in 1910, and the city fought for years over the idea of constructing a monument to him because city leaders *hated* him. The blog "Curbed Detroit" described Scott as "a cross between Donald Trump and Charlie Sheen." He was a bad boy, a wild, wealthy guy who delighted in taunting and often suing his rivals.

It was eventually decided that they shouldn't deprive Detroit of something that would beautify the city, even if it bore the name of such a jerk. According to Scott's terms, the site also had to have a sculpture of him. A contest was held, and the winning design was from Cass Gilbert, the architect who designed the Detroit Public Library and the U.S. Supreme Court Building.

I've seen Buckingham Fountain in Chicago's Grant Park, and I've even seen the Trevi Fountain in Rome. Both are magnificent. But the Scott Fountain has a certain grace and lightness as it sits there on an island in the Detroit River. The requisite sculpture of Scott was placed at the edge of the plaza. He perpetually sits there in his elevated chair, gazing past the fountain to Detroit's skyline in the distance. There is a satisfied look on his face, because, once again, he won.

Architectural gems on the island

Milene, Les, and I left the fountain and walked along the island's southern edge. Ancient weeping willows dot the island. The chimes of Belle Isle's Carillon Tower played as we walked. The structure was reflected in an island pond. We strolled next to a designated bike lane, and nearly every biker called "good morning" to us as they pedaled by that Sunday morning. This community feeling contrasted sharply with the isolation we felt as we drove through the ruined parts of the city. Belle Isle was not only an oasis from urban blight, but also a place for people to gather and connect.

We headed toward the conservatory, arriving just as the gates to the surrounding gardens were being unlocked. We strolled the groomed paths and saw another beautiful fountain topped with a bronze sculpture of a wheeling gazelle. Marshall M. Fredericks was the architect of this graceful piece (he also designed the "Spirit of Detroit" sculpture). The commission for this fountain was the first major competition that Fredericks won, launching his career. At the base of the fountain are stone carvings of four animals native to Michigan: rabbit, otter, grouse, and hawk. While the gazelle is bronze and hyper-realistic, the four smaller animals are semi-primitive in representation.

We strolled through the glass-domed conservatory, admiring the orchids and other flowers and plants on display. We then toured the adjacent aquarium that opened in 1904. Albert Kahn, called the "architect of Detroit," designed both the conservatory and aquarium. He also designed Ford's Highland Park Plant and the Rouge Complex, the Fisher Building, the original General Motors Building, and many other grand structures in and around the city.

Closed for several years, the aquarium had recently been re-opened on weekends, staffed by volunteers. Restoration is in progress on the historic building. Two of the original skylights – that hadn't been opened in 60 years – had scaffolding underneath them. Before the end of the year, these skylights were restored and opened once again.

The building is worth a visit even if you aren't interested in the fish. The pillared and arched entrance alone is worth the walk. The keystone is graced with the face of Neptune, the Roman god of water. Sculpted fish adorn the facade, and the seal of Detroit is at the apex. In the interior, Kahn created a long, domed gallery surfaced with shiny tiles in hues of green. The effect makes you feel like you are underwater with the fish swimming in the restored tanks.

We strolled the interior trails of the island park to loop back to our car. Restoration efforts had not reached here yet. The paths were severely overgrown, the pavement cracked or absent in places. We were soon on one of the main roads that ran along the island's zoo, an attraction that had been closed since 2007. There was clearly a lot of work to be done before that might reopen. Many of the zoo structures were nearly swallowed by vines. Les and Milene chuckled about their adventurous visit here over three decades ago.

We stopped at the Scott Fountain once more, and from the angle we approached we could see the Renaissance Center in the distance. At the edge of the plaza, I looked downriver. Belle Isle is the best place to see skylines of both Detroit and Windsor, Ontario, rising on opposite sides of the river. Even in the haze forming on this warm day, I could make out the Ambassador Bridge, that massive span of steel linking the two banks of this mighty Great Lakes river.

Thinking about the problems of Detroit, and walking along these paths, I realized that rebirth might be easier on an island. The edges are evident, so the extent of an island project is defined and contained. The work already undertaken to clean up Belle Isle had made visible and lasting improvements. Maybe the isolation of this distinct place, existing on the flowing river that surrounds and shelters it, nourishes the desire to attempt a renewal here. Restoration happens quickly, and tends to spur on further efforts. One crew cleans up fallen branches; another plants cherry trees that will bloom in the spring. Hope for this island oasis led to action, which then spurred on further restoration efforts.

As I walked, I hoped that the restoration, rebirth, and community connections happening on this island oasis would soon spill over to the city of Detroit.

Miles for Belle Isle:
Hike
5

LAKE HURON ISLANDS

Lake Huron was the first Great Lake to be seen by European explorers. As I mentioned in the Lake Ontario section, the major rapids on the St. Lawrence River made upriver travel difficult. Explorers instead ventured overland from French settlements like Montreal. Etienne Brule, a scout for Samuel de Champlain, was still a teenager when he took an overland route to arrive on the shores of this Great Lake in 1615. He is thought to be the first European to see these waters, even before Champlain saw them.

The majority of the Great Lakes islands are located in the waters of eastern Lake Huron. As always, there is a good geological reason. The Bruce Peninsula is a wedge of land thrusting upward into the southeastern part of the lake. This peninsula and a string of islands partition a lobe of water on the east side of the lake called Georgian Bay, and a narrow passage above it called the North Channel. The landforms making this division are all part of the Niagara Escarpment, that dolostone ridge running in a long arc through the Great Lakes. The Canadian Shield – the great slab of granite underpinning virtually the entire continent – forms Ontario's shoreline here and also produces some of the islands in the North Channel.

Both the escarpment and shield landforms are dense, erosion-resistant rock. This is why so many islands survived the grinding, crushing forces of the glaciers and still rise above the water here today. If you zoom in on a digital map of the eastern edge of Georgian Bay, you'll see that it is fuzzy with islands. There are areas where the shoreline looks like cheesecloth, raked and porous. Water reaches in and around these shreds of land, islanding them.

Most of these islands are too small to name. Many of the waterways are so shallow they are only accessible by kayak or by rolling up your pant legs and wading. The number of islands changes here depending on the level of the water, but it is estimated that there are nearly 30,000 islands in all of Lake Huron. Most of them are in Georgian Bay and the North Channel along Ontario's shoreline. While there are thousands of tiny islands in Lake Huron, the largest island in the Great Lakes Basin, Manitoulin Island, is also located here.

Many islands are also scattered around the edges of Lake Huron. And a group of islands gathers near the Straits of Mackinac, the place in the basin where the tops of Lakes Michigan and Huron meet. My next destination was this group, the Les Cheneaux Islands.

Lighthouse Tour, Northern Lake Huron

Lights on the lakes

As part of my exploration of these islands, I paused in Mackinaw City and took a boat tour of the area's lighthouses. This was a convenient way to travel around the edge of Bois Blanc Island (locally pronounced *Bob-Low*, an English corruption of the French). The western side of this island snugs up against tiny Round Island, adjacent to the more famous Mackinac Island.

The tour left the dock in Mackinaw City and headed past the historic lighthouse on the mainland, Old Mackinac Point Light, with its yellowish brick and bright red roof. Then, we sped to the Mighty Mackinac Bridge and paused underneath the elevated center span. I have visited this bridge on all three of my adventures – sometimes more than once – and have developed a deep affection for its beauty and grace. Passing underneath the bridge gives the true scale of the structure, something driving over or even walking over doesn't quite convey.

We then sped toward the space between Mackinac Island and Round Island. The Round Island Light is on the island (as one would assume from the name) and a passage light sits nearby on a shallow point in the channel. Most people taking the ferry to Mackinac Island will glance only briefly at these structures; soon the docks and hotels, historic fort, and many stores that await them at the landing on Mackinac Island will fixate them. And the breeze might even carry the enticing smell of hot fudge cooling on tables of thick marble.

On our lighthouse tour, we passed in between the islands and then chugged east along the shoreline of Bois Blanc Island. This name means "white wood" and refers to the stand of old-growth white pines that once grew along the elevated spine of the island. The U.S. Navy put an early claim on these trees, planning to use them in building wooden ships for their fleet. When the navy evolved from sailing to steam ships, the island's trees were no longer needed and the government released their claim. The massive trees were logged off for other purposes. Some of these giant pines were used in the construction of buildings that are now part of the Mission Point Resort on Mackinac Island.

As we headed along the northern shore of Bois Blanc, the Les Cheneaux Islands were about 10 miles north of us, far enough away to be hidden in the haze of the warm day.

A long peninsula reaches out into the lake from Bois Blanc, and a lighthouse has been located here since 1829. The current lighthouse is the latest in a series constructed here. This lighthouse is privately owned and serves as a summer home. A small group of around 50 people lives year-round on this island. The population swells during the mild months when more people take the ferry from the city of Cheboygan, Michigan, to their summer island homes.

We rounded the east end of the island, but could barely make out the lighthouse on Spectacle Reef in the distance. There are several "floating" or "crib" lighthouses in this area, marking dangerous reefs or shoals. Many of these structures were partially constructed in the Les Cheneaux Islands, then towed to these reefs and anchored. A crib is a square interlocking wooden structure (think of Lincoln Logs) that is then filled with stone. The lighthouse structure is built on this sturdy base.

It may seem odd that so many lighthouses are in one small stretch of Lake Huron (we would see eight during our loop), but until serviceable roads were constructed there was only one way to easily move goods and people around the region, and that was by water. The Mackinac Bridge wasn't completed until 1957, so passage between Michigan's two peninsulas was by ship until that relatively recent point in time. Before that, thousands of vessels were active on the lakes, so the government constructed many lighthouses for the safety of those vessels. Safe ports or dangerous peninsulas were well marked, but so were all shoals or reefs along an important route that could wreck a ship.

Today, GPS, sonar and radar allow vessels to travel these waters more accurately without the aid of these historic lights. Still, many of the structures are maintained, and some are automated to keep their lights shining, preserving this beautiful piece of Great Lakes history.

Miles on ship:
54

Les Cheneaux Islands, Michigan

The Snows

These islands are affectionately called "The Snows" (a short, corrupted version of "Les Cheneaux," which is French and pronounced *Lay-Shen-O*). They are located a dozen miles from Mackinac Island, nestled up against the southeastern edge of Michigan's Upper Peninsula. The foundation of these islands is based on a series of parallel rock ridges covered over with mounds of glacial till. In between the islands are the eponymous "channels" of water (*cheneaux* is French for "channel").

I confess that up until a couple of years ago, I had never heard about The Snows or even noticed them on a map. There are 36 islands in this group, and they fit like puzzle pieces in between a series of peninsulas reaching into Lake Huron. Unless you look closely at a map, The Snows seem at quick glance to be part of the irregular coastline. There are places where the islands are less than a thousand feet from the mainland, separated only by a narrow channel of water.

When I admitted my long ignorance of these islands' existence to residents there, they were fine with hearing that people knew little about their special archipelago.

"That's the way we like it," they said. They preferred to keep it the rather serene place it is today. I'll tell you a little about these delightful islands . . . just promise you won't tell anyone else.

The Snows weren't always this sleepy summer hideaway. These islands are located near the strategic juncture of lakes Superior, Huron, and

Michigan. This area was well travelled by Native Americans for centuries, long before Europeans contemplated crossing the Atlantic. The channels between the islands provided sheltered passage to small craft traveling through the Straits of Mackinac.

Many canoe flotillas of Native Americans, then in more recent times early European explorers, then French voyageurs or Jesuit priests, all paddled through these channels and took shelter on these islands. Jean Nicolet and Father Claude Allouez paddled here. Father Marquette did, too, and he drew the first known map of these islands. Father Charlevoix visited here, and Henry R. Schoolcraft frequented the area.

Schoolcraft had a long connection to the region. He was the Indian Agent – the representative of the U.S. government assigned to interact with native peoples – in Sault Ste. Marie and Mackinac Island for almost two decades in the early 1800s. He was a true renaissance man: a geologist, geographer, and explorer, an authority on Native American history and languages, a gatherer of the legends and stories of these people, and a writer. His first wife, Jane Johnston, was half Ojibwe, her grandfather a tribal chief. She is credited with helping Schoolcraft collect stories from the Native Americans in the area. Schoolcraft's publication *Algic Researches* explored and illuminated native cultures and peoples; it is the work that Longfellow drew from to write his epic poem, "The Song of Hiawatha."

The Les Cheneaux Islands had an especially active period from 1890 to 1950. It was during this time that a group of men from Bay City, Michigan, decided to establish a summer settlement here. These men had fished and hunted the area and thought it would be a wonderful retreat for their families. They bought a tract of land on the largest island, Marquette Island, and began developing it. Their idea was to build summer dwellings arranged in a loop around a clubhouse and to leave the rest of the island wild. The Les Cheneaux Club opened in 1890. Membership soon expanded beyond Michiganders. When the Arnold Ferry line began running a steamer between Mackinac Island and The Snows, it opened the summer resort to people from all over the region.

Boyhood summers in The Snows

While the Les Cheneaux Club became the summer destination for many rich and powerful people seeking a restful season, there was one young summer resident whose life trajectory was shaped by his time on these wild islands. His name was Aldo Leopold. His family began coming to the islands in 1900 from their home in Iowa because his mother had severe hay fever and found relief from her symptoms there. The entire family – Aldo was the oldest of four kids – would catch a train from their home in Burlington, Iowa, to Union Station in Chicago. Most of the family would then take a cross-town, horse-drawn coach to the lake steamer with their luggage for the summer. The older boys, though, would walk with the family dogs through downtown Chicago to the docks on the Chicago River. There, they would all board the steamer *Manitou* for the 24-hour passage to Mackinac Island. The family would then transfer to the local Arnold ferry, called the *Islander*, to get to the Les Cheneaux Club. This ferry made a daily loop among these islands, which fostered the building of many large hotels in the towns of Hessel and Cedarville on the mainland and even on some of the islands.

While the Leopold family had a lovely house on Marquette Island, the kids explored many of the other islands, especially after Aldo got a canoe. Aldo and his brothers would go on long hunting and fishing trips, camping for nights out on their own. The boys hiked all over the several thousand acres on Marquette Island, and Aldo drew maps of the trails including some paths that he had personally blazed. The islands were theirs for the summer, and Aldo was especially adventurous in exploring and learning about the plants and wildlife there.

It was at the Les Cheneaux Club that Aldo met the headmaster from the Lawrenceville Preparatory School in New Jersey where he would complete his high school years. From there, he went to Yale and got a masters degree in forestry.

An Ethic for the Land

Leopold's first post after graduating from Yale was to the Southwest, a region where he witnessed severe erosion. He speculated that overgrazing by domestic animals had caused the degradation of the land. He learned to observe the complex interactions of land, fire, wildlife, domesticated animals, and man. Here and in his subsequent assignments, Leopold began to develop a philosophy, a way to see the land as a living organism. He began to grasp the vital connections between the land, the animals and plants, and even the microscopic inhabitants of the soil.

One early formative moment in Leopold's development of his philosophy of land conservation was the day he watched, up close, a wolf die. This occurred in the Southwest, on a day he spotted a wolf crossing a river. At that time, the official policy of land management was to kill the "bad" species (predators like wolves, mountain lions, and bears) to promote the "good" species (like deer, whose beneficial aspect was that they could be hunted by man). So he shot the wolf. He then hiked down to where she lay dying.

Leopold relates the experience in his essay "Thinking Like a Mountain":

"We reached the old wolf in time to watch a fierce green fire dying in her eyes. I realized then, and have known ever since, that there was something new to me in those eyes – something known only to her and to the mountain. I was young then and full of trigger-itch; I thought that because fewer wolves meant more deer, that no wolves would mean a hunters' paradise. But after seeing the green fire die, I sensed that neither the wolf nor the mountain agreed with such a view."

Leopold went on to become the father of modern conservation. He also wrote the book – literally – on game management. His most famous work is a brilliant collection of nature essays called *A Sand County Almanac*. One essay, "The Land Ethic," articulates his philosophy about the earth, the land, and its creatures; to recognize that they worked as a system, to understand that all parts were vital to the success of the whole. Think about a working piece of machinery: pull a few wires and remove a couple of cogs and the whole thing will cease to work properly.

Leopold's writing were greatly influential. He was the first to make the science-based argument that the environment is connected, that it works as a system, and that all parts are valuable and necessary. He took the almost religious passion that the earlier nature writer John Muir had and applied scientific principles to studying, restoring, and conserving it. This laid the foundation for others, such as Rachel Carson, who would write the book, *Silent Spring*, that spawned the modern environmental movement.

The last decade of Leopold's life was spent putting into practice his philosophy of restoring the land. He bought 80 acres of exhausted and abused farmland in Wisconsin. He envisioned what the land had been before the loggers and farmers had arrived, before the wetlands were drained and the land overgrazed. He brought in native plants, planted thousands of trees, and coaxed the soil back to life. The first twelve chapters of *A Sand County Almanac* take the reader through a year on this farm as Leopold observes his land. The book is written with the keen observations of a scientist, a hunter, a forester, a wildlife manager, and of that boy that wandered the islands of upper Lake Huron. It is beautifully written and will transport you to walk his land with him at sunrise, a loyal dog trotting along at your side, through a landscape that is a living, evolving, always interconnected thing.

Leopold's children also loved the outdoors. All studied in related subjects: botany, geology, and wildlife management. His son, Starker Leopold, wrote a report for the National Parks Service in the 1960s that became a foundational document that has shaped the way our parks have been managed. I'll explore this later, in connection with the Lake Superior portion of this book.

The legacy of the Leopold family germinated during the long summers that Aldo spent as a boy and young man in the Les Cheneaux Islands. Today, almost 1,400 acres on Marquette Island are set aside as a preserve bearing Aldo Leopold's name. There are also designated reserves honoring his name in both the Gila Forest in New Mexico and on his farm in central Wisconsin.

Boats, boats, boats

The Islander ferry made its daily loop through The Snows until 1940. Then, a diesel ship called the *Ottawa* made runs to the islands until the late 1950s. By that time, roads in the area had improved, and construction of the Mackinac Bridge was finally complete, linking Michigan's two peninsulas. When the ferry service ended, the large hotels began to close, and the area became a retreat for those who had summer homes on the islands and boats of their own to reach them. Even the towns of Cedarville and Hessel that once bustled with people and shops soon shrank and quieted.

I packed my kayak and headed north to explore The Snows. As I drove the streets of Hessel and Cedarville, it was clear that this was a place for boats. There were boat manufacturers and restorers along the main road. I spotted many classic wooden boats parked in and outside their shops, including at least a dozen gorgeous Chris-Crafts. These wooden boats were made by a Michigan company for over 80 years. The older ones possess a grace lacking in modern boats.

I stopped to take a closer look at four of these wooden vessels, parked together. They were all beautifully restored, with exterior surfaces so clean and shiny that I took several photos of my reflection in their sides. When I looked closer, I could see that each screw had been counter-sunk and then covered with a wooden plug. Craftsmanship like this is difficult to come by today.

I drove the back streets in the area hoping to get my first look at the islands and happened upon the Great Lakes Boat Building School in Cedarville. I stopped in for a tour. The pleasant smell of cut wood greeted me. The school had just graduated a dozen students, so the place was deserted except for staff. John Mills, the administrator, gave me a tour.

In the first year of the hands-on program, students concentrate on traditional techniques, building wooden boats as they learn. The graduating class had built a Garvey-style workboat and a replica of an original Petoskey Boat Company 14-foot rowing boat from the early 1900s. The third vessel from this year's class, an 18-foot sloop, was about half done, still in the shop up on a supporting frame. The screws were still visible in the cypress boards of the hull, counter-sunk, awaiting their plugs.

In the second year of the program, more modern techniques are taught, including working with composites and yacht joinery. Overall, the school has 12,000 square feet containing workshops, a classroom/library, and offices. While I'm not much of a boater, I appreciate the craftsmen and craftswomen that this school produced each year and was glad I had stopped. And I do love the smell of a woodshop.

A geologist at the B&B

Today, you can drive onto two of the Les Cheneaux Islands. All others must be reached by water. A good-sized causeway connects Hill Island to the mainland, and a smaller one connects Hill Island to the adjacent Island No. 8. I wanted to stay on one of the islands, so I checked in at the only B&B, an establishment called Dancing Waters, on the southern tip of Hill Island.

After settling in, I did what I do best: I hiked. Even though these two islands are the most populated of The Snows, there were still very few cars on the road. And I saw more deer than people on my walk. The shoulders of the narrow road were abloom with forget-me-nots, with clearings in the woods a riot of these tiny blue flowers with yellow centers. The trees were so thick that I rarely saw the water, which was not far away. On these narrow islands, each had a main road running down the center, with homes fanning out along the edges. Almost all of the houses had access to the water.

When I got back to the B&B, I was introduced to the other couple staying there, John and Martha Groves. They were there because John is a geologist, working for the company that owns the dolostone mine near the islands, along with 15 other mines in North America. John examines the core drillings from new areas of these mines and develops a geologic model for each limestone or dolostone deposit.

At home, my desk and office are crowded with rocks I have collected along my adventures: Petoskey stones and greenstones, geodes and fossilized horn coral, lightening stones and crinoids. I rarely get to discuss limestone or geology. I asked John how he got into the field.

"I studied as a paleontologist and fell in love with the science of geology," he replied.

"Have you discovered new fossils?" I asked. How cool that would be.

"Many."

"Did you get to name them?" This, I've always thought, would be great fun, the best part of such a discovery.

"I named one after one of my professors, *Cylindrofolia Glenisteri*."

"What's your favorite rock in your collection?" I knew he had a collection. All rock hounds do.

He divulged that his favorite is a slab of chert banded with iron ore, a striped gray-and-red rock that is quite beautiful. I have some chert in my collection, but had never seen the banded form.

I was rock jealous.

Boathouses, boathouses, boathouses

I launched my kayak from the dock adjacent to the 60-year-old boathouse right at the B&B. The docks and boathouse foundations here are mostly the traditional crib-style with interlocking logs forming a structure that is then filled with rocks. Pilings driven along the edges and corners keep it in place. The channels of these Lake Huron islands are very protected, allowing boathouses and docks to last for decades. Mink, that semi-aquatic mammal related to the otter but with a more expensive coat, tends to take up residence in these structures, lending them an especially pungent smell.

Now, I have rubbed my boots with mink oil for years, and for some reason I'd always assumed this was a trade name for a synthetic product. *Mink Oil! Protect your boots and make them feel glamorous!* Turns out, it's actually the fatty layer that lies just underneath the pelt of a mink. This layer is collected and canned. Dipping my fingers into that golden sludge will never be the same.

I paddled the narrow channel between Hill Island and Island No. 8, passing under the causeway that links the two. It was a misty, gray day, and the tops of the trees were stuck in low clouds. Red-winged blackbirds squawked at me as I paddled by their nests. A great blue heron flew almost silently overhead, its neck curved in a perfect "S."

I rounded the northern end of Island No. 8, then crossed the channel to the big bay on the east side of Big LaSalle Island. Here I saw merganser ducks and loons, and a lone sandhill crane. There were no vessels in the bay except for my little kayak, and the water was barely rippled by the slight breeze. A large bird skimmed the trees, then landed on the top of the tallest spruce. I zoomed in with my camera to identify it – a mature bald eagle – a second before it called out with its identifying screechy-whistle.

From there, I paddled to Government Island. This island is a park today, part of the Hiawatha National Forest. There are trails and some designated campsites on the edges of the island, and I decided to return to hike it before I left the area. I paddled back to Hill Island, past Coryell and Boot Islands in the distance.

With the fog and the quiet surrounding my kayak, I imagined myself a voyageur paddling with a canoe full of pelts, slipping atop the waterways between these many islands, enjoying my safe passage so well protected from the waves of Lake Huron. I listened for the watery splashing of moose feeding on submerged plants. I imagined catching the scent of a fire made by an Ojibwe fisherman camped nearby, smoking fish caught in these waters. And I leaned forward, pulling hard on each stroke, feeling the weight of the heavy piles of pelts – mostly beaver, but also muskrat, mink, raccoon and one lynx – safely tucked down in my craft.

A builder of boats

That evening, I interviewed James Barryhill at his home on Island No. 8. Mr. Barryhill is retired from a long career in the U.S. Air Force. He and his wife have lived in their house in The Snows for over three decades now. While in the service, he was stationed all over the world. He could have retired anywhere, so why here, I asked.

"It's a sheltered environment, a safe place for a home. There are no earthquakes here, no volcanoes, no coup d'etats," he told me. "Just a bit of snow in the winter."

Barryhill hasn't been napping his retirement away, though. I came to talk to him about the Les Cheneaux Row Club that he founded.

"I saw an article about 'Build and Row Clubs' in Scotland," he told me. "Some people build a boat together, then they row it." Barryhill wanted to transfer the concept to the Great Lakes, so he started talking to people in the area. This was about more than rowing, though. Barryhill was looking for something to connect the people in his community.

"People started asking me, 'Are you building a boat'?" Barryhill said. "I'd tell them, 'Yes, but we're also starting a *movement!*'"

The club has built four dories. Two hold a single pair of rowers each, while the others require four people at the oars and a fifth person, a coxswain, at the rudder. Barryhill has built watercrafts most of his life. His first was a little duck boat he built on his kitchen table. And he builds a cedar strip canoe for each grandkid when they graduate from high school.

"Except this year. I thought my granddaughter might like one of the standing paddle boards instead, so I'm making one of those for her."

When I asked him to tally up all the vessels he's built or helped others build, he looked at the ceiling for a bit, finally conceding that it must be more than 20, but he couldn't give the exact number. "Would you like to see the shop?" he asked.

Barryhill showed me a boat in progress in the woodshop in the house, then we went to the garage that was also stuffed with boats and the nearly completed paddle board. One of the four-person dories filled one bay of the garage. I tried to imagine it out on the water with people pulling oars in unison.

My favorite painting by Winslow Homer is "The Herring Net" painted in 1885. It depicts two men clad in oilcloth slickers and hats pulling a net from the sea by hand. The net is loaded with herring, their gills slashes of red. The two men are in a dory, just like Barryhill's boat, its oars crisscrossed in the front, out of the water. The man in the bow sits and pulls herring from the net. The other man stands, bent over, hauling the net from the rolling sea. The day is cloudy and the men's hats are slick with moisture that reflects the muted light filtering through the clouds. On the horizon, several large sailing ships glide at full sail.

I couldn't imagine rowing such a tiny craft out on the rolling ocean, even for a net full of herring.

That night, a super-large full moon would rise in the southern sky. Called the "Honey Moon," it would glow deep yellow on this night. I'm usually dubious when I hear reports of a special moon, but this one did not disappoint. It rose over Lake Huron, leaving a trail of light rippling on the surface of the lake in a broad swath up to Hill Island's southern point. I stood on that wedge of land in silence, watching the Honey Moon rise into the black night sky above the lighthouse blinking on Martin Reef.

Row it like . . .

Mr. Barryhill picked me up early the next morning. It was drizzling and a bit foggy, but I was wide-awake. We parked in front of a new log house and went inside to meet Mike and Laurel. A college student, Jane Ann, soon joined us. Barryhill had assisted her in building a canoe as part of her independent study course in high school.

I looked out the wall of windows. The backyard sloped down to the long dock. Two rowing dories sat in the shallows, their bows lifted up onto shore.

We soon headed down and Mike handed everyone a float cushion. He maneuvered the larger dory into shallow water parallel to the dock, and we took turns getting in and sitting on the four built-in benches. Laurel took her place at the rudder, and I fit the pin of my long oar into the oarlock.

With four rowers, each of us would pull only one oar, which alternated on the sides of the vessel. Mike, at the bow directly behind me, pulled his oar on the right side. I was on the second bench, pulling on the left. Jane Ann pulled on the right, and Barryhill, again, on the left. The interior of the boat was medium-colored wood, and the fixed benches also served as foot rests for the person behind.

"Barryhill sets the pace," Mike said. And as Barryhill pulled his oar, we joined him. It took a few strokes to get into rhythm. Laurel set our course using the rudder. Proper rowing technique was reinforced by the mechanics of the process, because if you pulled early or late you would make contact with the person ahead of you with your oar, or lean into the oar handle behind you that was still in the forward position. When everyone was in synch, though, it was a beautiful thing and I was surprised how fast we sliced through the water. Even though it was cool and overcast and drizzly, it was exhilarating. I found myself smiling as I leaned into each pull of the oar.

We passed a shoal marked by grasses poking up out of the water, then made a long pass along Big LaSalle Island. Two massive Newfoundland dogs on a dock watched us row by, but couldn't be bothered to bark. Eventually, Laurel eased the rudder to one side allowing us to make a big loop back to their dock.

"We were really moving," I said to Mike as we walked up to the house. "How fast do you think we were going?"

"Probably better than seven knots," he answered. I didn't know what that translated to in miles per hour, but it sounded fast – *water* fast.

Back inside, we had coffee and chatted around the large dining room table. There were several carved birds in the house, and Laurel said they were learning this art from Barryhill. Before we left, Laurel gave me a bottle of wine, a "Merleaux" with a label from the Les Cheneaux Row Club. A photo of the boat we had just rowed was on the label.

Underneath was the motto of the club: "Row it like you stole it!"

May I borrow your duck boat?

Since the wind was picking up, and I wanted a shorter paddle to Government Island for my hike, I asked Mr. Barryhill if I could borrow one of his duck boats to paddle from Island No. 8 to Government Island. A duck boat is kind of a squashed kayak. There isn't a cockpit, but rather a wide, low-slung opening where you sit on a cushion with your back against the narrow cross-brace. You paddle it with a kayak paddle. This is a calm water boat, but this was not a calm water day.

The crossing was short, though, and the channel narrowed between the islands to the southeast. If it got any rougher while I was on the island, I would carry the duck boat to a more sheltered launching site and paddle the shorter, protected crossing.

"Are you sure you have it?" Barryhill asked as I launched out onto the water.

"I've got it!" I yelled into the wind, pretty sure I had it. With any boat on rough water, it's important to keep the bow pointed into the waves. With a duck boat with an open cockpit and a short sidewall, it is imperative. I paddled parallel to Government Island out into the water, then timed my turn between choppy swells to make a landing on the north end of the island. It was exciting. If the wind got any stronger, it could be dangerous.

I landed the boat and pulled it well away from the water's edge. I walked a few yards toward the east side of the island to confirm that the narrow channel was calmer than what I had just paddled. Sure enough, the angle of the islands cut off the waves so they didn't rush up the channel. I returned to the boat and pulled my boots out of my dry bag. I left my sandals with my life jacket and began hiking the perimeter of the island.

Building a light on the water

A thick layer of moss grew on the moist edges of the island. On the mat of dark green, I noticed the blue-black claw of a crayfish, probably the scraps from a voracious mink's dinner. I headed around the east side of the island and saw the remains of a large dock. It was here that the cribs for two of Lake Huron's lighthouses – Spectacle Reef Light (I had seen it on the lighthouse boat tour) and the nearby Martin Reef Lighthouse – were constructed before they were towed out to their sites. There was once a camp of a couple dozen men living on Government Island, working to construct these cribs and their lighthouses.

Spectacle Reef (the reef is shaped like a pair of glasses) is made of solid limestone, lurking less than ten feet below the surface. Two schooners were gashed open and sank there in 1867, making a strong case that a permanent light was needed. It was a period of much traffic on the Great Lakes, and between 1870 and 1890, around 150 lighthouses were constructed in key locations to improve the safety of traveling on these waters.

Consider the complexity of building a lighthouse on a submerged reef

16 miles from your construction site. Now figure out how to do this if you are living in the late 1800s. It took the crew four years to build the foundation, the lighthouse tower, and the living quarters for the lighthouse keeper.

Spectacle Reef Light was finally completed in 1874. It was the most expensive lighthouse ever constructed on the Great Lakes, and is an engineering marvel.

The crib was first assembled on Government Island. This structure was made of massive, interlocking timbers, reaching 24 feet high. It encircled an area of about a quarter acre. A cofferdam – a massive wooden-stave barrel structure, held together with iron hoops – was constructed in Detroit and then transported to the island. A base platform for the crib was built and then sunk into the deep channel at Government Island near the dock, and the crib was floated over it. Then the two parts were bolted together. The cofferdam was positioned in the middle of the crib and held in place there.

Now, the tricky part: you need to float this massive structure 16 miles out into Lake Huron, position it on the reef, and anchor it there with tons of rock. It took six hours to tow the structure to the site. In subsequent trips, workers ferried large quantities of stone to dump into the compartments of the crib to sink it on the reef.

The wooden staves of the central cofferdam were driven down to meet the surface of the reef. Divers plugged and cemented any gaps at the bottom, then the cofferdam was pumped dry. Masons shaped stones to snugly fill the cofferdam. They bolted the first courses of stone to the reef, then subsequent layers to each other. Gaps were filled with cement that hardened to stone, so the first 34 feet of the lighthouse there today is essentially solid stone.

The rest of the lighthouse has rooms for the keepers and thick, exterior stone walls.

To give you some idea of the forces this lighthouse has had to withstand, consider the gale-force storm that collided with it while it was still under construction. Housing for the workers was built on top of the crib at this time and a temporary light was on its roof. The superintendent of construction reported the damage after the storm:

The sea burst in the doors and windows of the workmen's quarters, tore up the floors and all banks on the side nearest the edge of the pier, carried off the walk between the privy and pier, and the privy itself, and tore up the platform between the quarters and the pier. Everything in the quarters was completely demolished, except the kitchen, which remained serviceable.

The lens, showing a temporary light and located on top of the quarters, was found intact, but out of level. Several timbers on the east side of the crib were driven in some four inches, and the temporary cribs were completely swept away.

A stone weighing over thirty pounds was thrown across the pier a distance of 70 feet, but the greatest feat accomplished by the gale was the moving of the revolving derrick from the northeast to the southwest corner.

At 3 o'clock in the morning the men were obliged to run for their lives and the only shelter they found was on the opposite side of the tower. The sea finally moderated sufficiently to allow them to seek refuge in the small cement shanty standing near the southeast corner of the crib. Many lost their clothing.

I love the line ". . . the men were obliged to run for their lives. . . ." Since they were on top of a structure of wood and stone in the middle of the lake, there weren't too many places to "run" to. And consider the force of wind and waves that could rip the clothing from men huddled against the outside of an unfinished lighthouse in the middle of Lake Huron.

Thankfully, this storm occurred at a time when there wasn't any ice on the lake. Reimagine that same storm if there had been slabs of ice to toss around.

The lighthouse on Spectacle Reef still stands today nearly 150 years after its completion. The crib has been reinforced, but the light itself has stood strong without further intervention.

Hiking Government Island

Today, there is little left on Government Island to tell the tale of the creation of the lighthouses. There are only the submerged remains of a large dock and a few foundations from buildings removed long ago.

I found the wide trail that stayed fairly close to the edge of the island and began hiking. A mixture of mature trees grows on the island, birch and spruce and others. Near the south end, I walked at the shore's edge for a while and saw cormorants and mergansers and geese in the shallows. This end of the island pokes out into the big waters of Lake Huron, and breakers crashed against a nearby shoal. I passed through rubble of limestone boulders, through swampy areas and swale.

The shoreline got increasingly rugged, so I cut inland to try to find the trail with the help of my GPS. The far end of the island is not visited as much as the north end, and dozens of trees had blown down with the force of the wind off the unprotected water of Lake Huron. Even when I was sure I was on the trail, the hiking was obstructed with felled trees or, in some places, completely overgrown.

I was almost back to the northern end of the island when the trail finally revealed itself again. There was a rise separating me from the water. When I hiked to the top, I was surprised to hear the wind screaming and waves crashing. I located my little boat, safely tucked away, and looked out over the water. Whitecaps frothed the entire stretch north of the island. I walked to where the waterway narrowed and was shocked to see whitecaps rolling up the channel. The wind had shifted enough so it was blowing unimpeded there.

This was bad news. If the water looked this rough when I was setting out for the island, I would not have gone. It was simply too rough to safely paddle the little, exposed duck boat. I had no spray skirt with this vessel, and I didn't have a wet suit, either. The water was still quite chilly, so getting turned over would be dangerous and possibly disastrous.

No other boats were out on the water on this rather dreary, pre-summer-season day, no one to flag down and request safe passage. I was pretty sure that Mr. Barryhill was working on the paddleboard for his granddaughter all day, absorbed in his work, likely unaware of the shift in the wind and waves.

So, I did what I had planned to do if the water got rougher: I carried the boat to the spot where I would have the shortest crossing of the channel. I set the small duck boat in the water near the old dock, secured my dry bag by fastening it around the cross-brace, got in, and was immediately swamped by a wave.

I got out, dumped the water, then straddled the duck boat as it danced on the water, watching the waves for my chance to launch again. When I saw a series of waves slightly shorter in height than the ones before, I jumped in and pulled hard with as rapid a stroke as I could manage, propelling the craft into the channel using only the right side of the paddle to keep the nose of the little craft turned into the waves.

"You're not going to flip," I said aloud to myself. I clenched my teeth and paddled for all I was worth. It took all my strength to keep the nose pointed into the whitecaps. Wave after wave crashed on the front of the boat, and a good bit of water splashed onto me and into the shallow cockpit. The current and waves quickly pushed me downwind, pointing me at a target landing spot several docks away from Barryhill's. I was almost at the shoreline before the current finally calmed enough that I could use both sides of the paddle without the waves flipping me.

Exhausted, I finally landed the little boat. I took the cushion and paddle up the hill to return them to the garage and check in with Mr. Barryhill. As I suspected, he was engrossed in his work on the beautiful paddleboard and quite unaware of the wild conditions on the water.

Artists, visionaries, and separatists

That night, I attended the annual island banquet with Jim and Betty Struble, owners of the B&B. In its 24th year, this event raised money for community projects like funding studies of whitetail deer, marsh birds, and frogs, or having the fifth graders grow up salmon from eggs. They also fund a scholarship for students going to college for degrees in environmental science or biology.

Over two hundred people showed up for this gala. This archipelago attracts a wonderful mix of artists, visionaries, and separatists – able people who can work with their hands and who want to live close to the water and to nature. Some even start movements involving people pulling oars in unison. The Snows call to people of substance, giving them a special place to live, only requiring that residents remain attuned to the watery edges of their lives.

Miles for the Les Cheneaux Islands:
Hike   Kayak/duck/dory
13   15

Manitoulin Island, Ontario

Swinging bridge

To approach Manitoulin Island, I drove into Michigan's Upper Peninsula and crossed the bridge over the Saint Marys River. This river carries the waters of the northernmost Great Lake – Lake Superior – down into Lake Huron. From the elevated bridge, I was able to see the expanse of Lake Superior funneling into the river. Massive shipping locks step freighters – some longer than three football fields – up and down the nearly 30-foot difference between the two lake levels. These locks are the busiest in the world, with thousands of vessels passing through them each year.

The bridge landed me in Ontario, then I drove east parallel to the shoreline of the North Channel, passing through the La Cloche Mountains. This area is rugged and forested, and the underlying Canadian Shield is often exposed where the road slices through the hills. Some of the cuts were dramatic. Slabs of rose or brown granite or white quartzite several stories tall bracketed the roadway.

This beautiful and wild area inspired many artists, including members of a famous collection of Canadian painters called the "Group of Seven." These painters captured Canadian wild places using bold colors and brushstrokes in the Post-Impressionist and Art Nouveau manner. A.Y. Jackson, a founding member of the group, was instrumental in protecting part of the La Cloche Mountains. When the area was slated to be logged off, Jackson wrote a letter to the government of Ontario making the argument that it was an essential part of wild Canada and should remain pristine. In 1959, the Killarney Provincial Park set aside almost 200 square miles here, protecting it forever.

During the mild months, Manitoulin Island disconnects from the mainland for the first part of every daylight hour. This is when the swing bridge pivots open on its central pedestal, allowing boats to pass through the narrow channel. This old railroad bridge, built in 1913, has been converted to handle a single lane of vehicular traffic. It is the longest swing bridge in the world. When first constructed, eight men would turn a capstan to slowly swivel the bridge open and closed. A capstan is the same rotating machine with vertical axle used on early ships to manually raise the anchor. Today, the bridge is automated, and the single stoplight on the island is here to control the flow of traffic across the bridge.

Manitoulin is a watery island punctuated with dozens of inland lakes. The largest is over ten miles at its widest point. A series of bays intrude into the edges of the island, sometimes creating gentle undulations of the shoreline, other times thrusting into the landmass threatening to slice the island into smaller pieces.

This island is a spiritual place to the First Nations people. A *manitou* is a spirit, a life force honored by the Anishinaabek (the native name of the people that include the Ojibwa, Odawa, and Potawatomi tribes). *Gitche Manitou* – the Great Spirit – was the greatest of all the spirits, and it was believed to have a home here on Manitoulin Island.

Little Current

The town of Little Current is nearest the swing bridge. If the dozen boats I saw slipping by the open bridge wasn't enough evidence that this is a boater's paradise, then the more than thirty large sailboats and cabin cruisers docked along Little Current's boardwalk or visible out in the North Channel certainly was. There is even a little cruise line offering tours of these waters. There were few small boats here.

Little Current is home to the *Manitoulin Expositor*, one of the oldest newspapers in Ontario. In the late 1800s, the settlement was dubbed "Sawdust Town" due to all the mills churning out millions of feet of pine lumber each year. Today, the marina and tourism are the center of economic activity. And Little Current is the largest community on the island.

I should note that the total population on the island today is just over 12,000, so even the largest community, Little Current, has 1,500 or so residents. The island also has large tracts that are First Nations land, and almost

40 percent of residents on this island are First Nations peoples.

Cup and Saucer Trail

One of the most famous hiking trails in all of Ontario is on Manitoulin: the Cup and Saucer Trail. This trail is named for the stacked limestone layers that have eroded in places to resemble the profile of a cup sitting on a saucer. The highest point on the island is on this trail as it climbs the spine of the Niagara Escarpment.

If you could go back to when the glaciers were on their final retreat from the region (roughly 11,000 years ago), most of Manitoulin Island would have been submerged in fresh, glacial meltwater. The top of the Cup and Saucer Trail, though, would still have poked above the water that formed ancient Lake Algonquin. As the waters receded, even 5,000 years ago, many sections of Manitoulin would have been underwater, effectively slicing it into many smaller islands.

The trail was fairly easy to hike, until it climbed the limestone ridge thrusting out of the land. Then, it became quite steep, nearly vertical for short stretches. The view, though, was worth every step. Along the top, the trail snakes along the edge of the escarpment, occasionally poking out onto slabs of limestone that hover hundreds of feet above the trees. From these outlooks, I could see wind farms and inland lakes, a small quarry, and the watery edges of the island.

And trees.

The island is lushly forested in second-growth trees. Much of the over-look was the dark green of treetops with an occasional flash of white birch bark. One islander told me that when the leaves change color in the fall, "Everyone becomes a poet, it is so beautiful." I could see the beauty even in mid-summer, the evergreens mixed with the leafed trees, the dozen shades of green undulating and mixing in the wind.

There are no railings on these rocks, and it was thrilling to step to the edge to feel the wind rising up the escarpment. Thrilling, but danger-ous since these formations are constantly being undercut by erosion. From many points, I could look up the escarpment, a huge spine of striated lime-stone lifting itself from the trees below and stretching toward the water. The tallest part of the trail is over 500 feet above lake level.

Dig into the past

Manitoulin Island has at least ten museums, or visitor/cultural centers to explore, and I went to most of them. The first was the Centennial Museum of Sheguiandah (*Shag-ooo-in-dah*) where I met Heidi, the manager. Heidi has lived on Manitoulin most of her life. I asked her to try to describe what was special about this island. She paused a while, then said that there is a sense of peacefulness on Manitoulin. This was something I had experienced immediately after crossing the swing bridge.

"There is a sense of being separated from time here. It is its own place," Heidi said.

I thought about the concept of time being different on an island. This is something I'd encountered on other islands: time elongating, slowing down in a relaxing way. There is the concept of "island time," something the Urban Dictionary tries to define as "The time vacuum created by the ocean's presence. . . . everything moves nice and slow." This concept is true for freshwater islands, too. Maybe it's all the negative ions released into the air by the lapping of all that water, the frisson of two natural forces: water against land.

One of the most significant archeological finds in the Great Lakes Basin is near the museum on a large stony hilltop. Hundreds of stone artifacts created about 9,000 years ago were discovered here, and many are on display in the museum. Early peoples frequented the quartzite outcropping here. They mined the stone and shaped it to create axes, scrapers, spear points, and arrowheads. Finding an accessible quartzite or chert deposit like this particular spot was essential for survival for early native peoples, as it yielded the tools necessary for life.

Never relinquished

The colorful map I had of the island showed First Nations land as patches of white on the green map. There are four small white patches spread over the island, and then the entire eastern end of the island – more than 100,000 acres – is all designated as First Nations land. It is labeled "Wikwemikong Unceded Indian Reserve." I drove over the narrowing of the island between South Bay and Manitowaning Bay to explore there. The locals have a helpful habit of shortening longer names, so Wikwemikong was known as just

"Wiky."

At one time the British Crown set aside all of the islands from Manitoulin up to Sault Ste. Marie for native peoples. White settlers inevitably coveted these islands. The British Government then employed some of the same shameful tactics that the United States used to remove native peoples from their land.

It's beyond the scope of this book to fully explore this topic, but Manitoulin Island provides a study of this pattern of betrayal of native peoples. The island is also a key place where First Nation peoples were partially successful in their defiance of the British Crown.

In 1836 the British Government wanted to free up land for an influx of settlers to Upper Canada (Ontario). They drew up the Bond Head Treaty, giving Manitoulin Island to native peoples. The government expected that many natives would migrate to the island of their own accord, giving up their farmland on the mainland to the new settlers. Most of the native peoples stayed where they were, though. And within a few decades, the settlers had their eye on Manitoulin Island as well.

The British claimed that since native migration to the island hadn't happened as expected, the Bond Head Treaty wasn't valid. They would now assign a certain amount of land to each native on Manitoulin, and the rest would be open for settlers. They also stipulated that natives had to relinquish land next to water: bays, inland lakes and even rivers. Native people on the island were primarily fishermen and boat builders, so this rule would effectively cut them off from both food supplies and their livelihoods.

This was a time still within the generation of native warriors who had joined with the British to fight the Americans during the War of 1812. Tecumseh – arguably one of the greatest leaders ever – had united diverse tribes to give the British the manpower they desperately needed in many battles during the war. Tecumseh was eventually killed on British territory (now Ontario).

Jean Baptiste Assiginack was also a great leader within the Odawa tribe. He once gave a speech lasting from sunrise to sunset to mobilize his people to fight alongside the British. After the War of 1812, many natives fled to British territory and settled on Manitoulin Island, including Assiginack.

Mookmanish was another warrior who distinguished himself in battles during that war. He also showed mercy to a wounded captive American soldier. The British Commander at Fort Mackinac, Lt. Col. Robert McDouall, was so moved by these actions that he presented Mookmanish with a sword for his bravery and compassion.

When representatives of the British Government met with the island chiefs in the fall of 1861, the chiefs stood firm. This was their island. They would not relinquish it. They would not allow the island to be surveyed. The British insisted that the survey would happen, even if they had to send soldiers to the island.

In October of 1862, a treaty was drawn up ceding most of the island to new settlers. It was presented to the chiefs and soundly rejected. An editorial in Toronto's *The Globe and Mail* questioned the removal of the natives from their island and recalled the War of 1812. The editor wrote, ". . . are these subjects of the Queen to be driven out of her dominions by violence? Thousands of Indians have with their blood, sealed their loyalty to the British Crown!"

Through coercion, threats, and other backdoor dealings, several native representatives (including some who had no authority to speak for their people) eventually signed the document. The chiefs of Wiky never signed, and so their land – the entire eastern end of the island – was never ceded, never relinquished, never opened to white settlers.

Crossing into Wiky, I was greeted by a large sign saying, "Aanii, Welcome." There was also a sign celebrating the Bond Head Treaty, the original treaty that had preserved Manitoulin Island and surrounding islands for the Anishinaabek. The sign explained that the island is a spiritual place, noting that a great spirit frequents an underwater tunnel at the heart of the bay.

I drove to the little village in the reserve and stopped at the visitor kiosk there. Three First Nations teenagers, one girl and two boys, were talking at a nearby picnic table. I studied the map posted there, and the girl walked over to me and asked if she could help. I had heard about a hiking trail on the northern part of the reserve, and she kindly gave me directions to get there.

At the parking area for the Bebamikawe Memorial Trail, three happy dogs greeted me. I looked at the trail map and then began hiking up the "Three Fires" route. One of the dogs stayed behind, but the other two trotted in front of me, excited to explore. One was a mostly black, shepherd mix, the other an all-white, medium-sized mutt. They vaulted in excitement off the trail frequently, crashing off into the underbrush trying to catch a chipmunk or mouse, but then they'd emerge ahead of me again and continue. They often glanced back to be sure I was following.

The trail steepened toward the top, and I travelled many switchbacks to get up the rise. The dogs headed straight up the hill, looking back at me like they weren't sure I knew what I was doing, since I was taking the long way.

The view from the top was a study in blues and greens. The island was many shades of green, the water of the bay many of blue. The sky was a lighter blue with clouds smudging the horizon. The bay looked like a splendid place for a great spirit to reside.

After a short break, I continued farther along the trail. The white dog stayed with me, but the other one headed back the way we'd come. I noticed fossils – horn coral and some fossilized plant – in the sedimentary rock on the top of the trail. I was at least 300 feet above lake level, but this land, clearly, was once submerged.

I drove around Wiky a bit more after my hike. I'd love to report that this is a thriving community with a strong economic base, a huge success. But Wiky is struggling. Unemployment is high, substance abuse is a problem, and there aren't many opportunities for the young people. This is similar to other rural communities, but this native community also has to deal with the scars from residential schools in the past where kids were taught to be ashamed of their own heritage.

One thing I noticed that was special to Wiky, though, was the use of the Anishinaabe language on many of the signs on their land. Stop signs had the traditional shape and color, but bore the long Anishinaabe word for "stop." Language immersion has also been recently introduced at the local schools. Grades K–3 are now taught in Anishinaabe. The high school kids learn to drum and sing traditional songs. The guidance counselors smudge the students with traditional plants and herbs. Leaders in the community hope that by reclaiming the pride in their native culture and way of life that healing and prosperity will return to Wiky.

Old Woman Lake

The village of Mindemoya is considered the central hub of the island. Lake Mindemoya is nearby and is the third largest lake on the island (after Lake Manitou and Lake Kagawong). Lake Mindemoya has the largest island on it, Treasure Island. The word "Mindemoya" means "old woman" and there are a couple of legends about the island. One says an old spirit woman was flung into the lake, and the island rose up where she sank.

Treasure Island is the largest island – over 80 acres – on a lake, located on the largest island on the Great Lakes.

It's an island on a lake, on an island in a Great Lake.

I inflated my kayak at the boat launch. The day was warm, and families with kids were splashing around at the nearby beach. Paddling away from shore, the lake bottom dropped away until I could see the beams of sunlight streaking into the depths, but could no longer see the bottom. The water was perfectly clear.

As I neared the island I could see the bottom again, a rubble of limestone blocks. Small fish schooled in the shallows and darted around. Some trees on the shoreline had blown over, their root mats exposed but still clinging to rocks they had been holding before they fell. Some trees leaned out over the water, and their branches reached for me as I paddled. As I headed back to shore, I saw huge fish in the depths. These pristine island lakes provided rich fishing in years past and continue to produce trophy fish today.

After packing away my kayak, I drove to the west side of the lake to explore a cave. A stream dissolved the limestone to form this cave, so entering it is like seeing the inner workings of the geology. Mindemoya Cave is on the private land of a resort, so there is a small fee to tour it. I went to the window where an elderly woman greeted me. She took my money and handed me a small key chained to a chunk of wooden dowel. On the cut surface of the wood, someone had written "Cave" with a black marker.

Scary tale

The trail to the cave is called the "Fairy Tale Trail" because little cabins along the way are staged with scenes from popular fairy tales. This sounded pleasant enough. But when I went up to the first tiny cabin and peered in the large window, I was stunned. Inside, I first saw two stuffed pigs – real pigs that had been to the taxidermist – looking back at me. This was weird enough, but when I got closer to the window and the glare of the sunshine on the glass diminished, I could make out a third pig, likewise preserved, standing on her hind legs and wearing an apron. She was at the table, fixing tea at the rear of the cabin. When I looked to the right of this pig, I stepped back in surprise because bursting through a door on the side of the cabin was a wolf, teeth bared, caught in mid-leap on his way to a pork chop dinner.

I guess the creator of this tableau didn't care for the "huffing and puffing" part of this story and empowered the wolf to crash through the door.

Let me emphasize: This wasn't a sculpture or a drawing of three pigs and a wolf. It was four actual dead creatures, stuffed and posed.

I stood there wondering who took the time to choose which pigs to stuff, then to pose them just right, and tie an apron on one of them. The other two pigs were naked, as most pigs are. These two gaze out the window at visitors, unaware of the wolf bursting through the door. And the wolf looked ferocious. His huge paw was a few feet from the aproned pig whose back was to the wolf.

I'm telling you, the next few moments in that cabin are going to be mayhem.

After staring at the scene for several minutes and getting progressively more disturbed, I continued down the path to the second tiny cabin. Inside, there were three taxidermied black bears. Two were close to the window sitting at a table with bowls of porridge, and one stood farther back near a tiny bed. As I got closer, I could also make out a small girl standing in the corner of the cabin: Goldilocks. I studied her for a moment, a bit worried. Of course, she wasn't a taxidermied real girl, but a large doll or mannequin. She held one hand up to her mouth in surprise. I'm sure we'd all be surprised by three black bears in the room, even stuffed ones.

There was one more cabin – I think it was Hansel and Gretel – but my brain was still processing the first two, and I didn't pause there for long. The trail curved and descended toward the lake, and I soon saw the iron gate that secured the cave. My cave key fit the padlock. I swung the gate open and flipped on the cave light. Water pooled on the floor, and drips fell from the ceiling in places.

At this point I wasn't entirely surprised when I noticed a human skeleton up on a ledge. I'm pretty sure it was plastic. When three duck-hunting Mennonite preachers stumbled upon the cave in 1888, they found the skeletons of at least a dozen Huron Indians, presumed killed by the warring Iroquois in the mid-1600s. One of the skeletons was measured to be more than seven feet tall. All of the bones and other artifacts were shipped off to a museum in Toronto, but were later lost in a fire there.

The cave was long and fairly tall (60 feet long and 15 feet high in places). It would have been a good place to hide from a warring tribe . . . at least until they found you.

Me? I didn't stay too long.

Where mists rise

The most beautiful and accessible waterfall on the island is in the town of Kagawong. This Ojibwa name means, "Where mists rise from the falling water." This little village is on the northern edge of Manitoulin Island at Mudge Bay. I took a long walk from the falls to the shoreline, around the village, then back to the falls. It was an enchanting spot, relaxing after the unsettling experience of Mindemoya Cave.

In 1862, the island of Manitoulin was opened to settlers after the government took most of it back from First Nations people. To encourage permanent settlements, lumber mills could only be established in places where companies brought in at least a dozen settlers and also built gristmills to grind grain into flour. The Henry brothers, Robert and William, built the first sawmill and gristmill in Kagawong in 1873 and purchased 700 acres of land. Five years later, the little town was thriving.

Fate was not kind to the Henry brothers. In the spring of 1882, Robert was aboard the steamer *Manitoulin* when it caught fire two miles offshore. The captain ordered the ship be run aground so people could escape onto land. As the fire raged, though, many people jumped overboard prematurely to escape the flames. The captain and crew were able to beach the ship and offload the majority of passengers, but at least 20 died either in the flames or by drowning. This was a time when women wore long, bustled dresses, made of heavy cloth. Jumping into the water was almost certain death when wearing such a garment, even if the woman happened to know how to swim. Robert Henry escaped death by fire and water. Instead, he was felled by a fatal heart attack while assisting fellow passengers.

The steamer brought in to replace the burned *Manitoulin* was the *Asia*. This ship was made of wood, 136 feet long and only 20 feet wide at its widest point. It sat high in the water and was originally used on the Welland Canal, a constructed passage of the St. Lawrence Seaway, connecting lakes Ontario and Erie and bypassing Niagara Falls. The *Asia* was suited to work on the protected waters of the canal, but would now be doing a route in Georgian Bay between ports in Ontario, stopping at Manitoulin Island, then steaming up the St. Marys River to Sault Ste. Marie. William Henry, brother of Robert who had died that spring, was on the *Asia* when it ventured into Georgian Bay in September 1882, colliding headlong with an epic storm.

A valley of endless length

On September 14th, the *Asia* left Owen Sound at the southern end of Georgian Bay and steamed north, parallel to the Bruce Peninsula. It chugged straight into the teeth of a frightening storm that swept down from the north, hovering over Georgian Bay as the *Asia* turned to cross it. Hurricane winds were reported from Manitoulin Island, and the wind direction switched as the depression swirled. These whirling, gale-force winds whipped up waves that were thirty feet tall – roughly three stories high. The steamer could not maintain its direction in the wild seas. Cargo was cast overboard to lighten the load. Horses onboard broke loose, thundered around the deck, and leapt or were cast overboard by the violent rolling of the ship. The *Asia* soon foundered and went down.

A survivor, Christine Ann Morrison, said of her last moments on board:

I saw people putting on life preservers. The boat rolled on her side, and I thought it was sinking, when I jumped up and went into the adjoining state-room, where a woman with two children was. I found her asleep and awoke her, but think she never left the cabin. I then put on a life-preserver and sat by the cabin door.

Before I went to my state-room I asked the mate if there was any great danger. He said there was a very heavy sea, but they had already thrown some horses overboard and would throw off all the freight they could. I had hopes the boat would be saved till I saw water coming into the cabin.

I was on the upper side of the boat. She lay now on her side. I took hold of the rail, slid down into the water, and sank. I came up by the side of the Captain's boat. He took me by the wrist, and the mate helped to pull me up.

Another survivor, Dunkan Tinkus, described the storm from the lifeboat:

The sea was now a mountainous whirlpool. . . . Notwithstanding the horror of the scene, it was incomparably grand and awe-inspiring. Every time we went down in the hollow we seemed in a valley of endless length with towering mountains on both sides. . . . all about was a mountainous sea and no land was visible from any quarter.

There were seven people in his lifeboat, including Christine Ann Morrison. She said:

I saw the other two boats tip over three times, and when I next saw them they were empty, no one even clinging to their sides.

The others in their lifeboat all died of their injuries or exposure in the many hours the little boat spent in the storm. Of the over 100 passengers aboard the *Asia,* only these two, Dunkan Tinkus and Christine Ann Morrison, survived to tell the tale.

Ten years after the tragic event, Tinkus recalled the time on the lifeboat:

I thought – we all thought – these would all live to reach the shore, although two hours before a French deck-hand had gone crazy and jumped overboard. As the light gleamed over the billows we all, led by the Mate, began singing "Pull for The Shore." But the song ceased, and one by one the singers fell into that sleep that knows no waking.

The Montreal man died at eight o'clock; Little went next and the Mate – who had been singing so joyfully, a little over three hours before – succumbed at eleven.

I felt the premonitory symptoms myself; an intense cold followed by numbness in the finger tips, and then the warm glow and drowsiness accompanied with an almost overpowering desire to dose. But I knew that 15 minutes of that meant the beginning of the eternal sleep and I resisted. Three times I aroused the Captain from his lethargy and told him he was dying, but it was of no use, and he too, crossed the bar about midnight.

Our boat was still full of water and as each one died I placed the body under the seat to prevent it from being washed out. There was no sleep for Miss Morrison or myself that night.

After they made it miraculously to land, the two survivors were eventually rescued by a native man and his wife. Tinkus and Morrison were both just teenagers, only seventeen years old at the time of the disaster. Christine Ann Morrison lived till the age of 74. Later in her life she said of the aftermath of the wreck:

I didn't get up for two weeks and I couldn't talk about the wreck to anyone. Reporters tried to see me but I avoided them. I have hardly ever talked about it. . . .

This isn't quite true. Morrison did give a statement that the *New York Times* that was published a week after the sinking of the *Asia*. She was proclaimed a heroine by her sheer force of will to survive this disaster that took so many lives, most of them able-bodied men.

A dramatically staged photo of Morrison survives. She stands against a painted backdrop of a rocky shoreline. Waves roll onto the land, and ominous storm clouds hover over the water. She stands there wearing a long, black dress buttoned down in front and bustled in back. The hem brushes the ground. Black lace decorates her wrists and neckline. Her long hair has a slight wave to it as it flows down to her elbows. In her hands, she holds a rope. One end of it curls on the ground to her right, while the other end is held off-camera to her left. She gazes in the direction of the rope. Her face is calm, her eyes sleepy, her eyebrows thick and dark. In her account to the *New York Times*, she said:

The mate told me to hold on to the lifeline whatever happened, and I never let go. When the boat upset I hung on, and came up with it.

For at least a short time, Morrison made appearances in the region, proclaimed as a heroine, selling copies of that photograph. *The Paisley Advocate*, a small newspaper on the Bruce Peninsula that separates Georgian

Bay from Lake Huron, announced: "Christy Ann Morrison, heroine of the *Asia* disaster, to visit Bruce to sell her photograph; speaks Gaelic." The date for this event was December 1, 1882, eleven weeks after the sinking of the *Asia*.

William Henry, co-founding brother of the city of Kagawong, was one of the passengers who perished in this maritime disaster. Most of the bodies of *Asia*'s crew and passengers were never recovered, though occasionally one would wash up on shore even into the following year. People stopped eating fish from these waters, afraid that the fish had fed on the dead.

It was a warm day when I visited Kagawong, and people were splashing in the cool waters at the base of the falls and swimming in the deepest part where the waters splashed down. Young kids balanced along a ledge behind the falls, followed closely by their dogs.

In the village, I toured the Heritage Center in the old pulp mill that had once produced paper for the Sears Roebuck catalog. Today, the falling waters of Kagawong are still harnessed, but not to saw lumber or grind grain. A generating station has a turbine that is rotated by the river, and the power is sold to the Ontario grid.

Bay of Providence

For the next few days, I camped near one of the best beaches in Ontario on Providence Bay. This scoop of shoreline is located on the southern edge of Manitoulin Island and looks out onto the big waters of Lake Huron. I set up my tent, then rented a bike.

During the day I biked the quiet roads, circling back to the bay in the evenings. Each night, there was a postcard-worthy sunset on Providence Bay. After dinner at camp, I'd wade out into the cold water. This was always chilling, but it refreshed my legs for the next day's ride. The lakes were slowly warming from the record cold we had experienced the previous winter. Icebergs had been spotted floating on Lake Superior well into June.

I biked back up to the village of Mindemoya one day, to Lake Kagawong another. On the final day, I biked east to Michael's Bay. This last day was especially free of road traffic because a bridge was being replaced in that direction, and all traffic was routed off Government Road.

An archeological dig at Providence Bay had revealed evidence of transient native encampments dating back as early as 500 A.D. Both Providence Bay and Michael's Bay had thriving native settlements in the 1600s, and the Odawa who settled here were hunters and fishermen.

I toured the exhibits at Providence Bay's Harbour Centre and found a photo of one of the early lumber camps. Forty men stand in the snow, some in shirtsleeves, some wear wool sweaters, others heavy coats. Two lucky fellows have black bear fur coats that extend past their knees. Every man but one wears a hat, varying from knitted stocking caps (called a "toque" in Canada), to bowlers to wide-brimmed hats. Some wear woolen caps with a little brim, and one stylish fellow wears a tam o' shanter, an Irish bonnet like a fat beret with two pom-poms on top. The hats reveal the diverse ethnic origins of the men.

Eight sturdy draft horses, probably Percheron, stand mixed in with the back row of men, the men grasping their reins or bridles. Huge cut logs are stacked behind them. Two men on the left side of the photo almost disappear into the snowy scene because they are the camp cooks and wear white aprons. They hold long tinhorns to their lips, the instruments used to call the men in from the woods for meals. Many of the men have smoking pipes clamped in their mouth or held in their mitten-sheathed hand.

Two individuals stand out in the photo: one small boy, and a young man with an armful of cats. First, I consider the little boy. There are no women in the photo, even the cooks are men, but this small boy stands in the front row. He leans against the arm of a man in a striped woolen sweater. The boy's face is either flushed from the cold or smudged with dirt. It's difficult to tell from the sepia tones. He wears mittens, but they are too large for him. He stares blankly into the camera.

The guy with the cats is in the middle row and on the right side. He leans back as he clutches two cats to his chest. If they had to stand there outdoors a while to pose for the photographer, this guy was probably glad he brought along two warm cats.

While pedaling the back roads, I often stopped to look at thick stands of milkweed. The variety growing on the island was taller and lusher than the types I'd seen elsewhere on my journeys. At times the plants were almost four feet tall, with more globes of flowers than I'd ever seen on a single plant. The individual flowers – each one resembles a five-pointed star

– were a deeper red than the other varieties. You may know that the milkweed is the only plant on which monarch butterflies will lay their eggs. It is the only plant that monarch caterpillars eat, so it is essential for the survival of this species. I was encouraged to see this plant on all of my hikes, and delighted to see this robust variety alight with monarchs on Manitoulin Island.

Another thing I noticed on my rides were the many cows on the island. There had been a progression here – as I had also seen on other islands – from timber to agriculture to livestock, shifting as the natural resources on the island were depleted. On Manitoulin, I learned, most of the cows are now brought over from the mainland for the mild months to graze the island. Called "feeder cows," these cattle are then shipped off-island once they've fed for months on the lush island grasses. Another striking thing was that often there were calves mixed in with the heifers. Since the cows weren't being milked, the calves were allowed to stay and feed on their mothers' milk. It was odd that something so natural had become rare to see because of the way dairy farms operate.

Fish dinner

The side road leading to Michael's Bay was dirt, so the pedaling was a bit tougher, but there was no traffic. The Manitou River paralleled the road. This river cuts its way through an ancient raised delta that used to be the sandy mouth of the river. Now it is a sandstone plateau that the river flows over, continuing to smooth and shape it.

At the end of the road I walked out onto the limestone slab at bay's edge. I sat and looked out on the water. The limestone was warm from the sun and felt good on the backs of my legs. I wet my bandana in the cold water and tied it around my neck again.

As I watched the ripples on the water, a little head poked up about a dozen feet away. My first thought was that it was a turtle, but as it got closer I realized it was a snake. And it had something in its mouth. The snake continued swimming, intent on landing its lunch: a round goby.

I've seen these fish up close several times in fish tanks. In one, they were all sitting on the bottom, big frowns on their faces (that's how they look since their mouths turn down at the corners). A crayfish in the tank climbed around on the tops of their heads and still they didn't move. They stayed there, glowering. It seemed to me that they wouldn't be the cleverest at evading predators.

The snake was a beautifully striped northern water snake, and it had a mouthful with this goby that was about five inches long. Gobies have a rather fat head, and the snake had clamped its mouth around the side of it. The fish looked at me with its left eye while the right eye looked down the throat of the snake, staring into its near future. The snake landed the fish like a pro, but when he tried to reposition his mouth on the head of the goby, the fish saw a chance for escape and thrashed, flipping back into the water. The snake paused, glanced at me, then swam back out into the bay on the hunt once again.

There were some impressive fossils in the limestone along Michael's Bay. Ancient plants were preserved in the slabs of stone as large, quartz ovals, unlike anything I'd seen before. On my way back to Providence Bay, I stopped to explore the Manitou River. Finding a place where the river widened, I waded in, hoping the water would be shallow and warmer than the bay. It was. I found a spot in the ancient sandstone carved into a gentle depression. Sitting down, I allowed the pleasantly cool waters to swirl around me like a whirlpool.

The day I discover "Double Up"

During my long bike rides – on my most ambitious day, I covered 38 miles – I kept an eye out for any store or gas station selling sports drinks and ice cream. The sports drinks were to replace electrolytes, and the ice cream because I was pedaling many miles in the hot weather. And ice cream is delicious. I discovered a Canadian ice cream bar called "Double Up." One part is a standard vanilla ice cream dipped in thick chocolate and sprinkled with almonds. The other part is an ice cream sandwich.

That's right: they stuck an ice cream bar directly to an ice cream sandwich. You hold onto the ice cream sandwich as you eat the bar. Then, when the bar is gone, you have half of an ice cream sandwich left. And there's no wooden stick to toss away when you're done.

I don't know about you, but there have been many times when I've been halfway through an ice cream sandwich and thought, *I wish I had chosen the bar dipped in chocolate.* The "Double Up" erases ice cream regrets. When you've had enough of one type, the other type is right there in your hand. This was a brilliant ice cream idea that I revisited several times while on Manitoulin Island.

Sometimes, the research for this book was challenging and exhausting. Other times, it was delicious.

Another fish dinner

For my last dinner in Providence Bay, I shunned my freeze-dried camping dinners and, instead, walked to the nearby fish and chips place. The whitefish on the menu must have been swimming in Lake Huron earlier that day, it was so fresh and delicious.

The place also sold *poutine,* a another Canadian culinary creation where they put brown gravy on fries, then top it with cheese curds, but that looked a little heavy for the hot weather. I did have fries with my fish, though and observed the Canadian tradition of splashing them with malt vinegar.

Porcupine hunter

Next, I headed to the far western end of the island. On the way, I stopped at Misery Bay to hike the provincial park there. On the long drive, I spotted a fisher – a member of the weasel family – lying dead on the side of the road. Within the weasel group, fishers are larger than weasels and mink, but smaller than river otters. Males weigh around eight pounds when mature. It's rare to see these creatures – this was the first I had ever seen – so I stopped to examine it. It must have been a glancing blow that killed it, because it was not bloody or broken in any way. It looked like it was napping on its side.

The fisher is an impressive hunter and the only successful predator of the porcupine. To get around the porcupine's defensive quills, they attack its face until they inflict enough damage to stun or kill it, then they flip it over to access the unprotected belly.

Fishers have a long, catlike tail that helps them balance when climbing trees. They have short, pointed ears and an elongated face. The body is lithe. The dead fisher at my feet was probably born earlier in the year. It didn't look like it weighed more than five pounds. It was mostly black and dark brown, with lighter brown patches on the sides of its head and neck.

The edge of each ear was rimmed with light tan hairs. The feet were remarkable for their fat pads and sharp claws that did not retract.

Imperiled habitat

The story of how Misery Bay got its name finds a farmer cutting marsh grass there in the 1880s for cattle feed. Two government surveyors call out from their boat, asking what the bay was called. The farmer has been working in the blazing sun and fighting black flies all day, so he yells back, "Misery!"

That name was put on early maps and it stuck.

Misery Bay Provincial Park is located at the narrowest part of the island on a stretch that was submerged for a long time. When the waters receded, much of the exposed limestone shoreline became a habitat called *alvar*. This is a rare environment, and in North America it only exists in the Great Lakes Basin.

Alvars are defined by the flat expanses of limestone or dolostone. These rocky plains offer a harsh environment for plants and animals. Soils are shallow, and grasses and other vegetation struggle to get established. These rocks heat up in summer and are often flooded in spring. Some of the plants that thrive here are rare, and most alvar habitats, according to the Environmental Protection Agency, are "globally imperiled."

There are some spectacular alvar regions on Manitoulin Island, and Misery Bay is arguably the most impressive. I stopped in at the visitor center and studied the map of the hiking trails. One of the young volunteers recommended the blue trail that crossed the head of the bay and then looped around the other side.

"It's underwater right now," she pointed to the trail at the head of the bay, "but it's just knee deep and sandy."

The day was warm, and hiking Misery Bay by hiking *in* the bay sounded like an immersive – and enjoyable – way to fully explore the park. I hiked to the edge of the water, crossing limestone flats still bearing scars from the glaciers. The head of the bay was normally a sandy outwash, but higher water levels in Lake Huron had submerged this feature. At the water's edge, I took off my boots and tied the laces together, draped them over my shoulder, and headed into the water barefoot.

The wetland extended inland, so this area offered several types of habitat for plants and grasses and wildlife. Small fish darted before me in schools, and a crayfish scooted backward in retreat. Clumps of marsh grasses poked out of the water, and ducks and geese paddled around. As I reached the other side of the bay, it got rocky underfoot, so I plotted the shortest distance to dry land. I hauled myself out of the bay and up onto a rocky ledge and retied my boots. A leopard frog jumped into the water below me and swam back to the rocks, staying partially submerged.

As I hiked south along the edge of the bay, I saw huge slabs of limestone submerged in the water, and the smoothed limestone shoulder of the bay clearly had been shaped by wave action. One erratic – a rock moved and deposited in a different place by the glaciers – in the water was a boulder of puddingstone. This is a distinctive conglomerate stone that consists of large pebbles held together in a sandstone matrix. Early British settlers thought this stone resembled their meat or berry puddings and so named the rock.

There were small caves and fissures in the jagged limestone that rose along the bay. Large fossilized coral were evident in the limestone. The largest chain coral I'd ever seen was here, measuring over five inches at its widest point. Blowing sand gathered in small depressions in the rock face and, miraculously, tiny plants took root in this shallow soil. Many cracks between the rocks sprouted grasses or flowers. When I put my palm against the limestone, it was warm to the touch. These alvar flats intensified the heat of the day, but the plants growing here have adapted to these harsh, arid conditions.

On the way back across the bay head, wading once again in shallow water, I saw a pitcher plant growing in a marshy area. I scared up a northern water snake. I watched a sand piper poking around in the shallows. On one sandy area, I saw the rare Pitcher's thistle thriving.

This park has many rare and endangered plants and animals, including Blanding's turtle. In recent years this turtle has been dying off in the park, and scientists are trying to find out why. Blanding's turtles have a unique feature that helps scientists to keep track of them: the plastron, or lower shell of the turtle, has a colorful pattern. And each pattern is unique. It's like their fingerprint. So scientists don't have to tag the turtles. They can just photograph this pattern and know which individual they have when recaptured in the future.

Some of the female turtles, however, have been fitted with radio transmitters, to allow scientists to track their movements in the park, helping them to locate and monitor nesting sites.

After my hike, I drove to Meldrum Bay and used the historic inn there as my base for the next few days. I had enjoyed camping at Providence Bay. But I knew that a large storm was heading for the island, and I didn't want to be in my tent when it hit. The evening was beautiful, though, and I ate dinner at the inn's restaurant, seated outside on their wrap-around deck. Hummingbirds visited the flowers in hanging baskets on the porch while I ate. My view was of calm Meldrum Bay, the westernmost bay on the island.

That night, the storm transformed the bay into a rush of whitecaps. Fog hovered on the water as the rain continued into the next day.

Manitoulin's oldest lighthouse is at the western tip of the island, shining its light over the Mississagi Strait. I drove through the wind and rain to the lighthouse, passing by the entrance to the Lafarge limestone quarry on the way. With over four million tons of limestone extracted yearly, this is Ontario's third-largest mine. Stone from this mine is used primarily in the concrete business as aggregate and in the process of refining iron ore. Lafarge plans to expand the mine since demand for limestone is increasing. The evening before, I had seen two young scientists who were also staying at the Meldrum Bay Inn while they studied the environmental impact of the proposed mine expansion.

A caped man?

On the rugged dirt road out to the lighthouse, I looked through the rain-streaked windshield and saw a caped figure run across the road. When the figure lifted off the ground, I realized it was an enormous bird, not a short man. It flapped its huge wings, landing on the low branch of a tree. I stopped the car. An eagle? I hadn't seen any white on the head or tail.

I leaned over into the passenger seat and looked out the side window just as the bird turned its bowling ball head to look at me. This was no eagle. This was the biggest owl I'd ever seen. Great horned owls top out at two feet tall. This one was bigger, and it didn't have any horns, just that gorgeously rotund head.

This was the tallest owl in the world: the great grey. Topping out at over 30" in height, its wingspan can exceed five feet. This owl stays in mid-Canada to Alaska and was not even listed on the pocket bird checklist I had picked up at Misery Bay. Manitoulin Island is at the far southeastern range for this bird.

I opened the car door and stepped out into the rain. The bird had silently glided off into the fog. I looked up at the bare branch where the owl had been sitting. I finished the drive to the lighthouse leaning over the steering wheel, scanning into the fog for another glimpse of that owl, my stomach jangly with excitement.

The fading lights of the island

The squat lighthouse on the western side of the island is the classic Georgian Bay design, where the light sits atop the keeper's house. It is built on the limestone slab that rises above the waters of the strait that narrows to about two miles wide between Manitoulin and Cockburn Islands. Because of a dangerous combination of submerged rocks offshore and a magnetic reef that interferes with compasses, many ships were wrecked in this channel until the light was lit in 1873.

I was surprised to learn that many of Manitoulin's lighthouses are leased to people who run them as tourist attractions. This lighthouse was in need of some work. Tarpaper was tacked to the roof, and paint flaked off the clapboards on the light tower extending above that. Inside, the keeper's quarters were tidy and recently painted, but on the upper level, water leaked into the tower and dripped inside.

After touring the lighthouse, I went to the edge of the water. The limestone formation here was comprised of stacks of refrigerator- to car-sized blocks abutting the channel. Fissures ran between the chunks, twenty feet deep in places. Waves crashed toward me, and water surged into these fissures and fountained up, spraying me. Even though Cockburn Island was only a couple miles away, the fog prevented me from seeing its outline above the water. On this day, the scene looked like a nasty setting for a shipwreck.

I drove back to the main road and headed toward Gore Bay to see another of Manitoulin's lighthouses. On the way, as I approached the narrows by Lake Wolsey, I noticed an osprey nest on a platform. From on top of a pole near where I parked, an osprey screeched down at me when I got out of the car. I took a few quick photos of the other parent feeding the chicks in the nest. I soon left, though, not wanting to disturb the hard work of the parents. On the drive north to Gore Bay, I was thrilled to see a live fisher cross the road. It was wonderful to see a live one the same week I saw one that had met an early death.

An icy dip

I rented a bike at the Gore Bay marina and rode around the village a bit before heading to the Janet Head lighthouse on the west arm of the bay. This side of the bay has a gentle incline that I felt in my thigh muscles. The east side of the bay, in contrast, is distinguished by a tree-covered limestone escarpment that rose hundreds of feet above the level of the water. I was glad they had located the lighthouse on the gentle side.

The Janet Head light has been the summer home for four generations of the Fletcher family who have cared for the lighthouse and property. Members of the family take turns living in the keeper's quarters during the summer months and are happy to give tours to visitors. Built in 1879, this lighthouse was of similar construction to the light on Mississagi Strait.

One of the Fletchers showed me around the upper level of the house. I told her I'd been to the Mississagi light and was surprised it wasn't being kept up as well as hers.

"There is talk that all of the lighthouses here will be taken down," she told me. "My family has a lease from the county, which in turn leases this light from the government." She paused. "Unfortunately, there's no guarantee that will continue."

She told me that her grandmother had a habit of taking a dip in the bay every day of the season, even if there were still ice chunks floating around. She did this until she was 90, when she decided she was a little unsteady on her feet and would stop. These Manitoulin Islanders are of sturdy stock. Just thinking about taking a dip in the frigid, rocky bay in the middle of August made *me* feel a little unsteady.

After the tour, I strolled the rocky shore. Waves pulsed gently into the bay, calming as they entered the sheltered waters. The shore was scattered with fossils: horn coral, crinoids, ancient shells, and softball-sized rocks that were fossilized sponges. On the ride back to the village, I saw an eight-point buck still wearing velvet on its horns. It stared at me for a bit before turning and walking away.

On the drive back to Meldrum Bay, I saw a curling club with an indoor practice facility. This is a winter game of Scottish origin that involves sliding polished, rounded rocks along the ice.

I also realized that every gas station I had seen on the island was full service. This island seemed to be keeping its own time.

That evening, I asked Shirin, the owner of the Meldrum Bay Inn, if she had a bird book. I was quite sure about the identity of the owl, but wanted to see it again. She brought me her book and I opened to the page with the great grey. There he was.

The two scientists working on Lafarge's land were seated at a nearby table.

"I saw a great grey owl out there!" I blurted to them even before introducing myself.

"We saw it too," the young man answered. He was a biologist. The young woman was an environmental engineer.

"That's quite a bird!" I said, still excited by the sighting like the bird geek I am. We chatted for a bit about their work gathering water samples from test wells drilled around the mine. They would test the water, then submit a report to both the mining company and the provincial government. This report would guide the decision about the expansion of mining operations on the island.

More Misery

The next day, I headed toward Misery Bay again, exploring some of the side roads and bays along the way. Down Burnt Island road, I found the dock for the boats of the Purvis Fishery. This is a fifth-generation family business founded in the 1880s by William Purvis. He first fished these waters using a small Mackinaw sailboat. This fishery supplies the fresh fish to restaurants on the island.

At Misery Bay, I hiked most of the trails on the east side of the bay. The rain had cooled things down, and the steady breeze kept the mosquitoes away even along the interior trails. The wind made little sandstorms on the surface of the limestone plains. Still, little plants and even flowers clung to bits of soil caught in depressions or fissures in the rock. Lichen grew in patches, and some moss even tried to hang onto the stone near the water.

To the Cup and Saucer once again

On my drive from the western end of the island to South Baymouth at the eastern end, I took a detour to the Cup and Saucer Trail to climb the escarpment once again. I knew the island intimately now. There is a gentleness on Manitoulin, and a sense that the past is still quite present. The plentiful split-rail fences here – called *snake fence* on the island – blend in with the scenery. The abundant wildlife also speaks to the natural quality of the island and to the commitment by islanders to maintain habitat for these wild residents and winged visitors.

From the top of the ridge, the trees cloak the land until it breaks off at the water. From one outlook, the only indication of man's presence were some wind towers. These didn't intrude so much, but rather flowed with the breezes blowing over the treetops. The island is an unsettled, settled place with plenty of wilderness to explore.

Time is altered on Manitoulin Island. The past overlaps with the present. The pressures of modern life fall away as you drive over the swing bridge. Island time here means time unto itself – unpressured, natural, and calm.

Miles for Manitoulin Island:

Bike	Hike	Kayak	Ferry
107	78	8	29

Flowerpot Island, Ontario

The *Cheech*

During my sojourn on Manitoulin Island, I took a daytrip to nearby Flowerpot Island. A car ferry, the *Chi-Chemaun* (affectionately called the "*Cheech*" by locals) runs from the southern end of Manitoulin Island to the quaint town of Tobermory, located 30 miles to the southeast at the tip of the Bruce Peninsula.

I boarded the *Cheech* for the nearly two-hour passage. The day was clear and warm. We passed many islands along the way, more fragments of the dolostone ridge protruding above the waters of Lake Huron. The largest were Fitzwilliam and Cove Island.

Tobermory is organized around a harbor filled with all sorts of water-craft – from tall ships to many tour boats, along with several boats with equipment to dive on the many shipwrecks here. Canada's first National Marine Conservation Area protects the cluster of islands around the tip of the Bruce Peninsula, the lighthouses, and the waters around them. It is called the Fathom Five National Marine Park, and there are two dozen known shipwrecks here. This designation and the clear waters and many wrecks have made Tobermory the freshwater scuba diving capital of the world.

I chose one of the many tour companies transporting visitors out to Flowerpot Island, buying a ticket that would give me three hours to explore there. The boat had an underwater viewing area, a boxed-off section with a glass bottom, providing a window to the submerged world. The tour boat traveled into nearby Big Tub Harbour to give us a look at two shipwrecks. The 119-foot schooner, the *Sweepstakes*, ran aground near Cove Island in 1885 and was towed here to have her parts salvaged before she sank. The steamer called *City of Grand Rapids* caught fire in 1907 and was towed out of Tobermory's main harbor and into Big Tub to keep the fire from destroying docks and other vessels. The steamer burned to the waterline before sinking next to the submerged *Sweepstakes*.

Both of these shipwrecks were visible under the surface of the water, and a small part of the steamer stuck above the waterline. Our boat maneuvered over the top of the wrecks and passengers took turns at the viewing area to look at the ships' ancient timbers.

Flowerpots and sea stacks

We then sped out to Flowerpot Island. The depth of the water was indicated by the color: black/blue where it was deepest, green-blue as it got shallow, and aquamarine near land where submerged limestone slabs were visible beneath the waves.

We sped clockwise around the island before docking. This allowed us to view the rugged shoreline and the two distinctive flowerpot formations from the water. These limestone stacks are 23 and 40 feet tall respectively. Visitors clustered around each formation, looking up at them and posing for photos. People from all over the world were making the trip to this island. I heard at least eight different languages spoken.

These flowerpot formations – also called "sea stacks" – were once submerged. Water and waves eroded softer layers of sediment away, isolating these towers of limestone from the rest of the shoreline. When the water level dropped, these sturdy formations were revealed as pillars. Today, small shrubs grow out of the sides of the flowerpots. The tops of these formations have been sealed with mortar to prevent water from getting into the cracks and fracturing the rock during freezing weather.

The first lighthouse on Flowerpot was built on the bluff, a bit past the flowerpot formations, over a century ago. I climbed to the top and looked down at the turquoise water near the shore. While this elevated site surely made the light more visible to ships, the climb up the hill was tough, and the keepers would have had to transport everything up the hill to live here and maintain the light. Another lighthouse and keepers quarters were eventually constructed closer to the shoreline, and a volunteer group maintains these structures today.

The islands in this passage indicate where the Niagara Escarpment lies, but this dolostone shelf is also submerged here. Long after the retreat of the glaciers, the level of the lakes was so low for a time that land was exposed between where the Bruce Peninsula is today all the way to Manitoulin Island. A river coursed over this ledge, flowing to the east, dropping over the dolostone shelf into Georgian Bay in a great waterfall that was equal to Niagara Falls.

Today, as water from Georgian Bay now flows west into Lake Huron, there is a vast lifting as these waters rise to flow over this submerged shelf. The movement of water from deep (over 500 feet deep in places) to shallow waters around the islands brings up rich nutrients. The water is filled with zooplankton and phytoplankton, nature's fish food. Small fish have a feast, and larger fish feed on them.

The sun set during my trip back to Manitoulin Island on the *Cheech*, blazing orange before extinguishing itself in the vast waters of Lake Huron. The surface of the water deepened from blue-black to black-blue, then, as the sunlight was erased, finally to solid, swirling, inky blackness.

Miles for Flowerpot Island:

Hike	Ferry/powered boat
5	70

LAKE MICHIGAN ISLANDS

The islands of Lake Michigan are found at the northern end of the lake. On the west side, the Grand Traverse chain of islands fit in the gap between the tip of the Door Peninsula reaching north from Wisconsin and the Garden Peninsula of Michigan reaching south. These landforms are the western part of the Niagara Escarpment.

The east string of Lake Michigan islands is found close to Michigan's Leelanau Peninsula (the "pinky" of Michigan's lower peninsula). This 14-island archipelago stretches from the Manitou Islands through the largest in this chain, Beaver Island, and a couple of smaller islands reaching toward the Straits of Mackinac. The foundation of these islands is a tilted ridge of limestone.

Many of Lake Michigan's islands were inhabited by Native Americans hundreds of years B.C., while others are too small to be more than a resting place on a long, watery journey. Some of these islands have year-round communities today – most notably Washington Island and Beaver Island – while many others have been protected as parks or nature sanctuaries.

My travels took me to several islands on each side of the lake.

Cana Island, Wisconsin

Kayaking on the "big" lake

Early in the summer of 2013, I traveled to Wisconsin with my kayak, heading first for the Door Peninsula, where I stopped to explore Cana Island. This island is northeast of the town of Baileys Harbor and is, technically, no longer an island since a land bridge has formed between it and the mainland as the lake level dropped. Islands can be ephemeral. Their separateness can depend on the season, on the precipitation of the recent past, of the build-up or erosion of sandbars or shallows from slow sedimentary action or sudden storms. There are even islands that disappear under rising lake waters only to appear again when those waters retreat.

I paddled out into the lake and floated along the edge where the limestone shelf underpinning the island fell off into deep water. Shafts of light streaked into the black depths of the lake. I had seen this effect before, but always from a much bigger boat. In my little kayak, I felt the rays pulling at me.

I paddled closer to the island and looked at its lighthouse, a white tower adjacent to a red-roofed keeper's house. Then I turned and propelled the craft toward the unprotected edge of the landmass. Waves were magically forming where the pulsing of the lake reached the limestone shelf. The water lifted and pushed my craft into a shallow area where I had to lean on my paddle to advance the kayak where it scraped the rock.

Once back in deeper water, I rode up and over several waves. One was large enough to splash over the bow of the kayak, soaking me from lap to hat. When I finally reached the protected bay on the backside of the island, I was able to surf in on the waves rhythmically heading toward shore. The paddle took less than an hour, but it was thrilling to be out on Lake Michigan – *my* lake – to feel it pushing me along, to connect with it in a new way.

The limestone shelf supporting Cana Island is a hazard. Before the lakes were mapped, boats would draw close, not knowing about the submerged ledge of stone extending out from the island. One minute they'd be in deep water, the next they'd have run aground – or worse, gouged a gash in the hull of the ship.

The lighthouse on Cana Island was built in 1869 to guide ships around this danger. The Coast Guard automated the light in 1944. Today, it still shines out on the waters of Lake Michigan.

Miles for Cana Island:

Hike	Kayak
1	1

Washington Island, Wisconsin

Too big to walk around?

After kayaking Cana Island, I drove on to the tip of the Door Peninsula. This wedge of land thrusting north into Lake Michigan is verdant, rolling country with large farms, many beautiful barns, and quaint towns. It is this peninsula, along with the Garden Peninsula reaching south from the Upper Peninsula, that forms Green Bay, pinching it off the west side of Lake Michigan.

I had never been to the northern tip of the Door. As I mentioned earlier, this peninsula is part of the Niagara Escarpment, the arc of dolostone running through the Great Lakes Basin. It is the reason that these peninsular and island landforms exist: Lake Huron's Bruce Peninsula and Manitoulin Island, Lake Michigan's Door Peninsula and Garden Peninsula, with a sprinkling of islands in the watery gaps (such as Washington Island and Rock Island off the end of the Door).

When I arrived at the tip of the Door Peninsula, I went to the ticket booth to buy passage on the ferry to Washington Island.

"One ticket. I'm leaving my car here," I told the man in the booth.

He held up his hands and shook his head. "The island is too big to walk around," he replied.

"I'm a long-distance hiker," I insisted. Besides, how did he know how far I could walk?

"Okay. Most people aren't." He took my money and slid the ticket across the counter, still eyeing me sideways.

Okay, I know I look like your average middle-aged woman, but I can hike all day long and could leave this booth worker in my dust.

I parked my car where he directed and shouldered my pack. Then, I grabbed a large box of books. I had told Kathleen, the owner of Islandtime Books, that I was coming to Washington Island and would be happy to do a signing of my second book, *A 1000-Mile Great Lakes Walk*. She said the book was back-ordered and asked if I could bring some with me to the island. This was new: blending a book tour with a new adventure, combining the role of hiker and book delivery service.

The ferry quickly filled with cars and people. Many families with small kids gathered with me on the top deck for the ride to the island. I stowed the box of books underneath the bench to make room for people and then stood with a hand on my white backpack.

Death's Door

The water was calm as we crossed the passage between the tip of the Door and Washington Island. This waterway is called "Death's Door" because the currents and waves can make for a treacherous crossing. This dangerous passage has claimed many lake vessels, from Native American canoes to 18th-century wooden sloops, to 19th-century steam ships. This day was calm and mild, though, and our transit across death's door smooth.

There is something about taking a boat ride to an island that confirms you are travelling to a place removed from your normal life. There is no rushing the ferry. It keeps its own time and schedule. Time on the ferry encourages everyone to pause and relax. As you are transported over the top of the water, that gliding motion calms you. The breeze resets the mind. We passed an identical ferry on its return trip to the mainland, and I felt the slippage of time as the boats crossed within sight of each other.

On the island, I decided that renting a bike would be the best way to deliver the books. The bookstore was several miles from the dock, a distance I don't mind hiking with a heavy pack, but with a pack and a box of books in my arms . . . well, I didn't care to try that. I situated the books in the basket, cinched the straps of my pack tighter around me, then took off pedaling. Once I had delivered them safely to Kathleen, I continued pedaling toward the northeast corner of the island, Jackson Harbor.

While gliding down one of the many hills on the island, I was reminded of the topography of Lake Huron's Manitoulin Island. Manitoulin is more muscular, though. It has taller hills, more exposed rock, and is, of course, much larger. These islands share the same geological underpinning, though – the dolomitic Niagara Escarpment. This magnesium-hardened limestone shines white in the sunshine.

I was on Washington Island in mid-June, a beautiful time to explore this outpost. The lilacs were in full bloom, scenting the entire island. A flash of brilliant blue flew across my path and into some low trees: an indigo bunting. I had seen the occasional bluebird on my journeys, but never the exotic blue flash of the bunting.

Icelandic heritage

Washington Island has a permanent population of just over 650 residents, many are descendants of the hardy people who tamed this island and survived the harsh winters here. These people were largely from Scandinavia and Iceland. Between 1870 and 1914, nearly one fifth of Iceland's population emigrated to the U.S. due to difficult times (including a devastating volcanic eruption) in Iceland.

In 1875, Oddur Magnusson erected a large, two-story building on Washington Island. Newcomers would often stay for a time in this structure, lovingly dubbed the "Icelandic Castle." It was a place to connect with island residents and to catch up on news from Iceland. It seems true that a certain type of person is drawn to dwell on an island. Why else would Icelanders driven from their home island colonize Washington Island?

I submit that it is this dynamic, watery force constantly rubbing at the edges of islands that draws people to these isolated landmasses. "Island people" are deeply attracted to this setting of land-surrounded-by-water. This movement, this frisson of water against land, this mirror to the weather captivates many. It creates a force that can be sensed. Island people feel it and know they are home.

The most striking example of this island's connection to its Scandinavian heritage is the Stavkirke, a Nordic chapel. It was built in the 1990s, largely by volunteers, and was patterned after the distinctive architecture of medieval churches in Norway. Since the Stavkirke is constructed of wood and is shingled and sided with wooden shakes, it blends into the surrounding forest. The overlapping lower roofs and overall proportions of the building call back to a different time and place. And the four carved dragons adorning the top roof bring Vikings to mind. In the days of early Christianity in Norway, the church builders still felt a need to invoke these ancient mythological beasts as guardians.

As I stepped through the chapel door decorated with wrought iron hardware, I was surprised at how much lighter the wood in the interior was. The exterior had weathered and darkened, blending with the woods, but the inside was protected from the elements. There were a dozen vertical beams or "stavs" (related to the word *stave* from barrel-making) in this little chapel; each was nearly 20 feet tall. All of these supports were made from trees harvested on Washington Island. The building was constructed using old shipbuilding techniques, and the interior of the chapel feels ship-like because of this. Turn the Stavkirke upside down and launch it out onto Lake Michigan, and it might prove to be lake-worthy.

There were a couple dozen wooden chairs in the central room of the chapel, and a wooden altar at the far end inscribed with the words "Han Er Oppstanden" meaning "He is Risen." In the middle of the room I looked up. From there I could see the interior of the topmost part of the chapel and appreciate the geometry of the construction: the tongue-and-groove joinery of the beams, the angles of each roof as they stacked on top of each other, the wooden trunnels locking the massive pieces of wood together. There were once over a thousand of these churches in Scandinavia. Today, only a handful survives. And this modern re-creation stands on Washington Island in Lake Michigan, far-removed from its Nordic brethren.

A living community

On Washington Island, there were many friendly people to chat with. Some had summer residences there or regularly ventured to stay at one of the island lodges or hotels or camps. Some made the island their home, a continuation of generations that inhabited the island. Some had left to go to college or find jobs, then had later been drawn back to their island home.

Julie Anderson fell into this last group. Generations of her family have lived on the island. She told me that her grandmother witnessed the steamer cruise ships that used to dock there when she was a young girl. The women passengers wore long dresses and hats and carried parasols to shade them from the sun. The black porters wore red jackets and ties. The porters would carry a carpet off the ship, then roll it out on the beach for passengers to take a stroll. The carpet, of course, was red.

"What's the best thing about living on the island?" I asked Julie.

"Nature. Living close to the land," she said.

For some this concept – living close to the land – is just an ideal. But here on the island, it was a way of life.

"And what's the drawback to living here?"

"Some things are not as accessible. Like choices for shopping. And car parts. You have to plan ahead when you're going to the mainland."

In our conversation, she called the water surrounding her island "the moat."

I had stopped by a store on the way to Julie's house to pick up a bottle of wine to go with the dinner she was making for me. The store not only stocked a great selection of wine, but also offered shoes, furniture, and of course many island-themed gifts. This was my idea of good shopping. No chasing around, everything in one place.

Island evolution

Washington Island evolved over time as man tamed this wild place. Initially covered with thick forests of virgin woods and surrounded by rich fishing grounds when only Native Americans roamed the lake, settlers transformed the island. They harvested the lumber and quarried limestone from its edges. Then, the stumps were removed, and the land was sown with crops like peas and potatoes. In 1907, the regional markets were glutted with potatoes, and some of the ships returned to the island with unsold cargo. The farmers, having no way to store them all, tossed the excess spuds into the lake.

The land was quickly depleted of nutrients, so some farmers turned to raising dairy cattle. This progression from lumber to agriculture to livestock is a pattern common with other Great Lakes islands. Today, there are still farms and livestock, but much of the economy is based on the mild months when tourists and vacation homeowners cross Death's Door to spend time on this tranquil outpost.

The isolation that an island inherently possesses is a quality that can give farmers an advantage. For example, Washington Island was the first place in the U.S. to be declared free of bovine tuberculosis. Also, crops could be raised in isolation, and strains of seeds could be perfected. Islands give farmers a degree of control over the environment that mainlanders don't have.

Over several days, I hiked and biked much of the island. I sat on Schoolhouse Beach with its thick layer of tumbled, pure-white limestone cobbles and looked out at the clear water. I rode my bike over the rolling hills and waved to cows and horses. I chatted with the friendly and fascinating people at the Red Cup Coffee Shop, the Islandtime Bookstore, on the docks, and on the front porch of the small grocery store.

One family I met had been coming to the island for decades for their annual reunion. They reserved a small resort for one week every year, a familiar spot where four generations gathered for games and fellowship and time to reconnect. Washington Island seemed like the idyllic place for this, removing people from their busy lives so they could concentrate on what was truly important.

Miles for Washington Island:

Bike	Hike	Ferry
24	2	9

Rock Island,
Wisconsin

Rock Island sits off the northeast corner of Washington island. Thin peninsulas reach toward each other from the islands like the two landforms had recently been pulled apart. Satellite images reveal a skinny sandbar underneath the water, connecting the two peninsulas.

In fact, the fall before my visit, people on Washington Island had been able to wade along this sandbar in thigh-deep water to reach Rock Island, as Lake Michigan was at an all-time low. Currents in the area can be strong, though, so even with shallow water this can be a dangerous crossing.

Collector of books

From my room at the Jackson Harbor Inn on Washington Island, I could clearly see Rock Island a mile away. And even at that distance, I could make out a huge stone structure on the island. It is impossible to talk about the island without talking about this structure – "the boathouse" – and the man who had the vision to build it: Chester Thordarson.

He was born in Iceland in 1867. His family immigrated to America when he was only six years old. They moved around a bit, so Thordarson was mostly self-educated. When he got his first job in an electrical shop in Chicago, he earned $4 a week. Each week, he put $1 of that into buying books. He eventually amassed a magnificent library of over 11,000 books covering a wide range of scientific subjects. Many of the books were rare and valuable, including a complete four-volume *Audubon Folio*.

While visiting North Carolina a few years ago, I went to an art museum that held a set of these books. Like most people, I was familiar with Audubon's bird art through reproductions, but had never seen the originals. This set is often called the "elephant folio" because the volumes are gigantic, sized at just a bit more than three feet tall by two feet wide. At the museum, each of the four books was on a platform, sealed in a glass case that could be opened to allow the turning of the pages. On each sheet, birds are depicted life-sized. Birds taller than the scale of the book, like the great blue heron, are depicted bent over, ready to strike at something in the water. Smaller birds are depicted in groups or even in dynamic scenes, like a cluster of Virginian partridges scattering as a hawk descends on them.

John James Audubon became obsessed with birds as a young man and devoted thirteen years of his life to tracking down birds all over America in the early 1800s. He developed a naturalistic style of posing birds in their habitats rather than the standard, flat depiction of the time. In all, Audubon created 435 engraved copper plates of his birds. Prints from the plates were then individually colored by hand. At least 180 sets of the four folios were produced and sold. Today only 119 are known to survive.

Over time, these gorgeous books have steadily increased in value. When a complete set comes up for auction, it usually breaks the record for the last time a set was sold. Most recently, a set sold for $11.5 million. I own a lovely, but downsized, reproduction of these books created from digital photos of the set held by the Natural History Museum in London. Thordarson, however, owned one of the original, gigantic four-volume sets.

Before Thordarson turned 30 years old, he opened his own business. The Thordarson Electrical Manufacturing Company made electrical parts for radios and cars, and Thordarson experimented with new inventions to control electricity. With his increasing wealth, he began looking for an island retreat. When the parcel of land he wanted on Washington Island was not available, he decided to buy Rock Island. In 1910 he bought his first acreage there and in two years purchased the rest of the island for less than $6,000. The only part of the 912-acre island that he couldn't own was the corner held by the government where the Potawatomi Lighthouse stood.

If I won the lottery . . .

When posed with the question, "What would you do if you won the lottery?" many people answer, "I'd buy an island!" The idea captures escape, of having somewhere to yourself, of owning and controlling the entirety of a place, a place where the only rules are the ones you make. Several of the islands included on this odyssey had once been owned by a wealthy person. Rock Island is in this group, joining Heart Island (with its grand Boldt Castle).

Thordarson didn't merely want a wild retreat, though. He had plans to reimagine Rock Island. The boathouse is the most obvious surviving part of his plan, but he altered the flora and fauna there, too. He introduced species like wild turkey and grouse and constructed large greenhouses to grow the plants he desired to reshape the island. He constructed large fences to keep deer from eating the new plants. He also manipulated native species: when he was sure that the fox had eradicated all of the rabbits, he ordered that the foxes be exterminated.

Thordarson was a powerful man in his time, and he entertained other powerful men on his island retreat. One of Chicago's mayors, William Hale Thompson, was a close friend and such a frequent visitor that Thordarson built him a personal cabin on the island. Clarence Darrow, the defense attorney of the Scopes Monkey Trial fame, also vacationed there.

Thordarson renovated the few sturdy buildings that were already on the island, but soon commissioned a boathouse to be constructed using stone from the island. You may be picturing a modest structure where boats are sheltered, but Thordarson had something more grand in mind. It took 20 masons three years to build it at a cost of a quarter of a million dollars. Today, it would cost many millions to build the same structure. The footprint of the building is 2,800 square feet. It is several stories tall, with immense, arched windows on the main level. His personal library was transported to the island and housed in the boathouse. Thordarson considered the stone building to be fireproof and therefore a safe haven for his cherished books.

I rode the Karfi ferry ("Karfi" means "seaworthy ship for coastal voyages" in Icelandic) from Washington Island to Rock Island State Park, and the boathouse loomed above us as we drew near. The structure is beautiful, the skilled workmanship obvious to even my untrained eye. Since the boathouse is built with dolostone from the island, it feels like it pulled itself out of the shoreline, organizing its stones as it grew in height, then settling itself firmly in place along the edge of the harbor.

I got off the ferry and admired the structure from all sides before hiking the perimeter of the island. The day was mild, and I had only a water bottle and a granola bar to carry. Hiking without my large backpack perched on my back was liberating, and I took more time to photograph the blooming columbine, lilacs, and forget-me-nots. I found a tree with evidence of pileated woodpeckers. Seven rectangular holes had been gouged out by their strong bills, marking the tree with a vertical dash from ground level to ten feet up its trunk. I took photos of the lair of a wolf spider, and took some time to capture the perfect close-up of a sunlit, glowing columbine bloom from below.

The shoreline was mostly dolostone, either tumbled into cobbles or still intact in large hunks, and cliffs, but on the east side it opened into a wide, sandy stretch, and I wandered out to the water's edge. This attractive beach made Rock Island an easy place to land boats. Archeological digs along this beach have yielded evidence of several Native American tribes, early European explorers, and settlers who lived here in the mid- to late-1800s. Some of these artifacts are on display inside the boathouse today.

The loop trail was wide and the hiking mostly easy, with only a few places where the elevation changed abruptly. I took a break at the lighthouse on the northwest corner of the island. This was Wisconsin's first light on Lake Michigan. The original structure was built in 1836, and the lighthouse standing today replaced it two decades later. It, too, is built from island stone.

I took a tour of the lighthouse and enjoyed chatting with the volunteer keepers. The lighthouse was furnished with period pieces and even housed an original "lighthouse library." These wooden boxes were filled with books and would be swapped between the lighthouses so there was always something new to read. Instead of the keepers going to the library, the library came to them. There is an overlook at the lighthouse to view the scattering of small islands reaching north to Michigan's Garden Peninsula.

The Boathouse

I finished my hike with plenty of time to explore the boathouse before the ferry arrived. The "great hall" is the main room. The ceiling is roughly three stories above the floor. The walls are stone on the inside, too, and massive beams support the roof above. Arched windows grace three sides of the great hall, allowing the light to stream in and illuminate the white stone.

A single wooden chandelier measuring nine feet tall by six feet wide hangs in the middle of the room. On each arm of the structure, a buffalo horn points up to the ceiling. The wooden structure supporting the horn is decorated with colored glass. A light bulb is seated into each horn. These chandeliers – there were originally five of them – were a marvel of the day. Each had seven electrical circuits and thirty-five switches, making many different lighting effects possible. Thordarson made his fortune with electricity, and these chandeliers put on quite a show for visitors to his island kingdom.

He also wanted to show off in the lower level of the boathouse. There he installed state-of-the-art restrooms, outfitted with porcelain fixtures hooked up to water and sewage lines. These would have impressed his guests on the island, likely even before they got to see the light show in the great hall. Wisconsin is where the plumbing company Kohler was founded, so Thordarson had access to some of the most modern plumbing fixtures in the nation.

A massive fireplace dominates the windowless wall of the great hall. Today, there are many displays to explore in the boathouse with diagrams or actual examples of Thordarson's inventions, and some of his personal notebooks. Thordarson gained fame when he won a Gold Medal at the 1904 St. Louis World's Fair for inventing a transformer that could handle a million volts. He built it in only 28 days. The framed certificate of this award hangs in the boathouse.

Thordarson was a complex, driven man, and a pioneer in the new age of electricity. He was brilliant and intent on reshaping an industry and an island. His heirs sold his vast library – possibly the centerpiece of his life – to the University of Wisconsin in 1946 for a small fraction of what one volume of the Audubon Folio is worth today. Then, in 1963, they sold Rock Island to the State of Wisconsin. Today it is a state park, open for all to explore for the day, or longer if they wish to camp at one of the designated sites there.

Miles for Rock Island:
Hike	Ferry
7	3

Power Island, West Grand Traverse Bay, Michigan

Summer island dancing

A month after my visit to Washington, Rock and Cana islands, I drove north from my home in Battle Creek to explore a few islands on the east side of Lake Michigan. Anxious to do more kayaking, I took advantage of an ultra-calm summer day in Traverse City, Michigan, to paddle out to Power Island in West Grand Traverse Bay. From Bower Harbor on the Mission Peninsula, it is a seven-mile round trip paddle to this 200-acre island.

This was the largest stretch of open water I had kayaked at that point, so as the sandy bottom of the harbor transitioned into limestone and then fell off into deep, dark blue water, this adventure took on new depths. I had a waterproof camera with me that I could plunge underwater to capture the play of the waves, refracting the sunlight into moving patterns in the shallows.

Power Island is another outpost that has been owned by a single person in the past. After I pulled my kayak up onto the sandy shore near the long, wooden dock, I walked to a metal plaque embedded in a stone. It gave the thumbnail history of the island.

Frederick Hall first purchased the island in the 1880s and named it Marion Island after his daughter. During the decades of Hall's ownership, he teamed up with Captain Charles A. Webb to construct a long dock and a dance and dining hall there. Captain Webb piloted his steamer in a loop around Grand Traverse Bay, transporting people to the island to dance the summers away. When the sun went down, they hooked up the generator on the boat to the lights in the dance hall so the party could go late into the evenings.

When the automobile became widely available, however, interest in the dances on the island diminished. People began vacationing with their own vehicles on the mainland and stopped venturing to Marion Island.

Ford Island

The next owner was, ironically, the guy who had killed the island fun: Henry Ford. He purchased it from Hall in 1917. There was wild speculation about what Ford would do with the island: *He would build a summer mansion – bring famous people to visit – set up a camp for underprivileged boys!*

There are stories still told around the Traverse City area about the grand happenings on the island when Henry Ford owned it. They say that Ford hosted several U.S. presidents on the island. There is even one amazing story that tells how Ford invited Babe Ruth to the island to instruct underprivileged boys on how to hit a baseball. The tale continues that Ruth showed up drunk, and Ford, a committed non-drinker, booted him off the island. In retaliation, once back on the mainland, Ruth proceeded to hit baseballs into the water toward the island from the Mission Peninsula . . . or so the story goes.

In trying to verify these tales, I went through the archives at the Traverse City Historical Museum. The local newspaper at the time – which followed Henry Ford's every move when he steamed into Grand Traverse Bay on his luxury ship, *Sailia* – concluded that Ford never even set foot on the island. He did, however, arrive in Traverse City in the summer of 1923 with Harvey Firestone (of Firestone tires), Thomas A. Edison (of . . . ah . . . the light bulb), and their respective wives. They didn't get to the island, though, as the Edisons opted for a night at the Park Hotel, and the rest of the party slept on Ford's well-appointed steamer. The next day they left for Escanaba without even stopping at Ford's island.

Castaway

I tried to track down the more fantastical stories, but could not verify them. These myths emerged from the locals' dreams and desires projected on the island. One event I found to be true, though, was that Natalie Schafer (the actress who played Mrs. Thurston "Lovie" Howell, III, on the TV show, *Gilligan's Island)* came to Michigan in 1967 to be in a play at the Cherry County Playhouse.

As a publicity stunt, Schafer was taken out to the island, which was renamed Gilligan's Island for the day. She was ceremonially "cast away" there. In the archives, I came across a photo of Schafer standing by a man holding a handmade sign (done in that wacky *Gilligan's Island* font) renaming the island. The castaway comedy had ended that year, and I'm sure all of the actors were wondering how long their iconic island characters would overshadow their future careers. Schafer's smile in that staged photo was a little strained that day.

Other notable actors who set foot on the Cherry County Playhouse stage are Maureen O'Sullivan ("Jane" in the Tarzan films), Vivian Vance ("Ethel Mertz" on the *I Love Lucy Show),* Ann B. Davis ("Alice" from *The Brady Bunch),* and even actor Burt Reynolds. What I wouldn't give to see a group photo of them collectively marooned on that little island in West Grand Traverse Bay.

Ford never did anything grand with the island while he owned it. He allowed the dining and dancing structures to decay and then be dismantled. The wood was taken to the mainland and reused. In 1944, he sold the island to the Power family. That family, convinced that the island should be preserved in its wild state and open to everyone, eventually conveyed the island to Grand Traverse County with the help of The Nature Conservancy and other organizations. Today, it is a county park with camping sites. A caretaker family spends the summer months on the island outpost.

I stretched my legs after the long paddle to the island in the bay, and hiked across the soft, sandy place. There were no remnants of "Lovie's" visit, and Henry Ford built no monumental structure there. Today, instead, you'll find a quiet county park island with a few camping sites, surrounded by the crystal-clear blue waters of Grand Traverse Bay.

Miles for Power Island:

Hike	Kayak
1	7

The Manitou Islands, Michigan

Both South and North Manitou Islands became part of the Sleeping Bear Dunes National Lakeshore in 1970. They are the southernmost islands on the east side of Lake Michigan, located off the Leelanau Peninsula (it's the "pinky" on Michigan's "mitten"). I spent a summer week on these two islands after my paddle to Power Island.

The Manitou Islands (the name is from the same Algonquin root found in Manitoulin, from the native word for a spirit force) have evidence of early habitation by native peoples and were later settled, logged, and farmed for a century. Most settlers had left the islands, though, before they were formally absorbed into the National Lakeshore designated district.

Most of my time was spent helping to monitor the Great Lakes piping plovers that nest on these islands. This subspecies is classified as endangered. The closely related Northern Great Plains and Atlantic Coast piping plovers are both listed as threatened. At the lowest point in the 1980s, the population of the Great Lakes piping plover had dwindled to only a dozen nesting pairs.

Habitat destruction is the primary cause of the decline of these diminutive shorebirds. Because of this, the Manitou Islands serve as protected outposts, vital to their recovery.

South Manitou Island, Michigan

Planning to camp during my time on the Manitou Islands, I prepared my large white pack, with my tent and sleeping bag and pad strapped to the outside. Inside, I stuffed plenty of dehydrated food, a compact stove, rain gear, extra clothes, notebooks, a sketchpad and color pencils. It weighed about 40 pounds. At this point, though, I was comfortable hoisting it onto my back, settling and cinching it securely, and looking forward to a long hike.

As I walked the long dock onto South Manitou Island, I passed several people. One gentleman looked me over from boots to pack to hat, and then asked if I was the woman who hiked around Lake Michigan. I nodded and shook his hand.

"Are you doing another hike?" he asked.

I told him about my exploration of the islands. He looked pleased with the idea. He explained he was with a volunteer group working to preserve the historic buildings on South Manitou.

Valley of the Giants

I headed straight to my campsite and set up my tent in the Bay View Campground. There were low, rolling dunes between my tent and the water, but it was only a short walk to the lake's edge. With a campsite reserved for my four days on this island, I would be able to leave most of my gear and explore without the company of my large pack.

I had heard about the Valley of the Giants on this island, an area where some of the largest white cedar trees in the world still thrive, and I wanted to see them before I did my first evening check on the piping plovers. I took my water bottle – since it was in the mid-80s – and headed to the southwest corner of the island. The trails on South Manitou are well marked, and many are wide enough for vehicles because there's a motorized tour available to day-trippers.

I strolled past Florence Lake, a small island lake on this island in a lake.

South Manitou had recently seen a population surge in rabbits and snakes, and I saw plenty of both as I hiked. The rabbits were alert, because there are coyote on the island. Most of the snakes were garter snakes, but their coloration was more vibrant than those I had seen on the mainland. I also saw a rare collared snake sunning itself on the path. It was slender and small, barely a foot long, and completely gray except for its black head and a cream-colored ring around its neck. I crept close enough to watch its tongue languidly poking out to sample the smells in the air.

I soon arrived at the Valley of the Giants and began to walk among the massive white cedars. Despite their name, white cedars belong to the cypress family. The wood from these trees resists decay, making it useful for fencing and posts, for cabin construction, and it can be split to use as roofing shingles. Native Americans used this wood in the construction of canoes, and they also used parts of the tree for medicine. The Ojibwa tribe called the tree "Grandmother Cedar" because it had so many uses. Today, you can buy the essential oil of the cypress for calming aromatherapy.

Deer love to munch its distinctive foliage, especially in the winter. Unlike most conifers, the foliage of this tree isn't so much a needle as a flattened, narrow, branching structure called the "leaf" of the tree. It is rich in vitamin C.

The thin bark of the white cedar grows in vertical strips that naturally tend to detach, making the tree look shaggy. One of the giants I saw had been snapped off about twelve feet from the ground. The weather had subsequently denuded the enormous stump of its bark, revealing the structure beneath. Places where branches had once attached were now elaborate, exposed burls in the wood, as if some master carver had inlaid distorted faces there.

I ran my hand over the markings, trying to read the hundreds of years of history the tree had seen. This group of trees in the valley had been spared from the ax, while most of the other giants on the island were slashed to build homes, sent off-island as lumber, or chopped to cordwood to power the steamers that once travelled all over the Great Lakes.

A boardwalk had recently been installed to keep hikers from packing down the soil around the base of the ancient trees, so the stroll was easy and flat. I was alone with the giants, so I took my time visiting with them. One of the felled trees had 528 rings. This means it was less than 50 years old when Cartier crossed the Atlantic and sailed up the St. Lawrence River.

The roots of the trees extended outwards, crisscrossing each other as they skimmed over the top of the earth before plunging into the soil. A felled tree was left with its tangle of spiky roots exposed, a burst of roots in the air. Some of the standing trees reached over 100 feet tall. Their canopy didn't start until near the top, leaving their long trunks exposed.

I ran my hand over the shaggy bark of one enormous tree – a true giant – and wondered how many other people had also walked up to this specimen in awe and done the same over the centuries.

A determined, charismatic leader

As I hiked back through the village on my way to check on the piping plovers, the man I met on the dock walked toward me. "There's someone you need to meet," he said. "Follow me."

I followed him inside one of the houses in the village, where he offered me something cool to drink. A woman came in off the back porch, with some others in tow, and stepped into the living room. The fellow pointed at me and said. "Gwen. She's here."

Gwen, a short, lively woman in her 70s, stopped talking to the people alongside her and looked at me in amazement as if I had just appeared magically in her living room. Which, in fact, I had.

"My daughter just read your book, and she told me I had to meet you. And now here you are," Gwen said, waving her hands around her head. "Things like this happen to me all the time."

I smiled and shook her hand. She introduced me to the others, all volunteers helping to restore and maintain buildings on the island. I could tell that Gwen was the center of action. Everything revolved around her. She had assembled an impressive group to work on the island.

Over the years she had corralled over 70 people to tag-team projects there. Many had made an annual summer trip to South Manitou a regular part of their lives. There were carpenters and handymen, cabinetmakers and plumbers, electricians, guys who hung drywall, roofers, mechanics, and painters. Many had first visited the island on vacation and had fallen in love with it, and then Gwen got a hold of them. One of the volunteers, Dorothy Cooley, was a folk singer who wrote songs about the island. There were even a few descendants of people who had lived on the island in the past.

I wondered how an island takes hold of someone, how it captures their imagination to the point that they not only care about it, but repeatedly return to give it something of themselves. I asked Gwen why this island, of the tens of thousands of islands in the Great Lakes?

"I started coming here over thirty years ago with friends," she said. "We loved camping here. Then, the volunteering started in the early 1990s. The Parks Service didn't know us or what we could do, so we had to prove ourselves. We paid our own way out here in those early years and camped while we worked."

I asked about their first project. She said that the Parks Service asked them to dismantle three dilapidated cottages on Florence Lake in the interior of the island. The workers had camped during this assignment, but once the Parks Service saw all they accomplished, Gwen's group was allowed to stay in the houses on the island, and members were given free passage on the ferry when they came to volunteer.

At first, Gwen's group worked for just a week or two in the summer, but in recent years, that had expanded to all of the summer months. Gwen spent most of the winter organizing the schedule of volunteers, planning the projects with the Parks Service, and getting materials like paint and caulk and lumber donated. Then she'd spend the summer on the island with volunteers, who rotated on and off as their schedules allowed.

Gwen's group had painted most of the buildings on the island, cleared trails, caulked and repaired, put up fences, helped to dismantle old buildings at the end of their usefulness, upgraded historic boardwalks, and helped to move buildings back to their historic sites. In their spare time, they gave tours to visitors.

This summer, one of the priority projects was to caulk and paint the fog signal building. South Manitou had the first steam-powered fog signal on Lake Michigan.

Gwen insisted that I come back to join them for dinner that night. "We eat around six. And you're camping, right? Come early if you want to take a shower."

I liked the sound of that but didn't want to intrude. "Should I set a time to take a shower?"

"Just come anytime. Treat this like your second home."

It was more than an invitation. It was an order.

So I did. I would check in on the piping plovers at Gull Point in the morning, then take long hikes around the island during the day. In the late afternoon, I'd take a quick shower and then have dinner with Gwen's volunteer brigade before checking on the plovers again in the evenings. It was a delightful schedule.

Many Parks Service workers also joined the group for dinner. The volunteers liked to tell how Gwen had roped them into working so hard on their vacations. It takes a talented, charismatic leader to get people to work on their time off from work.

A rye history

The island is about eight square miles. When viewed from above, it looks like a fat "C" – with the indented part forming the deep harbor and bay on the east side. The top of the "C" is Gull Point where thousands of herring gulls gather to nest each year. This is the largest gathering of this species of gulls on the Great Lakes, and the area is protected during the spring and summer months when the gulls are raising their young. Occasionally, piping plovers have nested within the gull rookery, but most of those shorebirds choose to nest on nearby North Manitou Island.

During my stay on South Manitou, there was only one nesting pair of piping plovers to monitor. I hiked the curve of the bay many times to check on them. The bay also gave a great vantage point to view the island's historic lighthouse. I sketched it from Gull Point, with the blue-green waters filling the space between the lighthouse and me.

I also visited the farm sites abandoned over a half-century ago. Many buildings remain, though some have been lost to time and neglect. Several of the farms grew crops for seeds. The most important seed crop was Rosen Rye, a variety that thrived in the sandy soil found here. This variety was highly valued because it doubled the yield per acre over standard strains. Seeds had to be grown in isolation, though, because rye is easily cross-pollinated by the wind with lesser varieties. Farmers on South Manitou had the perfect conditions to grow Rosen Rye seed, and they worked to improve the strain. This high-yielding seed led to more farmers growing rye in the heartland of America and effectively tripled the production of this grain nationwide.

Farmers on South Manitou, particularly the Hutzler family, were given awards for their exceptional seed. During my research, I saw an old black-and-white photo of a skinny farmer standing in his field on the island. He gathered a fistful of the tall, wispy stalks in each hand, and the fat heads of the rye hovered above his head.

A tale of two women

After seeing all the work that the volunteers had done, I wanted to explore Gwen's connection to the island a bit more. Gwen told me the story of Bertha Peth, a woman who had come to live on South Manitou in 1891.

"She was hired as a nursemaid, and she fell in love with an islander named John Hutzler," Gwen told me. "They married in 1893. They had one son, Sam, who died young after being trampled by a bull." Gwen told me that Bertha left the island for a few years, but eventually returned to help care for some island children who had no mother.

Gwen told the story like she knew Bertha, as if she were a dear friend, even though they had never met. How was that possible?

Gwen sized me up for a moment before continuing her story.

"It started when I was camping with friends," she said. "We each had our own little tent. At night, I always left my flashlight beside my sleeping bag. I would unscrew it partway, so I'd have to tighten it when I needed the light. Well, on this island, that light would come on all by itself in the middle of the night. This happened several times on that trip. The only way I could keep it off was to separate the two parts and put one on either side of me. It was odd, as I'd used the light for many trips before, and this never happened.

"Later, as we worked in the cemetery, my watch would stop working. I'd take it in to get a new battery at home, and it would be running fine again. Until I returned to the island.

"Then, there was the time my group was using a power auger to dig postholes in the cemetery. This heavy tool was leaning into the crook of a tree. There was no wind that day, but that heavy tool lifted off that tree, made a turn, and hit me in the back, almost knocking me down."

A ghost story, I thought.

"Everyone was shocked. It was inexplicable. Then someone said, 'Bertha is challenging Gwen.'"

"She was protecting the island?" I asked.

"I think so. These things stopped happening only after I visited her."

That startled me. "Where . . . did you visit her?"

"She's buried on the island," Gwen said. "I sat by her grave and told her that I only wanted to save some of the old buildings on the island, that I would never do anything to harm this special place or the history of all of the people who lived here. I told her that I wanted to honor their memory. And her memory.

"After that, I only had Bertha tap me on my shoulder and tell me, 'Thank you for being here and looking after my island.' And I believe she looked after my volunteers too, so none of us were ever hurt or injured in the work we did.

"We even had a ceremony last summer at her grave. We brought a guitar and sang some songs. The coyotes started howling. So maybe Bertha came back as a coyote so she could still live here and watch over the island."

I was intrigued by the story. "You seem very connected to her," I said.

"We have a lot in common. She played piano and harmonica, as do I. We're both German and determined. I wish I could have known her when she was alive. I think we would have been great friends."

The next day, I hiked to the cemetery and found Bertha's headstone near the back fence. By this time I had learned a lot about this formidable woman. Bertha's nickname was "Queen of the Island" and she lived most of her 83 years here. For one stretch of 22 years, she didn't go to the mainland at all.

Bertha made a meager living by finding fishing lures and floats along the shoreline, cleaning them up, repairing them, and selling them to fishermen. She also knew where a patch of ginseng grew. She would gather and dry it, then sell it to people in Chicago. Bertha would also stock cigarettes and chocolate in her home to sell to island visitors.

It was a subsistence life, lived close to the land and lake.

The isolation of islands makes for a firmer attachment and reliance on the land that rises from the depths of the lake. I believe that the personalities drawn to a life with watery edges are strong – even powerful – and I don't doubt that they can persist long after death.

A dark and stormy night

On my final night, a huge thunderstorm blew in and battered the island. There's nothing like being in a tent in a rip-roaring thunderstorm. You're really *in* the storm. I had brought along an ultra-light tent for this trip, one that set up in about two minutes and packed away almost as quickly. It was an expensive tent, and I had practiced setting it up before this trip and was pleased with its design. The tent even had a vestibule where I could set my boots so they would be out of the rain.

As I listened to waves crashing on the shore and my tent flapping around in the wind, I turned on my headlamp to read. The thunder was so close, I could feel the ground shudder beneath me. I knew that sleep was not going to come until the storm passed.

As I was reading, I noticed a dripping sound inside the tent. I shone my headlamp and saw little beads of water forming along the two long seams. The tent had been expensive, so this leakage upset me. The drips became more frequent as the rain increased. I centered my sleeping pad and whipped out my towel and placed it to catch some of the drips.

In my flailing around, I noticed that I had brought along the instructions for this high-tech, rainbow-shaped tent. I pulled the little booklet out and then turned it over to read the backside. The text at the top began, "To seal the seams of your new tent . . ."

Of course I had tested setting up the tent on a nice sunny day. And given the cost of the tent, well, I had assumed that the seams were sealed.

The rest of the night involved sleeping between the two lines of drips. Even after the brunt of the storm moved away from the island, I had to wake periodically to mop up puddles forming on either side of me, and then would scoot over to squeeze out my towel in the vestibule. As I did, I kept repeating in a sarcastic voice, "*To seal the seams of your new tent. . .*"

In the morning, it was still raining steadily. I mopped out the tent once again, heated water for my breakfast, and waited for the rain to let up. But it didn't, and since the ranger boat was coming to transport me from South to North Manitou, I broke camp and packed up my wet gear in the rain.

The lake was still pretty wild from the storm. I went to find a ranger to ask about the boat schedule and found Gwen's volunteer group doing some work in the Parks Services' garage. The boat was delayed by the storm, so I pitched in with Gwen's crew until the lake calmed. I was glad to have some extra time with them.

When the rain let up, they gathered their tools and supplies to head to their next project. Gwen gave me one last big hug, then I headed to the dock.

To crown her volunteer efforts for that year, I learned that Gwen organized a "coming home" gathering of the descendants of the keepers of South Manitou's lighthouse. This was a grand celebration of the rich heritage of the island. There were twelve descendants of keepers of the light who gathered for the celebration that day. After that summer, Gwen retired from this work, passing the role of coordinating the South Manitou Island volunteer projects to others. The work continues.

Many of our Great Lakes islands are wild places, but these may contain artifacts from the sojourns of Native Peoples or French voyageurs or early settlers. Islands like North and South Manitou have all of this, plus the remains of more recent settlements. There are people still alive that grew up on these islands, or who have parents or grandparents who plowed the earth there, or tended the lighthouse, or manned the lifesaving station. While we eagerly preserve the wild character of these islands, thought must also be given to preserving the cultural heritage.

Gwen and her battalion of volunteers had given action to that concept, and visits to South Manitou Island are more fascinating because of their work.

Miles for South Manitou Island:

Hike	Ferry
32	22

North Manitou Island, Michigan

Heading to Nico

After my time on South Manitou, I journeyed to North Manitou. There I would assist Alice Van Zoeren, a naturalist, in monitoring the many piping plovers nesting there. I first met Alice when I climbed onto the ranger boat and stepped into the small cabin.

"You must be Alice," I said. "I'm Loreen. Your volunteer for the rest of the week."

I sat across from her. She was a tiny woman dressed all in khaki and tan. Her dark hair fell in gentle waves to her shoulders, highlighted here and there with streaks of gray. She blended into the neutral colors of the boat's cabin, camouflaged even there. I thought I might lose track of her when we got out on the dunes.

After we had crossed the three miles separating the islands, the ranger boat slowed. The captain pointed the vessel toward Dimmick's Point at the island's southeast corner. I had expected to hike from the dock about five miles north, but we were going to be dropped off right at the nesting area.

The rangers pulled down an inflatable rowboat strapped on top of the cabin, dumped several inches of rainwater out of it, and slid it overboard. In the next moment, Alice had scrambled out of the cabin and jumped into the rowboat with her pack. The rangers proceeded to hand her, one after the other, a series of gallon jugs of white vinegar .

Vinegar? I wondered. *Would we be pickling piping plovers?*

The rangers started to hand my pack overboard to Alice, and I feared for her safety. The pack easily weighed 40 pounds, and it might crush her.

"Let me get in first," I told the rangers, "then hand it to me."

I clambered into the rowboat, which was crowded with gallons of vinegar, a big blue jug of fresh water, Alice's pack, Alice, and now me. My pack was added to the load.

"You're on the side to row," Alice said. The disappointment in her voice told me that she had wanted to row us ashore with her skinny arms.

"I'm happy to row," I said.

The only place for my pack was in Alice's arms. Every time I thrust the oars forward, I bumped into either the pack, or Alice, or both. If I took a shorter stroke, we'd still be out there.

"Sorry . . . oops . . . whoops," I said after bumping her repeatedly. "Tell me if I'm veering off course." When rowing, you face away from the direction where you're going.

"You're heading right to Nico," Alice said.

What's a Nico? I thought. *Short for something? Or an acronym? North Island Canoe Outpost? Nice Island to be Castaway On?*

I had continued to speculate as I pulled on the oars.

When we bumped into the shallows, a little guy waiting onshore pulled us the rest of the way onto the beach and began unloading the vinegar and backpacks.

He was Nico. As we jumped out, he tossed his gear into the little boat, and began rowing away, back to the ranger boat.

I had just watched a shift change on the island.

Alice waved to Nico and called out, "I'm not sure they'll let you on the ranger boat."

It was a running joke. He put on a shocked face and rowed like a madman. After five days alone on the island with only the birds for company, he was ready to get to the mainland.

Alice shouldered her pack that was larger than she was, then she picked up her sighting scope (another twelve pounds), and camera pack. "We'll leave the blue jug of water here for now," she said. "If you can bring some of the vinegar jugs, we'll have plenty of water with those."

So the vinegar jugs were filled with water, too. That made more sense than a pickling project.

I shouldered my pack and grabbed all four gallon jugs. Alice held out a hand. "I can take two if you'd like." What was she, the bionic woman, with all that gear on her back and wanting to take more?

"I've got it," I said with two gallons in each hand. But that was awkward, so I ended up giving her one and juggling the other three over the dunes into camp.

A *delightful* volunteer

Researchers monitor the birds from April, when they arrive on the island and begin nesting, through July, when all of the new chicks have fledged. So they had set up a rather luxurious camp back in the wooded dunes to shelter researchers and volunteers. Luxurious in that there were two tents already set up, each with two sleeping pads. There was also a screen tent with chairs and a two-burner cookstove with a propane tank protected from the elements by tarps hung off the back of the screen tent. As a long-distance hiker, I never had many amenities with me. I didn't have room for an extra sleeping pad or a chair in my pack. I *had* brought my own sleeping pad with me to the camp, though, which meant that I had three sleeping pads for my time on North Manitou. What luxury.

"Stow your things and we'll check on the birds," Alice said. I could tell she was anxious to get to work. I stowed my gear, grabbed a water bottle and the second spotting scope, and followed Alice along the path to Dimmick's Point. The southeast part of the island is restricted while the piping plovers are nesting. Signs along the beach and stakes with orange tape strung between them warn hikers to keep out. As I followed Alice, I noticed how slowly she moved, how attuned she was to every sound and sight and track in the sand. As a long-distance hiker, this wasn't my normal pace. I'm used to moving quickly, and I almost walked right up and over her a couple of times before I reined in my legs.

As we walked, I looked at Alice's gear. She had a medium-sized backpack slung over one shoulder. Inside was her large, heavy camera with telescopic lens. She balanced her scope expertly over one shoulder. I wasn't sure how she did it since I was constantly shifting mine from one shoulder to the other, adjusting the legs in and out, then finally gripping it in my hand at my side like a suitcase to keep it from digging into my shoulder muscle.

Alice stopped and turned. She pulled a radio out of her vest. "We need to call in to dispatch. They don't know your name, so I'll call you 'the volunteer.'"

"*Delightful* volunteer," I said, raising my eyebrows.

Alice was serious. "We don't say that on the radio," she stated.

Once she had checked in, she turned and continued walking, ever so slowly, along the water's edge. Again I almost trampled her since once I get by the water, I want to move, to hike, to get the miles rolling underneath my boots. I finally forced myself to stand still, putting a buffer zone between us, and was glad I did, because she stopped suddenly. She had seen something move way up the beach. She opened the tripod on her scope in one fluid motion, and had sighted and identified several birds by the time I reached her side.

"That's the West Two male, OYB:XL, and he's with two of his chicks," she said. "Red dot and blue dot." From the front pocket of her vest, she pulled a metal clipboard and opened it to reveal a complicated data sheet used to track the dozens of birds on this island. She recorded the sightings, then handed me one of the blank sheets to use. "Nico said he hadn't seen the third chick all week. So he may only have two now."

Nico only has two chicks? The male? Who has the dots? And what in the hell is OYB:XL? Is it an extra-large bird? The questions bounced around in my head, but I smiled and nodded. On South Manitou the assignment had been easier: try to find the single nesting pair of plovers and their three chicks – mixed in with hundreds of squawking gulls. Here, on North Manitou, the assignment was to locate, identify, and track all the plovers on the point. That number was around fifty birds total, counting the adults and the chicks that had already hatched.

I looked over the data sheet and decoded the symbols relating to the colored bands on the legs of the birds. All birds that had been banded in Sleeping Bear Dunes National Lakeshore would have an orange flag on the top of their left leg (a band with a little tag on it), along with a metal band on the top of the right leg. On each of their ankles, they'd have other bands giving a unique code to each individual bird. Usually these bands were a single color like dark green or blue or black. Sometimes – to keep it interesting – the band would be the same size, but would be striped, perhaps a light blue band with a center stripe of orange.

The code was verbalized: "O, little 'b', X 'bob'." On paper it looked like this Ofb:Xbob. It meant that he had an orange flag on his left leg ('Of'), on his left ankle is a light blue band (little 'b'). On its other leg is a metal band (the X stood for metal) and underneath that is one of the split bands: light blue and orange ('bob' is blue-orange-blue).

If this sounds confusing, it's because it *is*. And the birds were constantly darting around on their twiggy legs, making it difficult to decipher the color-coding. Their feeding strategy involves running around to disturb the little beetles and bugs that they eat. They may even stop in one place and jiggle one foot to make their intended meals scuttle around on the sand. These birds rely on their large eyes to detect movement in their prey. And you can't identify a bird by just seeing some of the bands, you need to specify all four of them on every bird. Did I mention that piping plovers are only about six inches long and weigh just a couple of ounces?

We walked slowly to the edge of the sandy point, Alice stopping every few steps like the plovers, scoping the birds, quickly identifying them, then moving on, often before I had my scope adjusted properly. Once when she had stayed in place long enough for me to set up beside her and actually focus on the birds, I called, "Show us your legs!" to the little birds. My joke got no rise out of Alice, and her sideways look made it clear that there were to be no more loud words directed at the little plovers on North Manitou.

"I hate it when the stones align to look exactly like a piping plover," I muttered into my scope later that first day.

"Well. That's kind of the point," Alice stated. The birds live a life of disguise on the sand and rocks. "There's a nest we need to check," she said, barely loud enough to be heard over the sound of gentle waves pulsing at the shore. "They're due to hatch while we're here."

Alice shouldered her scope and began the agonizingly slow walk over low dunes toward the caged nest. The researchers protect each nest from predators by putting a protective fence cage over it. It's called an *ex*closure instead of an *en*closure because it is not meant to keep anything inside it. The adults can get in and out to tend the eggs, but predators – like coyotes and merlins (a small, fierce falcon) – are kept out. This single measure taken to protect this endangered bird has almost tripled the hatching success of eggs. With this tool as part of an intensive conservation effort, the number of pairs nesting in the Great Lakes has rebounded from a low of only a dozen in the mid-1980s to five times that number today.

Alice adroitly identified several birds on the way to the nest, recording each sighting and noting that one chick was still hopping around on one leg. "We call him Hoppy," she said. The little bird was moving fast even bouncing along on just his left leg, his right foot tucked against his body.

Piping plover chicks begin feeding on their own soon after hatching; they are precocial as opposed to altricial. Altricial is where the parents have to tend and feed the chicks until they mature, like robins and blue jays who bring food to the hatchlings. Piping plover chicks begin running around soon after hatching, chasing down bugs.

We finally got close enough to see the nest from the rise of a small dune. I set up my scope and focused to observe the male on the nest. It was easier to find the birds when they were within the nest exclosure. I had something to focus on, and the bird was not constantly running out of my scope's field of vision.

"He's not acting like the eggs are hatching yet," Alice said.

"How do they act?"

"They look surprised," she answered, as if this should be obvious.

Monkeys

Back at camp that evening, I asked Alice how many birds she had on her life list.

"Oh, I don't keep a list," she said.

"What's your favorite bird?"

She blinked at me. "The piping plover."

That was a dumb question. "Okay, what's the most fascinating bird you've ever seen?" I hoped her answer would not be the same.

"I once saw a great shearwater here. In the Great Lakes. Along the mainland." She tilted her head toward Glen Arbor and the perched dunes along the shoreline.

She continued, "It's not normally found here. Ever. Hurricane Isaac blew it off course, from the Atlantic where it lives." She paused, remembering. "It was windy and rainy, not the best time to be out birding, but I was. And saw it." A sad smile showed briefly on her face. "I was the only one to see it alive. By the time others got there, it had died."

"Because of the storm?"

"Probably. It wasn't acting normally when I saw it. They are usually powerful in flight. I'd love to see one out over the Atlantic sometime."

A screeching in the treetops broke the moment. Alice tilted her head to listen, then looked at me.

"Monkeys," I said. That earned me a deadpan look from Alice.

"It's a red-eye vireo, upset with some blue jays," she stated.

I was astonished that she got all of that from a few screeches. "Sure," I said drawing on my comparatively scant bird knowledge. "Blue jays are bullies."

"And they'll eat the chicks of other birds," Alice added.

"And there's that," I nodded, conceding all points to the expert.

I was on North Manitou for four days. I learned to move at a slow pace, to adjust my tripod without wrestling it, to sight birds at a distance and get my scope on them before they ran off. I learned to be quiet and still.

The eggs in the West Six nest began to hatch, and we saw two chicks emerge. One was still wet from being inside the egg when we first saw it. The parents kept close watch on the hatchlings while taking turns on the nest incubating the remaining eggs.

Pre-dawn

On the final morning on the island, I woke before sunrise to accompany Alice on her pre-dawn walk. She did this every morning, but had assured me I didn't have to accompany her. It was not part of the volunteer job, this up-before-the-sun stroll. But it was part of her rhythm of being on the island.

"Really," she said waving her hands in the space between us, "you don't have to come."

"I'd like to, at least once. Maybe the last day?" I half-pleaded. She didn't approve, but she didn't forbid me. So, on that last morning when I heard her stirring, I dressed quickly and met her in the screened tent where our scopes were stored. It was so dark that we both wore our headlamps.

She gathered up her gear and scope. I grabbed a snack and a water bottle, shouldered my scope, and followed. She turned off her headlamp, so I did the same, stashing it in my pocket. There was barely enough light to make out the sandy pathway, bordered with dune grasses mixed with vigorous poison ivy.

I followed her to the lakeshore, where she paused over each set of fresh tracks in the sand. She was reading the events of the night, the history of the darkness. She pointed to some sort of track and said something I couldn't hear. I reached the place in the sand and saw some weird tracks. Sloth? Nope, more than three toes. A few steps ahead they were clearer, paws digging into the soft sand on either side of a tail. I knew this one.

"Otter," I whispered triumphantly.

We walked slowly, slowly, toward the point of land, that sandy hook that curves out into Lake Michigan.

"Why don't you stay here and look for the third unbanded chick?" Alice said softly.

I set up my scope so I could sit on the dune and sight up the point in search of three tiny birds I could have easily balanced on one palm. They were so newly hatched that researchers hadn't banded them yet. In a few minutes the top of the sun crested above the lake, giving enough light to find one of the birds darting at the top of the waves. Its sibling joined it a few minutes later when the sun had lifted itself far enough to balance on the edge of Lake Michigan.

The challenge of finding the third chick was to keep track of the two you had already found, while occasionally scanning the area for the third. If another chick appeared apart from the two, it was essential to quickly relocate the first two to make sure the third wasn't actually one of the first two trying to trick you. I enjoyed watching the two chicks for the next hour as the morning chill burned off and the sand began radiating the sun's warmth around me. I did not see the third tiny creature.

Alice materialized at my elbow, startling me. "I think a coyote got most of the chicks from West Six's nest. I saw tracks," she said. "Tracks, then a pounce mark."

I didn't want to believe it. I had seen one of the chicks when it was still wet from hatching. This endangered bird on the brink of extinction was born into existence on an isolated, sandy point reaching off a wild island – a bundle of hope running around on toothpick legs, a puffball of energy encoded with ancient migration paths.

"Did any survive?" I asked.

"I saw only one," Alice answered.

Of five eggs in that nest, only one chick had survived.

Hoppy needs a new name

We spent our last morning again recording the birds we had seen. When it was time to leave, Alice met up with me. "Hoppy is using both legs now. He's all better."

"He'll need a new name," I said.

Alice pulled out her metal clipboard. She transferred my sightings onto her data sheet. On this last day, I had finally gotten the hang of this work and was able to contribute. What I thought would be an easy week of watching birds had turned out to be some of the most meticulous work I had ever done.

We returned to camp to pack our things and straighten up for the next shift. Since most of the chicks on the island had fledged, there would only be another week or two of monitoring. Many of the female adults had already flown off, leaving the males to watch over the chicks and guide them south to their winter home in the Carolinas or along the Gulf Coast.

I took my pack to the beach where the ranger would pick us up, then I returned to gather more gear while Alice left meticulous notes about the birds – and especially about the coyote. Alice had taken many photos of the tracks and the pounce. She was sure the evidence was there, the tale of carnage clear in the sand. She wanted Nico to examine the scene, too, to get his reading of the story left in paw prints and missing chicks.

Alice shouldered her enormous pack and her scope, and we hauled the rest of the gear to the beach. As the ranger boat approached, we heard the announcement from the radio that the boat was on the way to Dimmick's Point to pick up Alice.

She looked at me. "You weren't mentioned," she said with the slightest tease in her voice. "They may not let you aboard."

"What?" I pretended to be shocked at the running joke. "They didn't mention the *delightful* volunteer?"

And Alice, the master birdwatcher, naturalist, and protector of the endangered Great Lakes piping plover, finally smiled.

Island havens

The piping plovers spend the warm months on these islands. They tend their nests, then watch over hatchlings until they fledge and are ready to fly south. It was a privilege to be with these tiny birds, to watch them hatch and grow, to scan the rock-scattered sands to find the darting birds chasing beetles and bugs. These little shorebirds have been successful nesting on these island outposts far from the crowds of the mainland. The islands provide safety from civilization, from domestic dogs (though not wild ones), and from habitat destruction. Afloat in Lake Michigan, these islands are the best hope for preserving this species.

Miles for North Manitou Island:
Hike   Ferry
33   27

Annual Lake Michigan Bottom Survey

*I*n 2011, I read an interesting research paper about Lake Michigan written by Dr. David "Bo" Bunnell at the Great Lakes Science Center in Ann Arbor. I had a few questions about his work, so I had emailed him asking if I could interview him at his laboratory. He graciously set up a time. After my interview and a tour of the facility, Dr. Bunnell mentioned that much of his work in the lab is done on samples of fish gathered each year in the annual trawl survey of Lake Michigan.

"You should come out on the boat with us and see how the survey is done," he said. "We start up in Manistique and then head down the west side of Michigan, stopping in ports like Ludington, Grand Haven, and Saugatuck before heading to the other side of the lake."

In 2013 I contacted him about coordinating to get out on one of these daytrips. Weather scuttled early plans, but on Saturday, September 14, I woke at 4 a.m., grabbed my sack lunch and drove to Grand Haven.

I arrived before sunrise, a time when the stars were still out. Despite the early hour, or more accurately because of it, dozens of fishing boats were in motion, motoring out of the Grand River and into Lake Michigan. A salmon fishing contest was underway, and these fishermen were heading out before dawn to set their lines. I parked, then stepped onto the walkway by the river, where I was almost trampled by three runners outfitted with reflective vests and headlamps. Honestly, as I see it, if you can't wait for the sun to rise before you have to run, you may have a problem.

I proceeded toward the ship at the dock. A few lights were lit on the vessel, and as I got closer I could finally make out the name on the back: *Grayling*. This ship is part of the fleet of research vessels operated by the United States Geological Service (USGS). Their mission states: "The USGS serves the Nation by providing reliable scientific information to describe and understand the Earth; minimize loss of life and property from natural disasters; manage water, biological, energy, and mineral resources; and enhance and protect our quality of life."

The USGS is the nation's largest water, earth, and biological science and civilian mapping agency. They collect, monitor, analyze and provide scientific understanding about natural resource conditions, issues, and problems. They employ around 10,000 people in 400 locations engaged in this important work.

Boats are not in my wheelhouse

"Permission to come aboard?" I called out from the foot of the ship's walkway. I had seen this greeting in naval movies, but the deckhand looked surprised and waved me aboard. Once on the ship, I found Dr. Bunnell down in the galley. Now, I've been on a few boats, but I'm not a "boat person" per se. I have a tendency to get motion sick unless I am able to keep the horizon within sight. Down in the galley, even the gentle rocking of the ship against the dock made me uneasy.

I met the crew and the technician for the survey, then was outfitted with a life jacket and shown where the "Gumby" suits were stored. These neoprene survival suits would keep us alive and afloat in cold water should the *Grayling* sink. They got the Gumby nickname because wearers look like the Gumby character, only in red rather than green. Captain Shawn Parsons gave us a safety session that covered things like:

What to do if someone falls off the ship. Point at them and yell "Man Overboard!" (which seemed rather obvious) while tossing floatables their way.

What to do if a fire broke out on the ship. Fight it with one of the many fire extinguishers.

And, the worst-case scenario, where to gather if the general alarm was sounded. Meet out on the deck in front of the wheelhouse – unless, of course, that portion of the ship was engulfed in flames.

It is prudent to be prepared for these sorts of mishaps, but the talk made me want to slip into my Gumby suit and sit at the place everyone would assemble if disaster struck.

By the time the crew had finished breakfast and checked that the ship was ready for the day's trip, the sun was beginning to erode the black from the eastern sky. The ropes connecting us to the dock were pulled in, and we were soon merging with the fishing boats heading toward Lake Michigan.

Super Bassomatic

The bottom survey of Lake Michigan has been done annually since 1973. To replicate the survey, the captain uses GPS coordinates to return to the same spots each year. Then, the crew lowers a net weighted on each side by "doors" that hold the net open and also keep it down at the bottom of the lake. The net is pulled along for ten minutes while the boat motors ahead for a set distance. Then, two massive winches haul everything up and the contents of the net are released into plastic bins.

The full bins are taken into the sorting space off the back deck, and the fish are identified, measured, and weighed. Representative specimens are frozen for later analyses. Stomach contents are studied for information on what fish are eating. The otoliths (hard, calcium carbonate structures located directly behind the brain of bony fish) are examined to reveal the age of each fish. Specimens can also be analyzed to determine and quantify any contaminates they contain, like heavy metals or polychlorinated biphe-nyls (PCBs). This manmade compound was once widely used as a coolant and freely discarded into the Great Lakes.

Back in Dr. Bunnell's lab, I had seen the high-speed blender used to process whole fish for analysis. It was Dan Akroyd's "Super Bassomatic" sketch in real life.

A trawlin' we will go

We motored out of the river, then Captain Parsons threaded our ship (at 79 feet long, the *Grayling* loomed over the other vessels) through the crowd of fishing boats congregating at the mouth of the river. Then he turned south and headed toward the channel at Saugatuck, where the Kalamazoo River flowed out into the lake. It took us two hours to finally arrive there after we had passed the power plant at Port Sheldon, then the Saugatuck Dunes State Park. The lake bottom gradually deepens here, in contrast to other places where there is an abrupt fall-off into deep water, so the survey takes a few passes to assess how the yellow perch are doing. These fish like the shallow waters closer to shore.

This year, Dr. Bunnell had brought along an underwater miniature camera to connect to the net in hopes of capturing what was going on as the net was pulled along the lake bottom. The technology on the *Grayling* was sophisticated: GPS coordinates to locate precise locations for the trawls, a bathometer to measure the depth and water temperature of each sample, and sonar and radar. And now they had an underwater camera to catch the expression on each fish face as it went into the net.

Our first catch at 5.5 meters pulled up many alewives (a member of the herring family that is native to the Atlantic Ocean) and two yellow perch. With the next trawls set at progressively deeper water, we again pulled up mostly alewives. As the trawls got deeper, we began seeing other fish in the haul: deep water sculpin, slimy sculpin, bloaters (all native to the Great Lakes) and some round gobies (that invasive species that water snakes enjoy for dinner). One thing that became a constant with the deeper trawls was the presence of quagga mussels in the net. This mussel is native to the Dnieper River that flows through the Ukraine. These two invasive species, the round goby and the quagga mussel, were transported to the Great Lakes in the ballast tanks of ships entering the Great Lakes Basin after visiting far-off ports.

Another fish collected in the deeper samplings were a few lake trout. One was determined to be a fish grown in a hatchery, the other two were bred in the wild.

How can you tell the difference?

Their accents.

No, their level of "street smarts."

Seriously, the answer is that the stocked fish have their adipose fin clipped before they are released into the lake. Fish spawned in the wild will have an intact fin.

"We haven't seen this for a long time," Dr. Bunnell said as he measured the trout and recorded his findings. "Wild trout."

Invasive species dominate

At the end of the day, we had pulled up ten different species (including quagga mussels) from the depths of Lake Michigan. Of those ten, five were invasive species.

As we motored back to Grand Haven, Dr. Bunnell loaded the underwater footage onto a laptop so we could watch what was happening during the trawl. I sat in the galley with the others to watch the net-view footage. We could see the net passing through schools of alewife, many of the silver fish easily eluding the net. We saw the sculpin startle off the floor of the lake and into the net. And we saw masses of quagga mussels. The deeper the trawl, the more the lakebed was covered with these invasive shellfish.

I could only watch a few minutes of the footage before the movement of the video clashed with the actual movement of the vessel, and I had to go on deck for some fresh air. Out where I could see the lake and the dunes along the edge, I felt fine.

"You doing okay?" Dr. Bunnell asked as he joined me on deck.

"I'm fine. Just need to see where we're going," I replied.

With the wind in my face and the sun lowering itself into the western side of the lake, I had time to reflect on the importance of this work. The data from one year is merely a glimpse at what is going on in the lake. It is only over a much longer stretch of time that vital insight is gained. And, as with any complex biological system, the more we learn about it, the more we realize how much more there is to understand.

As Aldo Leopold asserted in his writings, how can we ever hope to restore and conserve nature unless we understand the intricate connections and complexities inherent to each ecosystem?

Miles on the *Grayling* for Lake Michigan Bottom Survey:
55

LAKE SUPERIOR ISLANDS

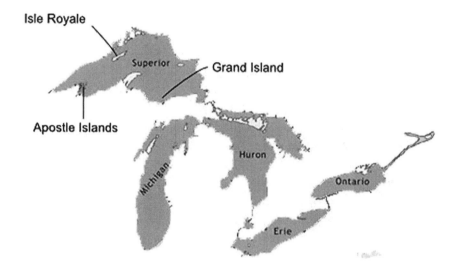

Isle Royale
Superior
Grand Island
Apostle Islands
Michigan
Huron
Ontario
Erie

*L*ake Superior was known by native peoples, the Ojibwa, as *gichigami,* meaning "big sea" or "huge water." But like so many other places in the region, Lake Superior was renamed by the Europeans, who chose the name to signify that it is geographically north of (or "superior to") the other lakes. It was the French explorers of the 1600s, traveling upwater from Lake Huron, who called it *lac supérieur,* which roughly translates as "Upper Lake." When the British took control of the region, they anglicized that to Superior.

This massive body of water is truly superior, though, in other ways. It is the largest lake in the world by surface area. It is third largest in the world in the amount of water contained in its basin. Compared to the other Great Lakes, Lake Superior is grander by every measurement you wish to apply. It is deeper and colder than the others, so vast that it contains more water than the other four lakes combined. In fact, you could fit the waters of the other lakes in its basin, then have room for a few additional inputs the size of what Lake Erie holds.

This largest Great Lake has many islands along its 1,400-mile shoreline. The Apostle Islands cluster around the Bayfield Peninsula in the southwest corner of the lake. Grand Island nestles in the harbor near the town of Munising along the center of Superior's southern shore. But the largest island on the lake is 20 miles from the western edge of Superior where Minnesota abuts Ontario. This island is Isle Royale. It's almost 50 miles long and nearly 10 miles wide at its western end. Curiously, early maps often had two large islands drawn here. One was called Isle Royale, and the other phantom island was called Isle Philippeaux. This double-island effect was due to explorers seeing the island from different vantage points out on the lake and thinking there must certainly be two of them.

Since the islands mentioned above are all located in Lake Superior, you might assume they'd be quite similar. But I discovered otherwise in my visits to them. The geology is quite varied. The wildlife inhabiting these islands differs significantly, too.

The islands I'd already visited in lakes Michigan, Huron, and Erie all had limestone as their base. Lake Superior's islands have different geological underpinnings. Along the southern part of the lake, the islands are based on sandstone, but the sandstone in the Apostle Islands is dark, reddish brown, while the sandstone at Grand Island is light brown. It's not the color that makes them different; the porosity of the sandstone also varies. The geology of Isle Royale is vastly different, as I'll soon explain.

Apostle Islands, Wisconsin

Iinvited my niece and nephew, teenagers Alison and Julian, to accompany me for my exploration of the Apostle Islands. They live in Atlanta, Georgia, so they hadn't seen much wilderness. Though they'd been to Michigan many times, they'd never made it over the Mighty Mackinac Bridge or seen Lake Superior. This trip would expand their sense of the Great Lakes and, I hoped after some time in the wild, their sense of themselves.

Due to my healthy respect for Lake Superior – especially after the exceptionally cold winter that left icebergs floating in the lake into early June – I coordinated our exploration of the Apostle Islands with a kayaking outfitter near Bayfield, Wisconsin. There are actually 22 islands in this grouping, not a dozen as the name suggests. They cluster around the Bayfield Peninsula in northwest Wisconsin.

We signed up for a three-day excursion, camping on the islands for two nights. They supplied the kayaking gear, including wet suits, and two guides handled our group of eleven. Seven of the people on this excursion were an adventuresome, middle-aged group from Minneapolis that often travelled together. One gentleman was from Oklahoma. Julian, Alison, and I rounded out the group. They both play soccer and are excellent athletes, so I was confident in their physical ability to complete the three-day journey.

Pondering your mortality

We had two guides for this trip: Nicole (a compact, dark-haired, able-looking woman) and Paige (a man with sandy brown long hair and beard lightened by the sunshine . . . yes, "Paige" is how he spells his name). They assisted us in choosing proper-fitting wet suits, life vests, and spray skirts.

This last piece of equipment was essential for safety in rough water. The spray skirt fit snugly at the waist and flared out like a strange, blue, oval tutu. When seated in the kayak, this skirt fit onto the raised edge of the cockpit, effectively sealing us in our seats. This barrier was essential for paddling in large waves. It would keep water out of the kayak and keep our lower bodies pretty dry even in the wildest waves.

After we were all wearing sleek, black wetsuits – well, Julian and Alison looked sleek and futuristic in theirs, the rest of the middle-aged group a little less so – we gathered near the shore where Nicole and Paige went over the itinerary for the trip. We would paddle out to Oak Island and stay there the first night. Then we'd paddle to Stockton Island, the largest in the Apostle archipelago, for our second night. On the third day, we'd paddle back to where we had started. Before heading out, though, we would all have to complete a "wet exit drill." This meant we would paddle out near the dock and take turns flipping our kayaks. Once inverted in 50-degree water, each person would have to demonstrate his or her ability to release the spray skirt, swim to the surface, right the kayak, and climb back into the cockpit.

When you're about to flip your kayak upside down into Lake Superior, it's helpful, I think, to take a moment to ponder your mortality. When you have a 17-year-old in the tandem kayak with you, however, there is no time for this. I had barely asked Julian which way we were going to flip – "To the left," he stated without debate – and we were upside down, underwater. You see, a heavy, long, low-slung tandem kayak doesn't roll lazily on its side. It flips happily upside down.

So, there I was sitting in the kayak, inverted, underwater. I blinked and realized I was pinching my nose closed with my fingers. Good move, I thought. The water was so shockingly cold that I pushed off with my legs to kick to the surface, but realized I had forgotten to release the spray skirt still sealing me in my seat. I grabbed the loop at the front of the skirt, pushed it forward, than pulled back to release it. I kicked to the surface and looped my arm over the bottom of the kayak. Julian was already there, patiently waiting. Paige, who was nearby, told us to flip the kayak right side up, and Julian did most of that work before I could even get hold of it to help.

Next, we had to get back in the kayak. This was accomplished by hooking the lower left leg inside the cockpit, using this connecting point to leverage up until the upper body was lying on the top of the craft, lifting the right leg inside, then twisting and sliding until once again in the seat. This sounds complicated – and it is – but it's amazing how motivated and focused one gets when bobbing around in 50-degree water.

Once we were back in the kayak, I felt my face and found my glasses still sitting on my nose. I had a strap holding them there, but my vision was blurry from the water on the lenses, and they had instantly fogged up after being chilled in the cold water. My wetsuit insulated me from the hypothermia-inducing water, though, and I was surprisingly comfortable. Our group all passed the test, so we returned to the dock to have lunch and dry out a bit before launching out for Oak Island.

Julian is tall and skinny with sandy brown hair and has the habit of looking off in the distance in photos instead of into the camera lens. I call it his "model pose." He's shy around people he doesn't know, but once you penetrate his defenses he reveals a quick wit and thoughtfulness. Alison is younger than Julian and a bit shorter. She is also slim, has shoulder-length, dark brown hair, and is more outgoing and outspoken. She has a wicked sarcastic streak that I appreciate. She looks directly into the camera and always gives a huge, open grin.

These two have played on the same soccer team their entire lives, so they are more than siblings. They are teammates and best friends. They watch out for each other, and there is little competition between them. They anticipate each other and often made decisions without discussion. People frequently ask if they are twins. I knew they were close, but until this trip I had no idea they were so in tune with each other.

Alison knew that Julian would want to paddle a tandem kayak with me instead of with a stranger, so she paired up with one of the Minnesotan women in a tandem kayak for the entire trip. The paddle out to Oak Island was a little choppy. Everyone in our group got used to handling the kayaks, finessing the rudders to help steer the longer tandems as we passed along the edge of the Bayfield Peninsula, then made the crossing. Soon, we were nearing the dock and landing our kayaks on the island.

We took all of our gear to the group campsite, when the guides instructed us to immediately lock up all food in the bear box. Oak Island, we learned, has the densest population of black bear in all of North America. On this 5,000-acre island, there are at least 17 black bears. We set up camp, and the guides cooked dinner. We began with warm bread topped with roasted garlic, and a wheel of brie softened to a puddle on the fire. Then, they grilled whitefish and made rice and stir-fried veggies on a cook stove.

After dinner, the kids and I went to the dock. The sun slipped into a dense cloudbank on the horizon, illuminating it from the inside, bouncing streaks of light upward. Wide ripples on the lake caught the light, bent and played with its reflection. The surface of the lake soon resembled molten metal more than flowing water.

Before the sun extinguished itself, it burned fierce red through a gap in the gray clouds. Then the full moon rose opposite the setting sun, hovering over the trees on Oak Island.

Did it awaken something?

The next day after an early breakfast, our group was shuttling all of our gear to the kayaks to be loaded for the day's paddle. I passed my niece and nephew on my way back to the campsite and they were smiling.

"We saw a bear!" Alison said. It was spotted near our campsite, just standing there. Nicole, the guide, watched it for a moment with them, then she made some noise and ran it off.

Once Julian and I had loaded our kayak and launched it out into the lake, I asked him about the bear. He told me it was only 25 feet away.

"Cool," I said. "Did you say 'Hello, brother bear?'"

Julian gave a slight laugh. "No."

"Did it awaken something wild in you?" I pressed.

Julian thought a moment, then said, "Yes. It did."

The lake was ultra-calm for this second day's long paddle from Oak to Stockton Island. It was so calm it was boring at first, but as we rounded to the south side of the island, we saw a black bear making its way along the shore. We slowed and watched him poking among the driftwood for something to eat. Bear on these islands tend to be smaller than those encountered on the mainland. The Apostle bears average only 150 pounds – "wrestling size," I joked with Julian and Alison. On the mainland, male black bears will average almost twice the weight of island males. This is a common trait of mammals isolated on islands. They tend to downsize, making it easier to survive on these isolated outposts with fewer resources.

Watery caves

The lake was so calm that we were able to paddle into some of the sandstone caves on the edge of the island. This was thrilling. Wave action erodes and shapes the base of these islands, forming caves and separating out sandstone boulders and pedestals. Some caves were a tight squeeze. We had to lean forward in our kayaks to avoid bumping our heads. If the lake had been wavy, we would have been bounced up and down, at risk of being crushed against the rock in a surge. But this day was delightfully peaceful on the water, making it easy to slip into the mysterious sea-caverns.

In many places, colorful lichen dotted the brown sandstone surfaces, or minerals carried by seeping water had streaked colorful washes – white, gray, black – onto rock faces. Water dripped through the porous sandstone in some caves, and tiny stalactites spiked an otherwise smooth cave roof. In the winter, these drips form enormous icicles, so the entire grotto is comprised of icy spikes.

Water moving through stone is also the reason that these formations tend to fracture in the winter as that water expands into ice. We saw many places where split sandstone had fallen into the lake. Trees clung to fractured boulders. Roots splayed out over the water at times, seeking an attachment point after rock below them had fallen away.

Most of the shoreline of these islands is stepped or sheer sandstone, so it was vital that the guides knew the few places where we could safely land our kayaks. Along Stockton Island, we paddled over the submerged remains of a dock, a remnant of an abandoned quarry operation. Many buildings constructed from this brownstone still stand in nearby towns, like Ashland's Union Passenger Depot and Marquette's City Hall. After the Great Chicago Fire of 1871, sandstone blocks the size of refrigerators were shipped south to rebuild that city. Growing Midwest cities like Minneapolis, Detroit, and Milwaukee used this brown sandstone for some of their grandest buildings. Detroit's original Chamber of Commerce building and some ornamental work on the long-gone Hudson Building was made of this stone. In Milwaukee, the original County Courthouse (demolished 1976) was built of sandstone from Basswood Island, as was the still-standing St. Paul's Episcopal Church (built in the late 1800s).

Quarry hike

We entered Quarry Bay at Stockton Island and landed our kayaks on the beach. Stockton is the largest of the Apostle group at almost 10,000 acres. We carried our gear to the campsite, where we were swarmed by more mosquitoes than I had ever seen in any one place on any of my hikes. The campsite abutted a marsh.

I had brought along head nets, but hoped we wouldn't need them. We slipped them on quickly, rolling down long sleeves and spraying bug spray on exposed skin. The guides set up lunch out on a nearby dock where a steady lake breeze kept the bugs away.

After lunch, Alison asked, "What time is it?"

"It's 3 p.m.," I said.

Alison looked stricken.

"Are you okay?" I asked.

She shook her head. "No, I'm not okay. I never knew a day could be this long."

It was only the second day out, but she was feeling the effects of being removed from the devices of modern life. I had asked them to leave their electronics behind, so there were no cell phones, no music or laptops. There were no distractions. Every moment had been engaged with and lived. Every bit of movement – both on land and water – was under our own power. And yes, the days tended to expand a bit.

Stockton Island had a quarry operation there in the late 1800s that was worked for more than two decades. We decided to explore the quarry site, so we pulled our head nets down over our hats, pulled our socks over our pant legs, doused each other with bug spray, and headed out.

The trail passed through the forest, but stayed close to the shoreline. Alison pulled her exposed hands up into her shirtsleeves so there wasn't an inch of skin for the mosquitoes to drink from. We saw a huge toad along the path, and I stooped to pick him up.

"Don't touch him, you'll get warts," Alison said.

I laughed, but then realized she was serious. "That's an old wives' tale. It's not true. Warts are caused by a virus, not by toads."

"Seriously?"

"Yeah, city kid," I teased.

"I had some warts once," she said. "Had to get them frozen off."

"And had you ever touched a toad?"

She shook her head.

I picked up the toad and he immediately peed on me.

"Yuck," Alison said, "Why did he do that?"

"It's a defense mechanism. Either that or he just lost it when the giant picked him up."

I let them look at the toad up close as I carefully held him, then I put him back down pointed in the direction he was heading.

We continued up a steep incline, then wove through the woods for a long stretch. The buzz of mosquitoes was constant, but we could also hear the wind in the leaves and the waves splashing against the base of the island. We had already seen mergansers and loons, eagles and cormorants, small-sized bear, and a large incontinent toad.

Unlike mammals, amphibians tend to get larger when isolated on islands. It allows them to store more resources for times when food is scarce.

The first indication that we were nearing the quarry site was a large metal rod anchored into the rock. Nearby, the sandstone had been sliced out in blocks, leaving a smooth wall scored with drill marks from the quarrying process. The bottom of the quarry had pools of standing water, and the whine of mosquitoes increased as they discovered us entering their territory. We clamored up the wall of the quarry, using roots and tree trunks to pull ourselves up. We arrived at the top, where we saw several perfect sandstone blocks ready to be shipped. But the noise of the hungry bugs made it nerve-wracking to linger, so we made a quick loop and headed back along the trail to camp.

During our hike, a painted turtle had left the marsh near our campsite, dug a hole in the sandy soil, and was now laying her eggs. There she sat, at an angle with her tail in the hole and her head sticking out of her shell, keeping watch. I took a few photos of her, using the zoom on my camera so I wouldn't disturb her motherly concentration.

After dinner, our entire group went out on the dock to get away from the bugs. The Minneapolis group was talking about their next trip and joking that they might want something easier, like a tour of wine country. They were all older than me, and I was impressed with their adventurous spirit, though some of them were doing slow stretches and groaning a bit.

The scattering of clouds lit up as the sun set on our final night in the Apostle Islands. Paige listened to the forecast on his mobile weather radio and informed us that we would have more wind for our final paddle – and it would likely be in the direction opposite to where we were heading. The days of easy paddling were over. The final day would see our longest distance traveled on the water, with three open crossings that were likely to be, well, exciting.

That night, the wind sharpened, and the tree branches roared over our campsite. Then – as quickly as that began – it calmed.

I laid down wishing there was a kayak that all three of us could paddle in together. If the lake was going to be rough, I wanted to keep tabs on both Julian and Alison. This was not possible, and I got little sleep this last night, especially when the wind picked up again toward dawn.

In the lee of the islands

Once we were done with breakfast and our gear had been loaded, the guides explained that on the return trip, we would loop around two islands – Hermit and Basswood – staying in the lee of these islands. This route would protect us from the wind and waves part of the time, making an easier paddle than if we kayaked a straight line back.

The first open crossing between Stockton and Hermit was fun, as we paddled through one- to two-foot rolling waves. By the time we made the crossing between Hermit and Basswood, though, the rollers had grown an additional foot tall.

This, too, was fun, and Julian paddled harder than ever and whooped it up when a wave lifted the front of the kayak then smacked it down with a splash. One of the Minnesotan women paddling solo took a strong wave on this crossing and had to do another "wet exit." Paige was nearby and helped her back into her kayak.

By the time we reached the southern tip of Basswood Island and could finally see the shoreline of the Bayfield Peninsula, the winds were growing even stronger. The sky darkened. Paige got an update from the weather radio. He and Nicole conferred and made the decision to proceed with the crossing.

"Stay together," Paige said, "And as the waves come up behind you, strike into it with your paddle and you'll be fine." Paige demonstrated the move: a swift, short stroke into an imaginary wave sneaking up on him.

Julian was in the front of the kayak. I was in the rear, controlling the rudder. With each paddle stroke, the wind and waves strengthened. Soon, we were paddling like crazy people, and not making any headway. The waves were turning our kayak off course, and I couldn't correct for it with the rudder, since it only worked if we had forward movement.

"We have to paddle harder," I yelled to Julian over the noise of the storm – it was a full-throttle storm now with rain and everything – "or else the rudder is useless."

We went from paddling like crazy people to paddling even harder. A micro-cell storm collided with us, pushing against us, pinning us down. We were barely making any headway. The wind was so strong that every time Julian pulled his paddle out, the water that used to stream down from it back into the lake was now blown horizontally into my face.

I looked behind us to see how close Alison's kayak was, but I couldn't see anything through my watery glasses. I yelled to Julian to look back, and he said that she was following and doing okay.

Meanwhile, Nicole was assisting one of the tandem kayaks in the crossing by using a rope between her life vest and the craft. She had her hands full with this task, when another one of the single kayaks was rolled by the strengthening waves. Paige went to the rescue, as Nicole shouted to the rest of us, "Paddle! Paddle! Paddle!"

This put the fear of Neptune into my soul, and Julian and I paddled like never before. I'm not sure how we kept it up for so long. We knew if we slackened or stopped, we might easily lose control of the direction of the kayak and get flipped by the waves. At one point I yelled, "It's like 'The Perfect Storm'! It's not going to let us out!" I tried to laugh to reassure Julian, but I recalled that the end of that movie was not so reassuring.

When we got part way across to a point where I hoped the winds would lessen in the sheltering effect of the hills on the still-distant mainland, the wind shifted just enough to keep it screaming directly at us. Julian was so parched from exertion that he scooped up some lake water with one hand and drank it. There was no way either one of us could reach for a water bottle. The wind would snatch our paddles if we tried to set them down for even a second.

It was still a battle. We seemed to be paddling to stay in one place, but in minute increments, we scooted our way across the channel. Finally we reached the protective shelter of the mainland. Exhausted, we watched Alison and her kayak partner continue to paddle for several long minutes to join us.

When the entire group was finally safe, I reclined as far back in my seat as I could and panted to catch my breath. This was the shortest open crossing we made that day, at just 1.3 miles, but it felt more like 13 miles.

By the time we got to the dock, the micro-cell had passed. It was a sunny, calm day, and the crossing seemed like it belonged to an alternate reality.

I looked at Julian and Alison. Together, we began laughing that "we didn't die!" laughter.

I don't have any photos from that crossing, no videos, not even any sketches. It is seared into my mind, though, and into the muscle memory of my arms and torso.

Did we get any real food?

We packed the car and piled in and drove to a nearby grocery store. I wanted to crash at our hotel and not hassle with getting cleaned up enough to go out to eat. We laughed our way into the store and started grabbing anything that appealed to us. We got fresh fruit and something to drink, then made a beeline for the desserts. We bought a frozen cake and a raft of chocolate éclairs.

When we got back on the road again, I asked, "Did we get any real food for dinner?" We all burst out laughing again.

When we pulled up to the hotel, I told them that it had a pool and whirlpool, then added, "And I think we have a view of Lake Superior!"

We burst out laughing again, because the last thing we wanted to see was the thing that had almost crushed us earlier that day. Our arms were so sore from paddling that we struggled with the luggage, prompting more bouts of uncontrolled laughter. There's nothing that bonds you to others like battling a storm in a low-slung kayak, struggling for inches against wind and waves – especially when you survive and can celebrate with baked goods afterward.

This defining feature of islands – that they are surrounded by water – is the feature that allows passage to these floating lands. This water also possesses inherent danger. Many an islander has perished during a watery crossing, surprised by a sudden storm.

Miles for the Apostle Islands:
Hike   Kayak
8   25

Grand Island, Michigan

After surviving our kayaking adventure, Julian, Alison and I headed east. We would cross the Porcupine Mountains on our way to Munising where we would explore Grand Island. I had seen many beautiful photographs of the Lake of the Clouds in Porcupine Mountains Wilderness State Park, but had never been there before. Since we had a little slack in our schedule, we took a short detour north to see this lovely lake, and can report it was well worth the extra miles.

The next day we awoke in Munising, and headed toward the bay to catch the noon ferry to Grand Island. This island is situated very close to the shore of the city. In fact, the name "Munising" means "Place of the Great Island." The island is truly grand at nearly 22 square miles (over 13,000 acres).

The day was chilly for July, with rain, and temperatures struggling to get into the 50s. We put our rain gear on and got in the car. We stopped at a gift shop on the way. By the time we got back into the car, the rain and wind had increased. I've hiked in all sorts of weather, but my adventures usually gave me little choice. I just had to keep going. On this day, though, with a car and Julian and Alison along, I made a U-turn back to the hotel. We had options. They could swim in the pool while I watched the radar for a better slice of weather. By the early afternoon, sure enough, the worst of it had passed and the rain stopped. The clouds even thinned enough to let some filtered light through.

We put on our rain gear once again and headed out.

Bear abuse

Julian and Alison bounced around the dock area while I purchased the tickets for our short passage, along with rental bikes on the island.

"I should probably tell you," the college kid said as he gave me a receipt, "about something that happened today." A family had gone over to the island. They happened upon a black bear, and one of their kids went toward the bear that was minding its own bear business, and sprayed it with pepper spray. The bear freaked and scared the kid plenty as it made its frantic getaway. The kid was not injured, but the entire family was upset, and the ferry had to make a special run to transport them back to the mainland.

I shook my head. "So you're telling me there's an angry, abused bear on the island."

He nodded. I spread my map on the desk between us and asked him to tell me where the encounter took place. It was on the east side of the island and I had planned to bike along the western edge. I figured there was enough distance and rough terrain between where we would bike and where the abused bear was nursing his inflamed eyes and snout.

We boarded the ferry.

Since it was only the three of us that were crossing to the island, the ferry service used their smaller vessel, a pontoon boat. We made the chilly crossing over the waves and white caps in a few minutes and were soon at the island dock. We chose bikes from the rack and headed north up the shoreline trail.

The island had served as a summer hunting and fishing and even farming location for Native Americans for thousands of years. They also prized a deposit of quartzite found on the island. Wherever outcroppings of this rock were found in the Great Lakes Basin – as noted before on Manitoulin Island – early native peoples would gather to make the tools necessary for survival.

Around the turn of the 19th century, fur traders shared Grand Island with the Ojibwa.

For most of the first half of the 20th century, the Cleveland-Cliffs Iron Company owned the island, and also operated a resort and wilderness area here. This actually protected Grand Island from large-scale logging during this period, and William Mather, the owner of the company, attempted to conserve some of the historic buildings there. After Mather died, though, many of the larger trees were harvested.

While there are a few summer residences there today (those that were built when the company owned the island), the vast majority of the island has been designated a National Recreation Area for over two decades.

Thunder Cove

The rain had softened the pathway and formed mud in places where it didn't drain completely, but otherwise the path was easy to ride and bordered by lush, green trees and ferns. We pedaled for several miles, stopping at some beautiful overlooks onto Lake Superior. I took several photos of the kids with their bikes. Alison gave her grin to the camera, and Julian looked like a model with his far-off gaze.

As we continued north, the waves on the lake grew stronger, crashing into the sandstone base of the island. We got off our bikes at Thunder Cove and hiked the trail there. Even before we reached the edge, we heard waves thumping inside an island cave. It was a deeper and more resonant crashing than when the waves hit a flat wall of sandstone. We walked the trail that was softened with pine needles and edged with lush moss to the lip of the island.

The drop to the lake was about twelve feet. Below, the waves were curling into a small cove and throwing themselves into a shallow cave. It sounded like thunder, but coming from the land instead of the sky. The sandstone was banded here, dark and light brown.

I handed my camera to Julian, then I climbed toward the cove along the edge of the island. Julian shot some video of me while I was clinging to a tree root with one hand and reaching out over Thunder Cove with the other. From here, we could look up the shoreline of Grand Island. It went north for a bit, then curved west out into the lake. Huge trees hugged the rocky shoreline. Several of them had bare roots reaching out into open air after the rock below them had been swept away by Lake Superior's rage.

As we hiked the looping trail back to our bikes, I took several selfies, positioning Julian and Alison over my shoulder in the shots. On the last photo, Julian finally looked right into the camera and gave a cheesy grin.

Playing dead is not appropriate

When we got back to our bikes, I told them the story of the pepper-sprayed bear. I said if we saw a bear we wouldn't make noise immediately or try to scare it away. We'd give it a lot of space, and we'd stay together. Enough time had elapsed to consider the possibility of encountering the animal the kid had sprayed. I didn't instruct them on the proper action if attacked by a black bear, which was to fight back (as the Grand Island info pamphlet stated, "Playing dead is not appropriate").

I hoped it wouldn't come to that. But if it did, I was just glad these island bears were "wrestling size" – and in my weight class – and not mainland size.

Thankfully, while we saw a rotten log that had been torn apart by the claws of a bear, we didn't see any bears, angry or otherwise, on our way back to the dock. We had to wait a few minutes for the ferry to return, so we walked the short beach there. The clouds were low and gray, obscuring hills in the distance, but the rain had stopped a while ago, and the day that had begun with such bluster had turned into a pleasant one.

It felt good to board the little pontoon boat and sit on the padded seats for the ride back to the mainland. I wished we had an entire day to explore Grand Island, but I was glad the weather had allowed us this slice of the afternoon to see the wild portion we had traveled.

Crazy-awesome

At dinner, I talked with the kids about their island experiences. Alison confessed to getting worried in the Apostle Islands, especially when the single kayak flipped in the waves. And we all laughed again about that final crazy crossing to the mainland.

"Would you do it again?" I asked.

They both emphatically nodded.

"How has this experience changed you?"

"Well," Alison laughed, "I've cheated death, so I can use it to do more adventurous things."

"Yeah," Julian nodded. "I want to do more crazy stuff."

"After that first day of kayaking, I thought, 'damn . . . two more days of this?'" Alison confessed. "But then we did it and survived."

"And what did you learn about me?" I asked.

"You're crazy," Alison said.

Surprised, I looked at her, not sure where she was going with that.

She continued. "Crazy-awesome – like someone I want to hang out with. You're passionate about this stuff."

"You make hard work look fun," Julian added. "I didn't know that was possible."

"I've created my dream job," I told them.

"Yeah. And it isn't boring at all," Alison said.

The wild inside

We had a long drive to get back to Battle Creek the next day. I expected Julian and Alison to fall asleep in the car, but they were both awake and looking out the windows as I drove. On a remote stretch of US Highway 2, I saw an animal approach the left edge of the roadway. I slowed and it crossed not far ahead up the road: coyote or wolf?

I pointed in its direction, but it had descended into the ditch and disappeared. If it was a coyote, it was the biggest I'd ever seen.

I continued driving slowly, and watched as the animal sauntered up onto the nearby railroad embankment, which paralleled the highway. The creature stopped on the tracks and looked around.

"See it?" I pointed. "That's a wolf!"

The head was broad, too wide for a coyote. And he was large and beautiful.

We had seen a wolf, and it stirred the wild inside each of us.

Miles for Grand Island:

Bike	Hike	Ferry
7	1	1

Isle Royale,
Michigan

This book began with the exploration of Montreal Island, the most east-ern and "downstream" island in this odyssey. Isle Royale is the most northern island explored, the most "upstream" that I set foot on for this adventure. The waters slapping the edges of Isle Royale will eventually flow into Lake Huron, through Lake Erie, then north up the Niagara River – plunging over Niagara Falls – before merging with Lake Ontario. This journey may take hundreds of years before the water that once resided in Lake Superior finally flows into the St. Lawrence River and slips past the watery edge of Montreal on the way to the North Atlantic.

While Montreal Island is distinctive for its development and popula-tion, Isle Royale is arguably one of the wilder islands in the Great Lakes. Though for a significant slice of time this remote island hosted transient populations of people and even some industry, since it was designated a National Park in 1931 the wilderness has been allowed to swallow much of the evidence from this period.

The archeological record reveals that native people frequented Isle Royale to fish, hunt, or to mine copper as early as 4,000 years ago. The Ojibwa called the island "Minong," meaning "a good place to be," and visited the island in the mild months. For several generations beginning in the mid-1800s, hardy fishermen of Scandinavian descent and their families populated seasonal settlements on the edges of the island. The men would row wooden skiffs out on the frigid lake to set nets or long lines to later haul in by hand. Commercial fisheries worked the island waters, but by the time the island was declared a National Park the commercial fisheries had over-harvested the waters, and many of the seasonal families no longer returned to fish. The invasive sea lamprey reached Lake Superior in the 1930s, further depleting the native fish that had provided life and livelihoods for so many for so long.

Larger-scale copper mining efforts were active in the late-1800s. This metal can still be found in nearly pure form on the island because of something that happened a billion years ago. A rift between continental plates opened where the middle of Lake Superior's basin is today. This rift spewed magma for millions of years, and the prolonged molten state allowed the copper molecules to find each other, to gather and settle out in a layer. When the lava finally cooled, the copper veins were sandwiched between strata of basaltic rock.

Eventually, the weight of all that magma caused the earth's crust to collapse. The crust of the earth elevated on either side of the collapse forming two landforms, Isle Royale and the Keweenaw Peninsula. This geologic occurrence of collapse and upheaval is called a *syncline*. The geology of these two landforms is almost identical, and the ridges found on them are actually the layers of the earth's crust exposed at the surface, then ground over by the glaciers thousands of years ago.

I explored the Keweenaw a bit for my last book, *A 1,000-Mile Great Lakes Walk*, and now I would hike the other side of this syncline isolated on Lake Superior: Isle Royale.

A long drive for a short boat ride

The longest-running predator/prey wildlife study ever done is based on Isle Royale. Scientists have been observing the interaction of wolves and moose here for over 50 years. This landmark wildlife study is the pride of Michigan Tech University where the researchers are based. When I began making plans to explore the island, I learned that they needed experienced hikers to help with this project. I applied and was accepted.

I wanted to be on an expedition that would leave from Grand Portage, Minnesota, right up against the border with Canada. This would mean a longer drive for me, but a shorter ferry ride to the island. I tend to get seasick, but I love to drive, so this plan worked for me.

I picked up another hiker, Cathy More, who had flown into Duluth and was looking to catch a ride up to Grand Portage. She was about my age with shoulder-length, sandy blonde hair, and round glasses on a round face. She spoke with a soothing, soft voice. On the two-hour drive north along the shoreline of Lake Superior, Cathy told me that the previous year, her group took the ferry from Copper Harbor, Michigan, to Isle Royale. On the five-hour return trip, Lake Superior was wild with waves cresting at 14 feet high. She said everyone on the ship hurled, including a Merchant Marine who had never been sick in all his years on the water.

Even the captain was seasick.

The captain driving the ferry had to take a break . . . to hurl.

I was pleased that I had chosen a shorter boat ride.

Since most of my hiking miles have been done solo, I had many questions for Cathy about the group experience. By the time we arrived at the hotel where we would stay the night before we traveled across to the island, my probing questions had been answered. I was reassured by Cathy's gentle personality and generous outlook. She deflected any chance at self-praise, always opting to credit her team and the scientists, especially Rolf Peterson and his wife Candy. If everyone who gathered on Isle Royale had this perspective, the team spirit would prevail during the weeklong expedition.

That first night, the team members and lead scientists gathered for dinner at the hotel. Participants ranged in age from around 20 to one man, Ron, in his 70s. His grandsons were also on this expedition. One of them was the youngest team leader. I was encouraged to see that almost a third of the hikers were women.

Most of those gathered had been on previous expeditions. Only five of us were first-timers. The group was friendly and inclusive of newcomers. The research team was there: Rolf and Candy Peterson greeted us warmly, and John and Leah Vucetich joined the group before dinner. The Petersons have been married for over 40 years now, and the thousands of wild miles they have hiked on Isle Royale have shaped them. They are both lean, almost wiry, and they move with purpose and direction even when off-island. They also communicated with few words. A look or motion would convey a message between them, something I'm sure they perfected while silently observing wolves and their pups in the wild.

At dinner, I was seated next to Rolf. He had been the lead researcher on this project for decades. He had recently retired, but was still closely involved with the work.

The wolf question

In May of 2014 when I joined this expedition, there were only nine wolves and slightly more than a thousand moose on Isle Royale. The wolf population, as you can probably surmise from its islanded status, is highly inbred. Recently, Isle Royale had been getting national press about the declining number of wolves. The population had taken a large hit in the early 1980s when a visitor on a private boat brought their dog to the island. That dog carried parvovirus. The wolf population was cut by 75 percent and then continued to decline.

In 2013, the one remaining wolf pack had three pups. They survived the winter. When an ice bridge formed between the island and mainland – something that hadn't happened since 2008 – researchers hoped that a new wolf would migrate from the mainland to the island and reinvigorate the weakening genetic pool. This had happened before. A lone male nicknamed the Old Grey Guy had made it to the island in 1997, and he injected fresh genes into the wolf packs on the island.

Unfortunately, Isle Royale didn't gain any wolves from the mainland in 2014. The only known crossing made that bitterly cold winter was that of a female wolf named Isabelle, who left the island using the ice bridge. She had not been able to integrate into any group, since the alpha female already in place will usually drive off other females. Isabelle ran into more bad luck when she crossed to the mainland and someone shot at her with an air rifle (legal there to discourage wolves from lingering near people and dogs). One of the pellets penetrated between her ribs, causing a fatal hemorrhage in her lungs.

Public input?

In 2013, the National Park Service (NPS) held a series of meetings seeking public input on the question of what to do about the declining wolf population on the island. I attended a meeting in Chelsea, Michigan. Several NPS staff were there along with the Isle Royale park superintendent, Phyllis Green. The rangers brought informational pamphlets, and Natural Resource Chief, Paul Brown gave a short talk about the history of the island and the wildlife there. Then Green spoke about the dwindling wolf population.

The concept of "Minimum Required Analysis" was explained. Green said that this idea has been one of the guiding principles of the NPS as part of their "non-interference" approach to wildlife management. For each situation, park management asks: 1. Is it necessary to take action? and 2. What is the minimum to be done to achieve the desired result?

While this principle may be effective in larger parks where ecosystems have the ability to correct for disruptions like severe weather events or disease, a more active management philosophy may better fit an isolated outpost like Isle Royale. Starker Leopold, the eldest son of famed conservationist Aldo Leopold, proposed a more active approach in his report commissioned by the NPS in the early 1960s, "Wildlife Management in the National Parks" (more commonly known as the "Leopold Report" and a link to it can be found under Related Reading in the back of this book). Starker followed in his father's footsteps, seeking methods of restoring and conserving natural biosystems. His report articulated many ideas that would guide the NPS's policies in the future.

The Leopold Report states: "Americans have shown a great capacity for degrading and fragmenting native biotas. So far we have not exercised much imagination or ingenuity in rebuilding damaged biotas. It will not be done by passive protection alone."

This report was revisited in 2012, nearly 50 years after the original. "Revisiting Leopold: Resource Stewardship in the National Parks" (a link to this report can also be found in the back) reinforces most of the conclusions of the original, and emphasizes the need for an increased role of science in maintaining our National Parks against "continuous change that is not yet fully understood, in order to preserve ecological integrity . . . provide visitors with transformative experiences, and form the core of a national conservation land- and seascape."

At the meeting in Chelsea, Superintendent Green asked for questions from the audience. She stood at the front of the room wearing her NPS uniform: olive-green dress shirt, dark green tie, NPS tie tack, golden NPS shield pinned on the left side of her shirt. Her gold nametag hovered over her right shirt pocket. Dark green pants, wide brown belt, and brown shoes completed the woodsy uniform.

One gentleman pressed the Superintendent for more precise language. Terms like "minimal maintenance" and "historical precedence" were being used, but it was unclear how they would influence action going forward. Superintendent Green let this concern go unanswered, moving on instead to the next question.

"You say that there are three components for making decision about whether to transport new wolves to the island," a young man stated. "These are: input from scientists, NPS guidelines, and public input."

Green nodded.

"But you haven't said how each of these is weighted. Is it equally? Or is one more important than the others?"

Green blinked and dodged that question, too.

The next question was about the Wolf-Moose Study and in particular if input from the Michigan Tech researchers would be considered in the decision-making process.

"No," Green said flatly. "We'll bring in other scientists to gather data on the island and make recommendations."

Honestly, this puzzled me. Why not take advantage of the peer-reviewed data from the Wolf-Moose Study? "Leopold Revisited" repeatedly states the importance of scientific data, and that data exists for 56 years of the island's wolf/moose populations and interactions.

When Green asked for a show of hands from the crowd of who wanted the wolf population to continue on the island, all hands went up. Several people who had been on Isle Royale spoke of hearing the wolves howling at night, recalling how that feral sound defined the island and a sense of wilderness for them. One person worried that the moose would destroy the vegetation on the island if there weren't enough wolves to keep their population in check.

At dinner the night before our Moosewatch Teams headed to Isle Royale, I told Rolf about the Chelsea meeting.

"They actually took questions from the audience?" he asked.

"Yes. After the presentation."

"They didn't take any at the first meeting," Rolf told me.

"Has the NPS made a decision about bringing new wolves to Isle Royale?" I asked.

"They have. Superintendent Green has stated that they will only take action if one of three things happens. 1: The wolves stop reproducing. 2: Wolf population loses all members of one sex. . . ."

"Which is actually number one," I observed.

"True. And 3: Moose over-browse the island vegetation."

"Why would they wait for a calamity to happen before acting?"

Rolf looked at me. "That's a great question."

To the isle

The dinner broke up and team members took to their rooms to re-check gear and get some sleep before the short early morning ride to Isle Royale. By 7:30 a.m. the next morning, all of our gear was loaded onto the ferry, the *Voyageur II*, including a dozen boxes filled with our food for the week, to be distributed once we reached the island.

The Windigo dock, our destination on Isle Royale, was only two hours from where I stood, and with the lake looking rather gentle, I debated whether to even strap on my anti-nausea wristbands. Erring on the side of not hurling, I put them on and then climbed onto the ferry. It was there that I learned that we would be getting off not at Windigo, but at Malone Bay.

"Where's that?" I asked.

"It's only about three hours from Windigo . . . but . . ."

I did the math. The two-hour ride had expanded to five. Thankfully, the lake still looked rather calm. The day was cool, in the 40s, but sunny with only light winds. I touched my wristbands compulsively. I could do five hours.

"But . . . ?" I asked.

"We're going to travel around the island clockwise, so it will be eight or nine hours to Malone Bay."

I almost hurled.

Although the ride to Malone Bay was long, it was a lovely way to see the island. Ice and snow still clung to the rocks at the edges. The deciduous trees were still in their dormant winter state, skeletal forms mixed in with the lush spruce. There are fir trees on the island, too, but this is the primary food source for moose during the winter, so smaller trees have their tops munched off year after year. Some trees that are only waist high may be decades old, their growth stunted by this yearly chomping.

The island is hilly, and it was easy to discern rocky shelves in the landscape that stepped down to the lake. In some areas, the edge of the island was a sheer rock wall that dropped off into the deep, blue water. We saw merganser ducks and kingfishers, bald eagles and loons along the way.

On the far eastern end of the island, we passed Rock Harbor. This is the most developed part of the island with a lodge, many park buildings, and a sprinkling of cabins. Even in this wild place, it's possible to have a rather civilized visit if you stay at the lodge. It's rare to find moose bones here, though. We were seeking something else: a true backcountry experience.

Lake Superior had a little more movement to its surface after we made the turn around the eastern end of the island. I went to the rear deck to take in the fresh air and sunshine, hoping to ward off nausea. The group had mingled and mixed while on the long ride, and I had chatted with almost everyone as the ferry finally entered Malone Bay.

Now you just need to see the middle

Once the ferry was tied at the dock, we each found our backpack after it was lifted off the boat and piled into a heap. We carried our gear off the dock onto the island proper, and looked to set our packs down in a place that wasn't covered with moose pellets. Oddly uniform, the winter poop from moose is almost two inches long, oval and black. The moose eat the foliage from fir trees to make it through the winter, which results in this pelletized poo. When their diet switches to fresher green growing things in the mild months, their poo looks more like a cow pie.

We hustled back to the dock to grab the cardboard boxes with food for the week, along with stoves, fuel, maps, and GPS units for each team.

We assembled around the NPS welcome cabin. They used to station a ranger near here (nicknamed the "Malone Ranger"), but there were so few hikers and boaters passing along this part of the shoreline that they no longer staff it. Candy Peterson oversaw the distribution of food from the cabin's small deck. It was clear that Candy had done this many times before. "You each get six blocks of cheese," she said, "and come up here to pack your hot drinks. Grab all the peanut butter you want for the week."

My group had two leaders, Wayne and Jason. Wayne was around 60 years old and from Iowa. He was a tall tree of a man with blondish-red wavy hair. He smiled mostly with his blue eyes. He had led many groups before on the island. Jason was in his 30s, his light hair buzzed close to his scalp, and he had wrap-around sunglasses that gave him an air of cool-ness. He had done a three-month wolf-moose internship on the island after graduating college. This trip was the first time he had been back to the island in over a decade. Isle Royale had made such an impression on Jason that he had named his son "Tobin" after an island harbor.

"Don't forget your chocolate," Candy called out.

I smiled to hear my cardinal hiking rule.

Wayne and Jason gathered our food, two cook stoves, and extra fuel containers, then began shoving most of it into their own packs. Eager to help, I grabbed a large bag of dehydrated dinners and another bag of hot chocolate and cider packets.

The two other people in our group were Bob from Oklahoma and Ifigenia "Ifi" from Costa Rica. Bob was around 60, a compact guy with silver hair and beard. Ifi was in her 30s, tan and thin. Ifi was a naturalist who worked at Corcovado National Park in Costa Rica. She had met Bob when he had recently hiked there. Bob had told tropical Ifi about this magi-cal island in Lake Superior, and she had come to look for moose bones with us. She was going to encounter low temperatures that her slight frame had never experienced before.

With team members from Iowa, Colorado, Oklahoma, Michigan, and Costa Rica, our group was the one from far-flung places, and the only group with *international* cachet.

It was sunny and around 50 degrees that first day, pleasant enough for us Midwesterners who had survived the ominously named "Polar Vortex" during the past winter. But to shivering Ifi, 50 degrees felt like a mini–polar vortex.

One of the other team members spotted a large moose antler, recently shed. It was an impressive one, and we took turns taking photos with it. Bull moose grow an annual set of antlers. This crowning structure emerges in May covered at first in "velvet," a fuzzy layer with a network of blood vessels that transports oxygen and nutrients to grow the antlers. Once fully formed, usually around the September rut, the moose will rub their new antlers against trees to remove the velvet. By the end of October, the mating season is over, and the antlers fall off before year's end.

The energy a bull moose puts into growing his annual crown is a huge metabolic drain and the main reason bulls have shorter lives than cows. In Rolf Peterson's book, *The Wolves of Isle Royale*, he notes that the oldest bull ever found on Isle Royale was 17 years old. The oldest cow was 20.

In comparison, wolves are lucky to live a decade. Peterson said the oldest he knows on Isle Royale lived a dozen years.

"I so want to see a moose on this trip," Ifi said, as she held the heavy antler.

"Well, you've seen the antlers. And the poop." I pointed to the nearby pile of oval pellets. "So now you just have to see the middle part."

Ifi nodded solemnly, agreeing that this was, indeed, true.

Once our packs were loaded with supplies for the week, we took a team photo with Malone Bay in the background. In the image, the five of us stand tall with our packs strapped on our backs. Jason and Wayne are on the right side of the photo, the tallest in our group. I am in the center wearing a new pack I got before the trip. My white pack was too small for a week in the wild gathering bones. Bob and Ifi are on the left side of the photo. It's no surprise that Ifi is bundled a little more than the rest of us. Bob's pack has an external, aluminum frame, the kind they don't make anymore, the one that he's hiked with for many decades.

Take care of each other

Since most of the daylight was burned getting to the island, we spent that first night in the nearby campground. That night, the almost-full moon rose over the bay. Jason and I tried to capture it with our cameras. It's amazing how much light is reflected off this dead sphere orbiting our earth. My photos captured the bright orb frosted with wispy clouds afloat in the inky sky.

Isle Royale is actually surrounded by a couple hundred smaller islands, and one photograph catches the winking light of the lighthouse on nearby Menagerie Island.

That night I still felt the gentle rocking of the ferry while tucked in my sleeping bag.

In the morning, I got up early to boil water for our breakfast. The stoves were two different models. I wasn't familiar with the old-school "pump the fuel" type, but I finally managed to get one lit and set a pan of Lake Superior water on top of it. Wayne joined me at the picnic table, watching me being so industrious. He nodded (which is "good morning" in Iowan), then he said, "That stove has legs."

This sounded like a riddle. I touched the water pan, and the whole thing rolled over on its side, spilling cold water on Wayne. (This is Michigander for "I don't know how to work these stoves.")

Wayne brushed off the water, then pointed to the legs on the bottom of the fuel can, the ones I had neglected to extend. I pulled them out and set it up again. Wayne pumped up the stove and lit it. I replaced the water pan with fresh water, sliding the whole thing far away from Wayne so I wouldn't scald the man if it tipped again.

After breakfast we went over our gear. Rolf stopped by to make sure that Wayne and Jason knew how to work the new radio/texting gizmo to check in each night, and reviewed the map of our route. Our team was the only one heading to the north shore of the island, the side we had spent hours looking at from the ferry. As Candy checked in with each group – making sure they had enough fuel, gathering trash from breakfast so they didn't have to carry it all week, smiling at everyone – she always left each group with one heartfelt admonition: "Take care of each other."

Our first skull

Our team left Malone Bay and hiked the trail through the black-and-white birch trees around Siskiwit Lake. Slabs of ice still crowded the edges of this island lake. We saw many moose tracks in the muddy areas and plenty of moose droppings. We even saw an occasional wolf track – dog-like prints, but wide and huge.

As we neared the western edge of Siskiwit Lake, we came upon a fairly fresh moose kill at the side of the trail. Jason estimated it at about two weeks old. All of the bones were there except the sternum, and the leg bones were very close to the otherwise intact skeleton. The hooves were still attached, and fur covered the lower part of each leg.

It was fascinating to see the entire skeleton presented like this. Wayne assured us that this was rare, to discover one with all the bones. And finding it on the trail was unique, too. We filled out a data sheet listing the bones found and inspected them closely for any signs of arthritis (none found here). We took photos of the site and bones, using special tags assigning it a number and our team's designation.

I picked up the lower jaw. It was still intact with all but one of the teeth still set in the bone. The scientists can make a pretty good estimate of a moose's age by looking at the extent of wear on molars, but the incisors give more precise data. Cross-sectioning these teeth reveals rings marking the interior tooth structure. By counting the rings, much like aging a tree, a researcher can pinpoint an accurate age for that moose.

I ran my finger across the smooth tops of the back teeth. Moose molars are rather beautiful the way they nest together and undulate in waves. They aren't solid white, but rather white on the outer edges with shades of brown and drops of black swirled through the middle. This moose – it was a female, a cow – was missing a molar in her lower jaw, and the abscess must have been painful because there was bone loss around the socket. Wolves will prey on the weak and the frail, and this cow was probably an easy kill with her missing tooth and the long, tough winter.

We gathered up the skull, lower jaw, and one of the long bones from the back leg. Jason wrapped it all in plastic, required since the skull was still juicy in places. He strapped it onto his pack.

Our first skull.

The Yoda route

Hiking Isle Royale lengthwise is easier because the ridges of the land – those exposed layers of the earth's crust – run the same way, so you can stay on one ridge. Moving widthwise is another story. If you hike the island this way, you will have to climb each of these ridges, one by one, up and down and up and down. You'll have to climb the highest ridge, the Greenstone, then the second-highest, the Minong. In between there are other ridges. And in between these I guarantee you there will be cedar swamps so dense and murky you will look around for Yoda to encourage you with the timeless advice, "There is no try, there is only *do*."

We had been assigned the Yoda route.

We were able to stay on the trail to the Ishpeming Point fire tower – which is 765 feet above Malone Bay, the equivalent of climbing the stairs of a 75-story building – but then we had to go off-trail for a long stretch before reaching the Minong Trail that would branch off to get to Little Todd Harbor. Once there, we'd set up basecamp for a few days.

When we came to the first of many rocky ridges, I was surprised at how steep it was and how much snow persisted in between huge lichen-spotted rock outcroppings. I scanned the drop-off, thinking that there was no way we were going to get down the ridge safely from that point. Then, I noticed Jason was already heading down. And the rest of the team was following.

Jason, as I mentioned, makes his home in Colorado. He lives at 5,000-feet elevation, and happens to work as a game warden. In effect, he climbs mountains for a living. In contrast, I am a flatlander, a hiker of shorelines with only an occasional dune or limestone outcropping to traverse.

I plunged down the rocky ridge with my 40-pound pack, often opting for the technique of keeping my bum in contact with the rocky face as I slid downward. I hoped the seat of my hiking pants was up for the challenge.

Wayne and Jason set a brisk pace. Bob had no trouble keeping up. Ifi seemed to be happy for the exertion that warmed her to her tropical norm. And I was trying to be safe while plunging over rock faces into snow that was thigh-deep in places.

Then we reached our first cedar swamp.

I don't have any photos of our swamp crossings because it was all I could do to balance across them, hopping from tree to tree, swinging out across deep, murky holes filled with icy water, slipping on mossy logs, stepping into deep mud.

"There is no try, there is only *do,*" echoed in my head.

By the time we finally reached the Minong Ridge Trail, my legs were rubbery from exertion.

"Yay," I gasped. "The trail."

This trail would take us all the way to Little Todd Harbor. Which meant not have to bushwhack through swamps and underbrush, climbing over deadfalls, thrashing through branches.

I had brought a walking stick along with me, one that had already been with me for over 500 miles of hiking. It was a simple, found stick that I had stripped of bark and topped with a black, rubber handgrip. I was thankful for the extra stability it provided on the rugged journey so far.

I felt something scratchy on my neck and pulled out a small dead branch that had lodged between my head and backpack. I took off my hat and shook other debris from my hair. This was a different kind of trek. Not the contemplative, my-stride-matching-the-waves hiking I had done so far. This hike would require that I focus on moving carefully and safely through the wild, rugged landscape, all the time scanning for a glint of white bone dispersed among persistent patches of snow and shreds of white birch bark littering the island.

We were all happy to have reached the trail. Jason set off at a brisk pace, and we followed, unimpeded, single file, toward our campground.

Where's the bridge?

We had one river to cross on the trail to Little Todd. When we reached it, we discovered that the bridge had been completely swept away during the spring melt.

Jason and Wayne scouted the river in each direction for a way to cross, but they returned to where the trail ended at the river's edge. Two long logs were almost submerged in the river here – a possible way to cross – but the river was wide and swift.

"There should be a bridge here with a railing," Wayne pointed out.

But there wasn't.

"I think we can cross on these logs," Bob said, stepping out onto them. He leaned on a long stick stuck into the river for balance. "Face upriver and make sure your feet are stable before moving your stick." He demonstrated a slow, cautious, sideways shuffle on the slippery logs, after which he moved his balancing stick against the current.

"Undo your hip belt before you cross," Jason said.

He didn't have to explain why. It was so if any of us fell in, we'd be able to quickly wriggle out of our pack while submerged in the frigid water.

I knew Jason and Wayne were great leaders; they had earned my complete confidence this first day over rugged terrain. And I knew they had a contingency plan to deal with a slip into this icy, rushing water – on a day where the air temperature had peaked at 50 and was now quickly cooling.

Disaster Plan: Fish the hiker out of the water. Some of us gather wood and build a fire. The rest of the group get the wet clothes off the soaked person and then cocoon them with dry sleeping bags from the packs of others. Help them to stand and do deep knee bends, until the fire is raging hot. Then dry their clothing and warm them by the fire until they stop shivering.

Also, retrieve their submerged pack.

Ifi watched the rushing water. She looked nauseated.

Bob crossed, side-stepping on the log, then he called out pointers as Wayne crossed.

I threw my walking stick across the river, where it got hung up in some branches on the other side. It was of no use to me for this balancing act. A much longer stick was necessary to reach down into the water and stabilize me during the crossing.

Moving sideways atop the slippery logs was tricky. And advancing the long balancing stick against the powerful current was a struggle. Moving the stick served to emphasize how deep the water was and how swift it was moving. I tried to not contemplate the force that would pin me against the logs if I fell in. I focused on sidling across the river.

Once safely across, I tried to retrieve my walking stick, tangled in some brush at the edge of the river, but only managed to poke it loose. It flowed swiftly downstream and disappeared around the bend out of sight.

We all crossed safely, so there was no need for the disaster plan.

We arrived at the campground and spread out to claim our sites. The relief of reaching our destination washed over me, and setting down my pack was a joy. As I moved around to set up my tent, I occasionally had to stop and stretch out a cramp in the muscle on the front of my thigh. This particular muscle had never complained before, but the day's hike with climbing up then jumping down countless rock faces, balancing through swamps, and shuffling over a slippery log –all with a full pack – had worked my legs like never before. It was the most rigorous day of hiking I had ever done, and it was only a nine-mile day.

We gathered to build a fire in the fire ring and boil water for our dinner atop our cook stoves. I noticed that Wayne had to stretch out his legs occasionally and knead the front of his thigh.

"Muscle cramp?" I asked.

He nodded. "I never get them here."

"Me either. That was quite the hike," I laughed.

Ifi stared into the fire, "I knew if I fell in the cold water of the river, I would die."

I assured her that we would have fished her out and warmed her over a big fire, but she looked unconvinced.

We spent the next two days searching for moose bones in the area. This may sound like a leisurely thing to do, strolling the woods in search of bones. But it was all off-trail, so it was more like doing gymnastics in the wild as we moved through the rough landscape, over rocks, down steep hills, and over and under enormous felled trees. And we had to cross that river several more times. But at least we were able to leave our large packs at camp.

The first time I crossed back over the river, I walked downstream a bit and was surprised to find my walking stick waiting for me, caught up in some reeds. I fished it out and shook it off.

Good as new.

Gotta have the skull

Finds of moose bones only counted if we located the skull. A leg bone was usually found first, then the team would fan out and search for more bones. Several times over the week we located a few bones in an area, but couldn't find the skull. This was disappointing.

In one swampy location, we were nearly ready to give up. We had found a few bones and had been searching for the skull for almost an hour. The swamp still had snow piled in places and the water was slushy with it. We had been reaching down into the water, probing for bones and finding a few more, but no skull. We were all wandering around in looping circles, searching, but without much hope. Then I noticed something small, white, and rounded, barely coming up out of a patch of snow. Round is an odd shape in nature, so I swiped away the snow, revealing a molar. A moose molar. The rounded part was the base of the skull where it sits atop the spine. White like the snow, the skull was upside down, nestled there under its white shroud.

"I found something," I called out. "And you're all going to be happy. It's the skull."

I continued brushing the snow away as the team gathered around. It was a lucky find.

The moose had significant arthritis, so we packed up all bones that had signs of deterioration to take to the scientists. The pelvis revealed that the right rear hip had come out of the socket, rubbing a painful groove into the pelvis. This moose had been another easy kill for the wolves.

A landmark study of moose bones gathered on Isle Royale had determined that nutritional intake when moose are young correlated with the prevalence of disease as the moose aged. If early nutrition was poor, then the likelihood of developing arthritis was greater. Nutritional intake is assessed by the severity of winters when the moose was a juvenile. This study was later repeated in humans, and that correlation of early nutrition predicting later health also exists for us.

The last night we spent at the Little Todd camp, I woke in the middle of the night. When camping in the wild, I usually sleep pretty lightly and often awaken if an animal crashes around or if the wind suddenly picks up. This night, it was the sound of wolves howling to each other that woke me.

I shivered at the sound – at the incredible wildness of it – and felt something wild awaken in me in response. Aldo Leopold, in his essay "Thinking Like a Mountain," said that wolf country "distinguishes that country from all other land. It tingles the spine of all who hear wolves by night, or scan their tracks by day."

Our next camp was near a stream, off trail. A snowshoe hare lived in the area, and it would hop around the perimeter of camp in the evenings while we cooked dinner. We usually tried to choose a place for our "kitchen" that had downed trees to sit on. One night while we were eating dinner, sitting on these logs, our friend the hare came rushing toward us. It took a leap over the log I was sitting on, passing by so close to me I could have stuck out my hand and grabbed it out of midair.

We all burst out laughing at the comedic feat. Then Wayne said, "I wonder what's chasing it." We fell silent, looking in the direction that the hare had come from. But if there was a wolf stalking it, we never saw it.

Why Isle Royale?

That night I asked each of my team members why they were on this expedition, why they had come – or returned – to Isle Royale.

Bob answered first. He told me earlier that he rarely explores the same place twice. But he made an exception for Isle Royale. He had returned to join the Moosewatch expedition many times. "This place is remote, pristine. It's difficult to get to," he said. "That's what makes it special."

Wayne, the most soft-spoken person in our group, answered next. He said in college he hadn't known what he wanted to do, that he had kind of stumbled into engineering, a field he would now, decades later, soon retire from. "If I could go back and relive those years," he said, "I'd be a park

ranger or a wildlife researcher. I would have liked to study grizzly bears."
His eyes flashed with this revelation. "Time here on this island fulfills that
part of me." He also felt it was a test to come to the island and complete a
week in the wild, and he needed to know he was up for the challenge.

"Well," Jason said, "I've thought about this island every single day
since I did my internship here. My wife knew that, and she finally told me
to do it, to return. I love working with the Petersons. They are so wise." He
said that Isle Royale gives a true backcountry experience, that on this island
we were truly in the wild. "Time here makes you stronger. It makes you
more confident in your life," he said.

"And I love finding bones." He grinned.

Jason was on to something there. It's difficult to convey the joy that
comes with finding a moose bone. It was a high-stakes treasure hunt; a
moose had to die for you to win. There was that sense that we were competing with other teams in a macabre scavenger hunt, while helping scientists
with important work.

I know I felt bonded to my team in a strong, essential way after surviving that first difficult day of hiking and hunting for bones. This connection
was new for me. I'd been a solitary walker for most of my past Great Lakes
adventures.

Ifi said she was grateful and happy to come to the island. For her, the
solitude reflected and revealed her inner thoughts. And she loved hearing
someone call out that they had found moose bones. She added that she
thought Rolf and Candy were special people.

Bob was quick to agree with that. "When I've asked people why they
return to help with this project," Bob said, "most people say 'Rolf and
Candy' as a major factor. I know that's true for me."

The allure of Isle Royale was that of a pristine wilderness, a chance to
experience the patterns of life on a rugged slice of land surrounded by the
lake with the largest surface area in the world. But it also involved a sense
of people, a unique community of bone-seekers, a gathering of colleagues
concerned with the ecological health of the island, coming together, over
years, to do something important. Islands hold a promise of learning much
about a tiny place in the world. And perhaps learning a little about yourself,
and about those who hike an island at your side.

On Sunday, we awoke to a steady light rain. By the time we had packed up, it had mostly stopped. But our gear was soggy and heavier on our backs. We hiked the day along the most rugged part of the Minong Trail to a new camp near a beaver pond. This section of the trail has repeated ups and downs even though it runs along the Minong Ridge. Huge bumps of stone – some were four stories tall, a few even taller – populate this section of the trail. Each one had to be scaled, then descended. I got "jelly legs" going up the largest of these bumps and had to stop for a short break a couple of times on the ascents. Wayne and Bob usually took a break with me, stopping to chat, while Ifi kept pace with Jason.

"Sorry I keep stopping," I said during my third break.

"Don't ever apologize for that," Wayne told me, saying it was always fine to rest. I wondered if he and Bob also wanted to take a break but didn't want to be the first to stop. Either way, it was nice chatting with them.

We hiked through a burned section of the island on this stretch. Many of the trees were blackened and twisted. Some were nothing but a charred shell with a hollow core that we could look through. The burnt ash mixed with the mud, making the trail extra slick.

There was also a wonderful variety of lichens on display. There are over 600 species on the island, and they were more exposed and visible in this burned area. Some rocks were a mosaic of lichen in muted colors: light gray and greens, browns and tans. Occasionally, a rust or orange lichen made a splash among the rest.

We crossed ponds by traversing the tops of old beaver dams. One dam had a large chunk missing, and we spotted each other as we leapt over the gap with our heavy packs. Moving through this rugged terrain, we covered only an average of a mile each hour.

Beaver pond camp

Our final camp was near an active beaver pond, six miles from the Windigo dock, our ultimate destination where we would meet up with the other groups at the end of the expedition. In the evening, we watched the beaver swim around and hoped for a moose to emerge from the woods. In the mornings, the pond was misty and mysterious, and yellow-bellied flycatchers flitted in the tree branches. One moose visited our camp on our last night, crashing around the edges a bit, looking for newly sprouted things to eat.

On our final day, the group went out to assess the growth of fir trees in a nearby area while I elected to stay near camp and do a few last sweeps looking for more bones. I was tired from waking so much at night and, honestly, sore from the rugged week of hiking. I thought it best to save my strength for the final push to Windigo.

When I had finally peeled off my long johns the previous day, when the temperatures had finally gotten up to 60 degrees, I was shocked at the number of bruises my legs had accumulated. My shins had more bruised than normal skin, and several of the spots were turning all sorts of weird colors.

I had also discovered a hairline fracture in my old walking stick. I bound it up with cloth tape I had along and hoped it would make it to Windigo. If it did, I could retire it with style. If it snapped in two along the trail, well, then I'd have to set it free.

The rest of my group took off to check out the fir trees, and I began my sweeps along the edges of the beaver pond, then arcing out in loops to swing into the woods and then back to camp. I tried to stay on the ridges, since anytime I descended into lower areas there was sure to be swampy land. Looping through the woods that the beavers had worked, I was struck by their ambition. Often they whittled away at a tree at one level, then, when it didn't fall, they would start a new cut lower on the trunk. Some of the trees they took down were significant in their girth, and the ground was littered with the uniform shavings from their sharp teeth.

Tree feet

Much of Isle Royale is rocky, so the trees have to spread their roots out horizontally and grip the rocks against the storms that buffet the island. There are deadfall zones, proving how the trees are often unsuccessful in maintaining their vertical attitude during winter gales and ice storms. While making my loops around camp, I noticed two such wind-felled trees lying in opposite directions from each other.

The root mats, now sticking straight up and down, were massive; one was over six feet tall, the other about nine feet. The space in between them was only a few feet wide. It intrigued me, and I wanted to stand in that space between the feet of the trees, so I headed down into the swampy area and stood there with twisted root walls on either side of me. I reached out my hands and touched the roots, appreciating the intricate weaving they had done over and under each other.

When I stepped out of this narrow corridor, I looked around the swampy area for the best route to make it back to camp, when I saw it: a huge moss-covered moose skull lying there in the swamp near one of the massive tree trunks. On closer inspection, I realized that the antlers of the moose were underneath the skull. They had come off, but had certainly been attached when this bull moose died.

I took off my coat and hung it on the roots of one of the trees and went to work. After an hour, I had found about a dozen bones, but the leg bones, oddly, were still missing. These bones are usually found first, and I wondered where they had gone.

I knew that the rest of my group would return soon and I needed their help to finish processing the find. They had the data sheets and tags we used, so I returned to camp and took down my tent and assembled my pack. Then, I made pudding for the group to eat when they returned.

About the time the pudding had set, I heard movement in the forest, so I whistled to help them locate camp. Jason whistled back and was first to emerge from the woods. I asked how it went, and he said that Bob should tell the tale.

Bob arrived walking a little strangely, and I realized that he had a bull moose skull with large antlers draped on his back. He set down the heavy find, and then I noticed his arm was bleeding. Ifi sat down next to me, hanging her head between her knees. She couldn't stand the sight of blood. Wayne helped Bob clean and dress his wound while Jason began packing up his gear.

"I made pudding," I said. Ifi brightened and scooped some out. She was hungry. When she had earlier seen the blood from Bob's arm, she hadn't been able to eat any of the lunch they had taken along with them.

Once Bob was patched up, I learned the story. He had been celebrating the find of the excellent skull with antlers – and had stumbled and impaled his arm.

"I found a skull, too," I told the group. "Back there, over that hill. I can't find the leg bones, though."

Since I was all packed up, I returned to continue looking for more bones while everyone else ate pudding and packed up their gear. Wayne gave me his knife and said he'd be over to help me soon. By the time he arrived, I had probed into all of the deep watery holes around the one where I had found the skull. A few more vertebrae had turned up, but I had still not found any of the long leg bones.

Wayne looked around the swampy site, with a puzzled expression. "Why did you even come down here?"

I pointed to the massive root mats. "I wanted to see the roots up close."

And then I took a closer look at the top of the tallest root mat.

Was I hallucinating? Was it a mirage, a side-effect of exhaustion from long, tiring days in the wilderness?

No, there were clearly two leg bones tangled in the roots high above me, about seven feet off the ground.

"Leg bones!" I shouted.

Wayne looked at the bones, then back at me, then again at the bones.

It took Wayne a half hour to cut the bones out of the roots. They must have been there a long time, since they had to have been on the ground lying on top of the roots before the tree toppled, and long enough for the roots to entangle them.

By the time we processed the skeleton and packed all of our bones for the final push to meet up with the other teams, it was getting late in the day. When Wayne mentioned that he didn't have a skull to carry, I asked him to carry the swampy skull since he had extricated the leg bones from the roots. It was as much his find at that point, and I wasn't sure I could manage the extra weight of that bull skull on top of the arthritic moose bones already strapped to my pack.

The island had awakened during our week there. We saw the first bat of the season flutter around a day before we saw the first mosquito. Skunk cabbage, a rare thermogenic plant that can melt the snow as it grows, was already emerging when we arrived. Patches of wild flowers bloomed toward the end of the week.

A few birds were already on the island when we docked, and more arrived during our stay. Flies hatched and buzzed around. Snakes emerged, slow to move as they shook off the months of living dormant under the thick snow. Frogs began singing in the ponds. Slugs slimed my tent the last couple of days.

Of course there are those island residents that never completely disappeared: wolves and moose, beaver and otter, fox and marten, and our comic leaping friend, the snowshoe hare.

Retirement

It was a six-mile hike to meet up with the rest of the Moosewatch teams and the researchers. We were all pretty tired by this point, after the work of recovering the two skulls on this last day. Our packs were the heaviest they had been on the trip. Thankfully, the trail was gentler than on previous days, but the light was fading when we finally reached the structure where the other teams had already gathered.

Some of us weighed our packs before dropping off the bones. My pack was 45 pounds. Jason's weighed in at 75 pounds.

After a week on the trail with freeze-dried and dehydrated and packable stuff to eat, I can tell you that I got a little choked up when I saw the massive bowl of salad on the table. It was in the middle of an amazing spread of lasagna, corn bread, and other great food, but what I most craved at that moment was a plate piled with fresh salad with thick slices of tomato and cucumber. When we walked into the main room filled with the other hikers, they cheered for us. And it felt like coming home.

The next morning, Rolf catalogued our moose bones. The very first skull had been collected on the island in 1958. Our final skull found, the one I found in the swamp on the last day, was skull number 4,955. Rolf examined this moss-covered skull, then the long metatarsal leg bone. He said it was the largest one ever found on Isle Royale.

"That's how big they grow on the mainland," Rolf told our team. "He would have been 1,200 pounds at peak weight."

My stick made it to the end without breaking, but I knew it had seen its last adventure. I found a black marker and passed the stick around for everyone to sign before I retired it. Rolf signed it "Isle Royale Forever. Rolf Peterson."

That's how I feel about this special island, too. It had seeped inside me during this week, challenging me more than any other place I'd explored in my three thousand miles journeying in the Great Lakes Basin.

May Isle Royale thrive and remain wild. And may the howling of wolves at the moon never be silenced.

Miles for Isle Royale:
Hike   Ferry
43   125

GRAND FINALE

Great Turtle

I invited family, friends, and followers to join me in walking the final miles of this adventure on Mackinac Island. This island is located in Lake Huron, east of the mighty Mackinac Bridge. The tops of Lake Michigan and Lake Huron connect underneath the bridge at the Straits of Mackinac.

This island is unique for several reasons, but the most prominent one is evident when you set foot there: cars are not allowed. Instead, there are over 500 horses doing the work of vehicles.

Mackinac Island has been part of all three of my adventures. I took a break there with my sons, Ben and Lucas, and my brother, Phil, during my first hike. I had completed half of my journey around Lake Michigan, walking from Chicago all the way to Mackinaw City. While I was thrilled to have made it that far, I was worried about the much wilder stretch of shoreline in Michigan's Upper Peninsula that still stretched out ahead of me. We biked the island and played miniature golf on the shoreline course. In between putts, we watched lake freighters passing so close that we could feel the vibrations from their thrumming engines in our lungs.

On my second hike, a few islands were included in my exploration of all five Great Lakes. I came Mackinac Island with a larger group this time: my mom, Ben and my sister-in-law, Mary Jo, and her kids, Alison and Julian. We rode bikes and explored the island's unique limestone formations.

The Native Americans who lived in this region long before Europeans ever entered the St. Lawrence River thought the limestone dome of the island resembled a giant turtle rising from the water. They named the island "Great Turtle." The Ojibwa word for this is *mishi-mikinaak*. The French adapted this word to Michilimackinac, and the British later shortened it to Mackinac.

There are many places on Mackinac Island that invite a visitor to explore the human history there. There is a bark lodge, one like native people would have constructed on the island. A statue of Father Jacques Marquette – intrepid explorer and priest who ministered to Native Americans in the region – overlooks Main Street. Fort Mackinac sits on the bluff overlooking the harbor, while the ruins of Fort Holmes (the first fort) are found in the interior of the island. You can bike to British Landing, the site where British and Native American forces came ashore to capture the island during the War of 1812.

There are also spots to explore the natural history of the island. Limestone outcroppings poke out of the forested hills all over the island, with delightful names like Skull Cave, Devil's Kitchen, Arch Rock. Arch Rock is a natural arch of limestone that is almost 150 feet above the level of the lake.

After the War of 1812, John Jacob Astor built a hub for his fur trading company here on Mackinac Island. You may be inclined to dismiss fur trading when you think of big businesses, but consider that Astor not only had a network to harvest furs in the Great Lakes and Canada, but he also funded expeditions to the Pacific Northwest to extend his enterprise coast-to-coast. Astor was the first multi-millionaire in America, the wealthiest man in the United States when he died. His descendants built the Waldorf Hotel and the Astoria Hotel in New York City, while George Boldt (who you may remember from the story of Heart Island at the beginning of this book) brokered the deal to merge these properties into one of America's finest hotels, the Waldorf-Astoria.

A truly GRAND Finale

Another one of North America's most famous hotels, the Grand Hotel, is on Mackinac Island. Billed as "America's Summer Place," this truly grand hotel, which opened in 1887, was financed by railroad and steamship companies. These companies had a vested interest in this "destination hotel" that could offer luxury accommodations to the people their companies transported to the island. This impressive wood frame structure was built in only 90 days, using white pine lumbered from Michigan's Upper Peninsula that was towed to the island over the ice during the winter.

Of the more than 1,200 large wood-frame hotels once found all over America at the turn of the 20th century, the Grand Hotel is one of only a dozen still operating. Imagine keeping any business afloat through two World Wars, prohibition, and the Great Depression. Then isolate that business on an island and try to imagine how much more difficult it would be. But this historic resort has thrived. It has hosted five presidents and many other famous people, such as Mark Twain, who lectured here, charging a dollar admission, and Thomas Edison, who gave a public demonstration of his phonograph on the porch.

There should be another name for the Grand Hotel's porch. At 660 feet, it holds the record for being the world's longest. There is enough room for dozens of white rocking chairs. Over thirty massive, white wooden pillars support the porch's overhang. The underside of this structure is painted sky blue, to trick birds into thinking the sky is still above them (so that they don't build their nests there). Flagpoles are secured to the base of every other pillar, with American flags flying from each pole, jutting out at an angle over the roadway. Flower boxes line the porch filled with the signature flower of the hotel, the red geranium.

Since the Grand Hotel closes for the winter, there is a special set of festivities and traditions associated with the end of the season. I timed my final miles with this "Closing of the Grand," and was thrilled to see my group gathered on the front porch on Sunday morning, October 26, for our hike around the island.

Walking stick elevated to art

For the final miles of this adventure, I brought along a custom walking stick that a woodcarver, Bette Hartig, had crafted for me. She lives in Big Rapids and had heard me speak at the bookstore there. When I met her, she told me, "I'm going to carve you a walking stick." Through the following months, she contacted me asking for measurements so she could customize the grip on the staff. In the summer of 2014, she said it was done and when I returned to the bookstore to do a reading, Bette presented it to me.

Now, I almost always hike with a stick, often just some fallen branch that I find along the way. I snap it off to the proper length, whittle the bark off, and then use it. The stick that Bette made for me isn't in this category.

It is art. On it, she carved the Mackinac Bridge, my initials, and then maps of my first two adventures. On the bottom part, she carved Michigan's state bird, flower, and flag. The grip is shaped to the size of my hand and wrapped in leather. The bottom has a post of metal topped with a rubber foot. It's beautiful. I wanted to honor her by walking the final miles of this journey with her gift.

This walking stick is so beautiful that strangers gathered around me at the Grand Hotel to hear its story. I stood with that beautiful staff on the porch on the final morning of my adventure and shared a few thoughts with the group of people who would set off to hike the island with me. We then walked the long porch and up the road to a set of stairs that took us down to the road that traces the perimeter of the island.

This Sunday in late October was breezy and chilly, but also gorgeous with a bright blue sky featuring a few fluffy white clouds. The leaves on the trees had changed into their fall colors, and most still clung to their branches. We set out along the road that stays at the edge of the water – I always enjoy walking close to the lake – and the group stretched out as people settled into their individual paces. We regrouped at British Landing, which was the 3-mile point, and shared snacks and refilled water bottles, then began hiking again.

Another few miles brought us to Arch Rock, that limestone formation that hovers high above the lake. From there, we were soon walking through the main shops and hotels before heading back up the long hill to the Grand Hotel. We took a short break before climbing the final hill. My sister and cousin, Leslie and Milene (who are serious shoppers), took advantage of the short break to duck into a store.

Since most of the island shuts down for the winter, the horses are ferried to mainland farms at the end of the season. Handlers walked their teams of horses past us to the docks. As much as the smell of freshly boiled fudge is the fragrance of Mackinac Island, the clacking of horse hooves is the sound of this unique place.

We regrouped to start up the wide avenue to the hotel. Leslie, Milene, Mary Jo and I hiked the final steps with our arms linked. My mom and my Auntie Marlene greeted us first, then we merged with the others waiting to welcome us. This gathering encircled and enfolded me.

To salute the end of this last day's wondrous island circle walked with friends and family, I lifted my walking stick at the base of the Grand Hotel.

The planning and hiking and biking and kayaking and boating of my 1,000-Mile Great Lakes Island Adventure was complete.

Miles for Mackinac Island:

Bike	Hike	Ferry
9	9	14

EPILOGUE

On a mild January day while I was working on this manuscript, I took a break to stroll the streets in Chicago. The wind was almost absent, and I found myself drifting toward the lakeshore to walk the pathways there. I headed toward Navy Pier, which had been the starting point for my first adventure.

The day was incredibly clear. Plumes of smoke rose along the southern lakeshore from South Chicago, Whiting, and Gary. Directly across the lake, billows of steam hovered above the nuclear power plant in southwest Michigan. Though I couldn't see the distant shoreline, this triangle of stacked steam marked it for me.

Thinking back to that starting point on Navy Pier, I remembered how insane it seemed to think I could hike from Chicago back to Michigan – 72 miles in 5 days. There were rivers to cross, industry to navigate through, decaying urban areas, and frozen stretches of lakeshore ahead of me. I wasn't sure it could be done. And even if it was possible, I wasn't sure I was up for the challenge.

Now, six years later, I have completed three journeys totaling over 3,000 miles. My fascination with and connection to Lake Michigan had led me to explore all of the lakes, the watery connections between them, and, finally, to launch out onto their waters to discover the islands.

This latest adventure spanned from Isle Royale (the most northern and "upstream" island I set foot on) and several others in Lake Superior, to many islands in Lakes Michigan and Huron and one afloat in the Detroit River, to the Lake Erie islands so rich with history, to young islands in Lake Ontario. I had kayaked in between the Thousand Islands in the St. Lawrence River and explored Montreal Island (the most eastern and "downstream" island visited).

These waters are ever-flowing to the North Atlantic, and by hopping from island to island, I got a new perspective on the Great Lakes Basin and its freshwater seas. This last undertaking challenged me the most – physically and mentally – and had the most complex planning logistics of the three journeys.

It has been a joy and a struggle and a thrill to complete these odysseys. Our Great Lakes still fascinate and captivate me.

This will be my final Great Lakes Adventure. Well, at least the last one I'll undertake on this scale and write a book about. Small adventures are good, too. I leave you this trilogy about my explorations with hope that they encourage you to seek out your own journeys in your own time. I hope these books also foster a deeper connection to these waters, these vast inland seas, these Greatest of Lakes. We need to care for these waters, to monitor their health, and to work toward their restoration and conservation.

They are vital, essential waters.

Thank you for going on these journeys with me by reading and sharing my books.

I hope to meet up with you along the shoreline one day when you are walking one way, and I the other. When our paths cross, I'll lift a hand and nod, knowing that you, also, cherish these waters.

Live your life as an adventure.

Acknowledgements

An adventure of 1,000 miles is not accomplished without assistance. I am grateful for the many people who allowed me to ask questions, cheered me on, walked by my side, or housed me along the way.

Thank you to the experts who took time to enlighten me about the Great Lakes islands I explored: Kristin Stanford (aka "The Island Snake Lady) at Ohio State University's research center on South Bass Island. Dr. David "Bo" Bunnell at the Great Lakes Research Center in Ann Arbor who invited me to go out on their research vessel for their annual trawling survey of the lake bottom. Alice Van Zoeren, the naturalist who I assisted on North Manitou Island while with the piping plovers. Ranger Ethan Scott who coordinated my time on the Manitou Islands. Rolf O. Peterson, Candy Peterson, John Vucetich, and Leah Vucetich, who are all involved in the moose-wolf study on Isle Royale. Jason Duetsch and Wayne Shannon, the able leaders of my Moosewatch team.

Thanks to the Archive Department at the History Museum in Traverse City. Robert Brown, retired General Manager for the Arnold Transit Company, provided details on the ferries that the Arnold Company ran between Mackinac Island and the Les Cheneaux Islands.

I conducted formal interviews with these experts, and quotes in this book are from my notes. Casual conversations are related as I remember them.

Thanks also to Mickey and Lynn for letting me stay with them while I explored the Lake Erie Islands. And to Gwen Glatz who welcomed me to her volunteer group dinners on South Manitou Island and told me stories of the island. Julie Anderson invited me to dinner and told me about her family and their connection to Washington Island. Mr. Barryhill and the Les Cheneaux Row Club gave me insight to life in that quiet archipelago.

In addition, I am thankful to Maija Stromberg who took the time to read early versions this manuscript and to give insightful editorial comments.

The Grand Hotel was the perfect place to celebrate the completion of this adventure. Thanks to the staff who coordinated our stay and my presentation in the theater.

My family and friends have supported me throughout these three adventures, and I am overwhelmed by your constant enthusiasm and support.

Crickhollow Books under the direction of Philip Martin has been the best of homes for these books about my Great Lakes adventures.

Great Lakes Bookstores

I encourage readers to support their local independent bookstores. These are special places where literature, regionalism, and community come together to celebrate where we live and what we care about. The success of my first two books is due in large part to independent bookstores embracing the work and telling their communities about it.

These are the independent bookstores I visited along my route this time (or on my way to and from the islands):

Apostle Islands Booksellers, Bayfield, WI
Islandtime Books & More, Washington Island, WI
Passtimes Books, Sister Bay, WI
Novel Ideas, Baileys Harbor, WI

Island Books & Crafts, Sault Ste. Marie, MI
Safe Harbor Books, Cedarville, MI

Ben McNally Bookstore, Toronto, ON

In addition, these bookstores have been strong supporters of my first two Great Lakes Adventures books and deserve your support.

Furby House Books, Port Hope, ON, Canada

The Book Exchange, Port Clinton, OH

Unabridged Bookstore, Chicago, IL
Women & Children First, Chicago, IL
The Bookworks, Chicago, IL
Sandmeyer's Bookstore, Chicago, IL

57th Street Books, Hyde Park, IL
Powells, Hyde Park, IL
Quimby's, Chicago, IL
Barbara's Bookstore, Chicago, IL
Book Stall at Chestnut Court, Winnetka, IL
Lake Forest Bookstore, Lake Forest, IL

Between the Covers Bookstore, Harbor Springs, MI
Black River Books, South Haven, MI
Book Nook & Java Shop, Montague, MI
The Bookman, Grand Haven, MI
The Bookstore, Manistee, MI
The Bookstore, Frankfort, MI
Book World, St. Ignace, MI
Brilliant Books, Traverse City, MI
The Cottage Book Shop, Glen Arbor, MI
Dog Ears Books, Northport, MI
Falling Rock Café and Bookstore, Munising, MI
Forever Books, St. Joseph, MI
Great Northern Books and Hobbies, Oscoda, MI
Horizon Books, Traverse City, MI
The Island Bookstore, Mackinaw City & Mackinaw Island, MI
Kazoo Books, Kalamazoo, MI
Log Mark Bookstore, Cheboygan, MI
McLean & Eakin Booksellers, Petoskey, MI
Readers World, Holland, MI

Bayshore Books, Oconto, WI
Frigate Books, Gladstone, WI
LaDeDa Books & Beans, Manitowoc, WI

Organizations Working to Protect the Great Lakes

These are some of the leading organizations working to protect the Great Lakes. They are worthy of your support, and they can assist you in understanding the complex challenges facing our Great Lakes.

Individually, we can do only a little; together, we can make a real difference in the health of the Great Lakes for us, our children, and future generations.

Alliance For the Great Lakes
http://greatlakes.org

Great Lakes Echo
http://greatlakesecho.org

Great Lakes United
http://www.glu.org

Healthy Lakes.org
http://www.healthylakes.org

Nature Conservancy
http://www.nature.org

Sierra Club
http://www.sierraclub.org

Related Reading

Carson, Rachel. *Silent Spring*. Boston: Houghton-Mifflin, 1962.

Crutchfield, James. *Grand Hotel: America's Summer Place*. Franklin: Grandin Hood, 2012.

Dennis, Jerry. *The Living Great Lakes: Searching for the Heart of the Inland Seas*. New York: Thomas Dunne, 2003.

Eyles, Nick & Clinton, Laura. *Toronto Rocks: The Geological Legacy of the Toronto Region*. Markham: Fitzhenry & Whiteside, 2012.

Fairburn, Jane M. *Along the Shore: Rediscovering Toronto's Waterfront Heritage*. Toronto: ECW Press, 2013.

Grady, Wayne. *The Great Lakes: The Natural History of a Changing Region*. Vancouver: Greystone Books, 2007.

Grover, Frank R. *A Brief History of Les Cheneaux Islands*. Evanston: Bowman Pub. Co., 1982.

Howard, Hugh. *Mr. And Mrs. Madison's War: America's First Couple and the Second War of Independence*. New York: Bloomsbury, 2012.

Jenkins, Mark Collins & Taylor, David A. *The War of 1812 and the Rise of the U. S. Navy*. Washington: National Geographic, 2012.

Leopold, Aldo. *A Sand County Almanac*. New York: Ballantine, 1970.

Leopold, A.S. (Chairman), "Wildlife Management in the National Parks" (known as the "Leopold Report"). *History of the National Park Service*. National Park Service, December 29, 1999. Web. July 28, 2014. <http://www.cr.nps.gov/history/online_books/leopold/leopold.htm>

Linteau, Paul-Andre. *The History of Montreal.* Montreal: Baraka Books, 2007.

National Park System Advisory Board. "Revisiting Leopold: Resource Stewardship in the National Parks." NPS.org. National Park Service, 2012. Web. July 28, 2014. <http://www.nps.gov/calltoaction/PDF/LeopoldReport_2012.pdf>

Peterson, Rolf O., *The Wolves of Isle Royale: A Broken Balance.* Ann Arbor: University of Michigan Press, 2007.

Pittman, Philip McM. *The Les Cheneaux Chronicles.* Cedarville: Les Cheneaux Ventures, 1984.

Purinton, Richard. *Thordarson and Rock Island.* Washington Island: Island Bayou Press, 2013.

Tanner, Thomas, ed. *Aldo Leopold: The Man and His Legacy.* Ankeny: Soil and Water Conservation Society, 1995.

Utt, Ronald D. *Ships of Oak Guns of Iron: The War of 1812 and the Forging of the American Navy.* Washington: Regnery History, 2012.

Williams, Brenda Wheeler, Arnold R. Alanen and William H. Tischler. *Coming Through with Rye: An Historic Agricultural Landscape Study of South Manitou Island at Sleeping Bear Dunes National Lakeshore, Michigan.* Omaha: National Park Service, 1996. Web. June 12, 2013. Manitou Islands Archives. <http://manitouislandsarchives.org/archives/ebooks/ctwr/ctwr-web.pdf>

Sivertson, Howard. *Once Upon an Isle: The Story of Fishing Families on Isle Royale.* Mount Horeb: Wisconsin Folk Museum, 1992.

Additional Links

Videos from my adventures

Please subscribe to my YouTube channel, where I will continue to post videos from my Great Lakes Adventures.

YouTube.com/LNiewenhuis

More links for news, book-related events, author events, etc.

The blog of my adventure with many photos is at:

LakeTrek.Blogspot.com

Author website

LakeTrek.com

Facebook Author Page

Facebook.com/LakeTrek

Favorite B&Bs

I sought out B&Bs and lodges along my route because owners of these unique and often historic places are always knowledgeable about their communities and the history of the areas in which they live. Much of my research was informed by conversations with these gracious hosts along the lakeshores and by poking around many of their libraries.

Please check the sidebar of my blog (http://LakeTrek.blogspot.com) for links to my favorite B&Bs along my route.

Sponsors

This adventure was sponsored in part by KEEN Footwear (Keenfootwear. com) and Advanced Elements Kayaks (AdvancedElements.com).

Statistics from this Adventure

Miles hiked: 295
Miles biked: 173
Miles kayaked/other human-powered boat: 65
Miles on other watercraft (ferry, research vessels, tall ships, etc.): 489

Total miles traveled: 1,022 miles in 52 days

My longest day (on Manitoulin Island):
I biked 38 miles, hiked 4 miles = 42 miles total

Percent of journey alone: 51%

Contact Loreen Niewenhuis

If you would like to host an author event, have me appear as a speaker, or have me engage with your book club, contact me:

LakeTrek@gmail.com